D0143359

# Morals, Rights and Practice
# in the Human Services

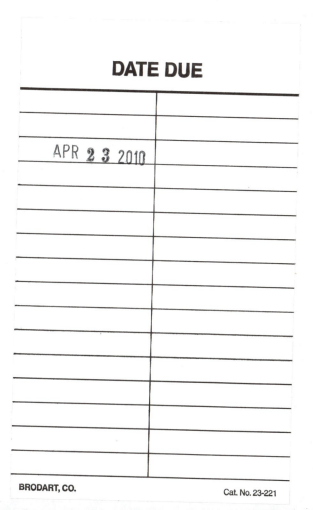

## DATE DUE

| | |
|---|---|
| | |
| APR 2 3 2010 | |
| | |
| | |
| | |
| | |
| | |
| | |
| | |
| | |
| | |
| | |

BRODART, CO.                    Cat. No. 23-221

*by the same authors*

**Culture and Child Protection: Reflexive Responses**
*Marie Connolly, Yvonne Crichton-Hill and Tony Ward*
ISBN 978 1 84310 270 0


*of related interest*

**Handbook for Practice Learning in Social Work and Social Care**
**Knowledge and Theory**
2nd edition
*Edited by Joyce Lishman*
ISBN 978 1 84310 186 4


**The Post-Qualifying Handbook for Social Workers**
*Edited by Wade Tovey*
ISBN 978 1 84310 428 5


**Competence in Social Work Practice**
**A Practical Guide for Students and Professionals**
2nd edition
*Edited by Kieran O'Hagan*
ISBN 978 1 84310 485 8


**Planning and Support for People with Intellectual Disabilities**
**Issues for Case Managers and Other Professionals**
*Edited by Christine Bigby, Chris Fyffe and Elizabeth Ozanne*
ISBN 978 1 84310 354 7


**Social Work Theories in Action**
*Edited by Mary Nash, Robyn Munford and Kieran O'Donoghue*
*Foreword by Jim Ife*
ISBN 978 1 84310 249 6


**Developments in Social Work with Offenders**
*Edited by Gill McIvor and Peter Raynor*
ISBN 978 1 84310 538 1


**Law, Rights and Disability**
*Edited by Jeremy Cooper*
ISBN 978 1 85302 836 6


**Professional Risk and Working with People**
*David Carson and Andy Bain*
ISBN 978 1 84310 389 9

# Morals, Rights and Practice in the Human Services

## Effective and Fair Decision-Making in Health, Social Care and Criminal Justice

*Marie Connolly and Tony Ward*

Jessica Kingsley Publishers
London and Philadelphia

First published in 2008
by Jessica Kingsley Publishers
116 Pentonville Road
London N1 9JB, UK
and
400 Market Street, Suite 400
Philadelphia, PA 19106, USA

*www.jkp.com*

Copyright © Marie Connolly and Tony Ward 2008

All rights reserved. No part of this publication may be reproduced in any material form
(including photocopying or storing it in any medium by electronic means and whether or not
transiently or incidentally to some other use of this publication) without the written
permission of the copyright owner except in accordance with the provisions of the
Copyright, Designs and Patents Act 1988 or under the terms of a licence issued by the
Copyright Licensing Agency Ltd, Saffron House, 6-10 Kirby Street, London EC1N 8TS.
Applications for the copyright owner's written permission to reproduce any part of this
publication should be addressed to the publisher.

Warning: The doing of an unauthorized act in relation to a copyright work may result in
both a civil claim for damages and criminal prosecution.

**Library of Congress Cataloging in Publication Data**
A CIP catalog record for this book is available from the Library of Congress

**British Library Cataloguing in Publication Data**
A CIP catalogue record for this book is available from the British Library

ISBN 978 1 84310 486 5

Printed and bound in Great Britain by
Athenaeum Press, Gateshead, Tyne and Wear

ACC LIBRARY SERVICES
AUSTIN, TX

*To my parents, Teresa and Patrick Connolly,
who taught me about fairness. MC*

*To my mother, Sonia Heeney, for getting me excited
about ideas all those years ago. TW*

# *Acknowledgements*

Many of our colleagues have contributed to the development of this book. In all sorts of ways these chapters reflect the important conversations we have had over the years as people have shared their experiences and insights with us. In this regard we thank Astrid Birgden, Theresa Gannon, Bill Marshall, Shadd Maruna, Pamela Yates, Eileen Munro, Dorothy Scott, and the late Steve Hudson. We are particularly grateful to Claire Stewart, Gabrielle Maxwell, Nigel Parton and Eric Blyth who have read over chapters for us and provided advice with respect to their specialist area of scholarship. It goes without saying that any errors that may be found within these pages are entirely ours.

We are deeply grateful to George Hook whose keen editorial eye and intelligent critique have improved our manuscript. We appreciate the hours it has taken from his work.

We also thank colleagues at Child, Youth and Family, particularly staff in the Office of the Chief Social Worker and on the Executive Team, whose commitment to working in the interests of children and family is outstanding. They keep us grounded with their important work. Finally, we thank Victoria University of Wellington and the Ministry of Social Development for their ongoing support.

# Contents

# *Preface*

While much is spoken and written about *human rights*, in some respects it repre-sents an underdeveloped area of professional concern. It is not that human services and the practitioners working within them do not appreciate or under-stand rights. Indeed, as we will explore throughout the pages of this book, practice and service delivery have become increasingly rights-conscious – but the focus tends to be on legalistic and often adversarial interpretations of rights and what service users can reasonably claim. Neglected, however, is the mean-ingful integration of rights-based ideas, the subtleties of rights-based thinking, and an appreciation of the ways in which a rights-based analysis can help us to negotiate the complexity of competing interests and claims. This book, then, is about these subtleties and the integration of a rich resource of rights-based ideas into multiple aspects of practice, including the ethical behaviour of practitioners.

There has been considerable debate relating to the relative value of rights-based ethics and the ethic of care (Meagher and Parton 2004). The *ethic of care* represents well the relational dimensions of practice, and feminist thinkers such as Noddings (1984) have argued that moral issues are intimately related to our capacities to care and to feel, and that natural hierarchies in the world revolve around the degrees of intimacy that people experience with others. Noddings' support for the ethic of care has been in strong opposition to *rights-based ethics*, which she sees as being individualistic and adversarial. Meagher and Parton note, however, that other feminist theorists have sought to move beyond the rights-versus-care debate, seeing them both as critically important to the understanding of rights and relationships – a position that we share. Insights from both perspectives will ultimately strengthen human poten-tial and the realization of fair and just responses to people in need. It is not our intention in this book to explore this debate. Our focus will be on rights, although it will become clear that our ideas have been influenced by the rela-tional dimensions that rest at the heart of the ethic of care. For a fuller discus-sion of the ethic of care and its relationship with rights and professionalism we refer you to Sarah Banks excellent third edition of *Ethics and Values in Social Work* (2006). In that text you will also find a particularly good discussion of rights and citizenship in the context of service delivery.

While we focus primarily on the notion of the rights of the individual in this book, we also write a good deal about families and their moral rights.

Families have been identified as 'one of the great, enduring institutions …persist[ing] over history across extremely different kinds of society and culture' (Archard 2003, p.65). Families are diverse and family formations increasingly complex. What we understand by the term *family* is often influenced by our own personal experiences and the cultural environment in which we live. When we talk about families in this book we are generally referring to families in the wider sense of extended family or broader kinship networks. So when we talk about family-led decision-making, for example, we are talking about it in the context of the extended family and other significant members of the kinship network coming together to sort out family issues. While this broader interpretation of the 'family' may not be the first association that springs to mind when you read the word 'family', we would like you to keep it in mind as it plays a significant role in our analysis of the nature of family relationships, obligations, duties and rights.

In this book we will take a broad look at human rights issues across a diverse set of practice domains and at the tensions that exist between rights and religious and cultural values. In doing so, we hope that the book will be of interest to practitioners, policy analysts and researchers.

In Part One we build a foundation of rights-based ideas, which we can then use to explore the nature and impact of rights in practice. Chapter 1, our theoretical chapter, begins by briefly considering the concept of *moral status* and its connection with *moral rights*, and then outlines a theory that derives the core human rights goods of freedom and well-being from the fundamental conditions required for *agency*. From the core goods a set of human rights objects is derived, which can be mapped onto the lists of human rights found in documents such as the Universal Declaration of Human Rights (United Nations 1948). Finally we construct a robust model of human rights with a strong theoretical justification, which can be productively applied to many fields of practice and also used to resolve many of the practice dilemmas associated with competing interests and rights.

We then move on to look at *human rights and culture* in Chapter 2. Here our focus is on the implications of multiculturalism for the application of human rights in a particular society, and the mediating role of culture when determining the entitlements of individuals from minority ethnic groups. By adopting a pluralist perspective on what constitutes acceptable social behaviour, we argue that human rights are devices designed to protect the minimal conditions required for a chance to live worthwhile lives, and that there are multiple ways of living such lives, all equally valid providing they do not infringe on the right of other individuals to realise their conception of a *good life*.

Continuing the theme of diversity and rights, in Chapter 3 we look specifically at *religious and spiritual values* and the ways in which they have influenced the development and delivery of human services over time. There are ambiguities in the relationship between the state and state-funded, faith-based human services. Here we consider how rights fit into this context – in particular how the right of the service provider to embed religious values and beliefs in the services they deliver, and the right of service users not to have those values or beliefs imposed upon them, can be reconciled.

We then move on in the second part of the book to navigate diverse practice areas in which the application of humans rights ideas is invariably productive but often contentious. The chapters in this section explore the complex interdependencies between the rights and needs of different individuals. Chapter 4 takes a broad look at human rights issues that occur across the life course, and we use examples of *life course* transitions or phases to illuminate issues related to moral claims versus human rights. The examples include family formation, bringing up children, adolescent maturation in the context of youth offending, and parenting grandparents. Each of these examples provides us with a rich opportunity to consider the contestable rights and responsibilities of children, young people and adults and the ways in which these are negotiated within the context of the family.

Chapters 5 and 6 then look specifically at the human rights of marginalized people. We discuss the rights of people who offend against the law in Chapter 5. *Offenders*, and particularly those people who offend against children, are frequently vilified in public opinion and largely unwanted in their communities. Yet, like everyone else, they have rights and many are keen to live a worthwhile life. Our aim in this chapter is to apply our human rights model to the correctional arena. While the ideas we present may challenge some conventional notions about the rights and needs of people who have themselves violated the rights of others, we argue that a rights-based approach can provide the ethical foundations of a liberal and flourishing community and a fairer and more humane criminal justice system.

*People with disabilities* have, throughout history, been denied the dignity and value attached to the status of being human. In Chapter 6 we explore rights-based approaches to practice and apply the model of human rights outlined in Chapter 1 to the domain of intellectual disability. We argue that it is the role of the practitioner to facilitate the translation of the interests and goals of people with disabilities into tangible outcomes, and this chapter looks at ways in which it can be done.

In the last two chapters of Part Two we return to the family and its relationship with the state. Here we concentrate on the contestability of rights. Drawing on our earlier cultural chapter, in Chapter 7 we explore the impact of *cultural values on child-rearing*. We consider some of the strongly held views about children and how they should be cared for, looking particularly at the issues of child discipline. Corporal punishment of children has been at the centre of heated debate internationally and we look at how countries have positioned themselves in this regard. Relatedly, our final chapter in this section, Chapter 8, looks at *service-user rights* in the context of child welfare, both with respect to children and their families. Over time we have seen services for children and families become increasingly forensic and risk averse. We explore the impact that this has had on the services provided to children and families and focus specifically on the impact that those services have had upon the rights of service users.

In our final section we look at the embedding of rights-based ideas in human service work. Chapter 9 explores *practice systems* and how the principles of inclusiveness, participation and shared responsibility can shift us toward a greater emphasis on rights within practice. We sketch out the reasons why we think it important to integrate rights-based ideas into service design and include a set of practice frameworks that can act as effective instruments through which rights-based ideas can be introduced. In providing these practice frameworks we suggest the potential for developing similar rights-based frameworks in other fields of practice. We believe that refocusing attention on rights, and linking this with critical perspectives that are based on principles such as participation, inclusion and empowerment, creates opportunities for practice to be more responsive to both the needs and rights of service users.

Finally, in Chapter 10 we consider how rights-based ideas can be integrated across *practice, policy and legal domains*. We consider the role that law and policy have played historically in the furthering (or otherwise) of human rights, and we consider some of the challenges to implementing rights-based initiatives in practice. We argue that creating systems whose components mutually reinforce critical ideas will be more likely to have the kind of depth of influence required to shift thinking toward human rights-based practice and reinforce its endurance over time.

The theory of human rights outlined early on in our book provides a coherent framework for thinking about practice in multiple domains and has focused our discussion on the conditions required to enable individuals to function as purposive agents. Human dignity follows from listening closely to what it is that people truly value and allowing them the opportunity to translate their vision of what constitutes a good life into a reality.

In presenting these ideas we have sought to refocus practice attention on the issue of human rights. This is not to swing the pendulum away from the relational dimension in professional practice. Rather, we seek to weave together the interdependencies of care, needs and rights and to support the development of fair, just and humane services for the people with whom we work. As humans we seek fairness and justice in our own lives and value being treated respectfully. Paying greater attention to rights-based ideas in practice will help us to ensure that those goods are not denied to those with whom we work.

# Part One
# Exploring the Territory

# Chapter 1

# *Understanding Human Rights*

In recent years there has been a surge of popular and academic interest in the subject of human rights (Churchill 2006; Donnelly 2003; Dunn and Wheeler 1999; Gewirth 1998; Li 2006; Nickel 2007; Orend 2002). Media reports on human rights and their violations appear on a daily basis and there are literally hundreds of books published each year on this topic and even more scholarly articles. The claim that every human being has intrinsic value has ignited the international political community, and countries are increasingly eager to publicize their human rights successes and to hide their failures (Donnelly 2003; Dunn and Wheeler 1999). Different nations have become galvanized by the idea of human rights and are prepared to monitor its abuses and to intervene to stop violations elsewhere. Of course, there are limits to the willingness of individual states to fight on behalf of the victims of abuses of human rights and it is clear that they modulate their responses to violations depending on their own economic and political interests (Freeman 2002; Morris 2006). Nevertheless, the topic of human rights has become a moral cause and declarations such as the United Nations Universal Declaration of Human Rights (UDHR), (United Nations 1948) and the two associated United Nations covenants are increasingly utilized in the evaluation of international and national laws and political processes (Donnelly 2003; Orend 2002).

People respond passionately to issues related to human rights, partly because they frame our expectations of fair treatment, equity and justice. How we respect the rights of others can determine how harmoniously we live together. It can also influence feelings of equality or discrimination. Increasingly, work within the human services is influenced by rights-based discourses. Decisions concerning how best to educate, protect and care for children, and how to resolve conflicts among individuals, are crucially dependent upon underlying assumptions about human rights and moral status. It is only because we take the interests of other people seriously that we bother to debate and explicitly consider what action to take in a given set of circumstances. In other words, knowledge about the nature and scope of human rights and their attendant moral assumptions are essential theoretical resources for human service workers faced with the complexities of practice in a post-industrial world.

In this first section of the book we want to build a foundation of rights-based ideas from which we can then explore the nature and impact of rights in practice. After briefly considering the concept of moral status and its connection with moral rights, we will then develop a model that derives core human rights values such as freedom, equality and well-being from the requirements of human agency, and link those values with the human rights listed in documents such as the Universal Declaration of Human Rights. It will not be our intention to provide an in-depth analysis of human rights. Rather we will provide what we consider to be the fundamentals necessary for understanding human rights, and in doing so clarify their relevance for practitioners. For a more in-depth discussion about the origins of human rights, analyses and justifications, we encourage readers to consult some of the excellent texts available, such as Donnelly (2003), Freeman (2002), Nickel (2007) and Orend (2002).

## Moral status and rights

In this book we argue that human rights serve an important function for practitioners. They serve to orientate workers to the necessary conditions for a minimally worthwhile life for service users – the prerequisites for a life of dignity and a chance at happiness. Respecting a person's human rights will not guarantee that they will actually have a fulfilling life or behave in an ethical manner. However, it will ensure that those individuals have the space to formulate their own beliefs, and are able to incorporate into their life plans, cherished values and goals. *Moral rights* are a more extensive category than human rights as this category includes human rights as well as other less essential moral claims: human rights are a subset of moral rights and should not be confused with broader ethical ideals.

The concept of *moral status* enables people to identify who has moral standing in a particular situation. The application of multiple criteria such as sentience (capacity to experience pleasure or pain), agency (capacity to act in pursuit of personal goals), and relatedness (connectedness between individuals and their social/ecological environment) can be used to distinguish between individuals who have moral status and those who do not (Warren 1997). Those with moral status in a particular situation are able to make moral claims upon others. So moral status clarifies who are the relevant moral agents and what kind of obligations they have to each other. In contrast, human rights zero in on the most fundamental needs that human beings possess – needs which if not met are likely to result in lives of desperation and misery.

Adapting the words of Mary Anne Warren from her important book which discusses the wider theoretical criteria used to identify entities which possess moral status (1997, p.3):

> to have moral status is to have moral standing. It is to be an [individual] towards whom moral agents have moral obligations. If an [individual] has moral status, then we may not treat [him or her] in just any way we please; we are morally obliged to give weight in our deliberations to [their] needs, interests, or well-being. Furthermore, we are morally obliged to do this not merely

because protecting [them] may benefit ourselves or other persons, but because the [individual's] needs have moral importance in their own right.

Hence the concept of moral status is the basis of a broad set of moral claims that people (and other entities) can make upon each other in their daily lives. It helps us to identify the individuals toward whom we have obligations and duties; that is, to determine who has moral standing and whose interests and concerns ought to be factored into the decision-making of a community, family or individual. Moral imperatives, such as respecting the feelings of others, behaving in a sensitive manner, being a responsible and loving parent, and behaving in a considerate way toward your partner, reflect the fact that morality is directly designed to facilitate social cooperation. While failure to meet such moral claims may cause offence and some small degree of harm it will not typically cause people to suffer radically impoverished lives.

## Human rights versus moral claims

Human rights are strong claims that individuals can make for the provision of a fundamental set of conditions that if not realized result in the experience of great harm to the persons concerned. Individuals possess moral status in specific situations and are able to make moral claims on each other and can expect certain entitlements, but in addition, all human beings are also the holders of the significant entitlements guaranteed by human rights. In our daily lives typically we are content to assert these lesser rights (moral claims) and do not need to assert our human rights. It is only when our fundamental interests (i.e. our welfare is severely threatened) are at stake that the issue of human rights arises. The two concepts are not always well distinguished and sometimes practitioners respond to situations as if they involved human rights when they are really (less fundamental) matters of lower urgency involving moral claims. In a sense it is a question of establishing different moral thresholds. A moral claim (lesser right) requires a lower threshold for what constitutes unacceptable behaviour and is concerned with regulating the day-to-day conduct of human beings toward each other. However, human rights, which are strong claims, require a higher threshold to be reached if they are to be activated and result in corrective action. In such cases it is a question of protecting the core interests of human beings and may indeed directly reflect matters of life and death, for example, access to adequate medical care. We will discuss this in greater depth later in this chapter.

The concept of human rights provides a way of reaching across the deep divisions of country, ethnicity, gender, class, and conduct in a search for what is common to all people of the world (Churchill 2006; Donnelly 2003; Gewirth 1998; Li 2006; Orend 2002).

It is an important insight of liberal democracies that people speak with different voices and thus have distinct conceptions of what constitutes a 'good life'. By the term 'good life' we mean a life that is lived in accordance with an individual's fundamental beliefs about what is important and valuable, in which they are able to formulate their own plans and realize them. Living a good life gives individuals a sense of identity and purpose.

In this book we also use the term 'good' and its plural 'goods'. Human goods refer to prudential goods that enhance human well-being. Thus *goods* are states of affairs, states of mind, personal characteristics, activities or experiences that are sought for their own sake and are likely to increase psychological well-being if achieved (Kekes 1989; Ward and Stewart 2003). That is, they have intrinsic value and represent the fundamental purposes and ultimate ends of human behaviour.

## The nature of human rights

Human rights can create a protective zone around people and allow them the opportunity to further their own conception of a 'good life' without interference from others. They are important devices for safeguarding the judgments of individuals concerning what beliefs, values and practices they endorse and wish to participate in.

Human rights are devices that facilitate individuals' pursuit of their own goals, and as such, defend their own interests and the interests of others. Summarising the key properties of human rights, Nickel (2007) asserts that human rights:

- are universal and extend to all peoples of the world
- are moral norms that provide strong reasons for granting individual significant benefits
- exert normative force through both national and international institutions
- are evident in both specific lists of rights and at the level of abstract values
- set minimum standards of living rather than depicting an ideal world.

The realization of human rights will not guarantee that people will live fulfilling lives but rather facilitates the possession of the basic capabilities required for individuals to advance their own projects and dreams. In other words, human rights are intended to ensure that individuals have the essential equipment they need to have a chance at happiness. Human rights give the individuals in question considerable moral status and mean that other people, including practitioners, must consider their interests when pursuing outcomes that are likely to harm or benefit those individuals. As we have already indicated, human rights represent a subset of moral rights, those that function to protect the fundamental interests of individuals. Lesser or general moral rights also represent claims people can make against each other but they are ones that ultimately involve a lesser degree of harm if violated. It is human rights that underpin basic human dignity and set out the conditions required for a minimally worthwhile life.

# Definition of rights

Defining rights is a complex endeavour, but it is helpful if we begin with an exploration of the concept of a *right*. A right is basically an entitlement – something that we can rightfully claim. According to the seminal analysis by Hohfeld (1919), there are essentially four kinds of rights: claim rights (somebody has a duty to you), liberty rights (absence of personal duties, freedom to act), power rights (institutional authority to act), and immunity rights (freedom from obligations that generally hold, for example police officers are allowed to exert force on others to make an arrest).

It is the notion of a right as a claim that is most relevant to the discussion of human rights (Orend 2002). In this sense of the term, a right is a claim asserted by an individual for something that is owed to him or her by another person or institution (e.g. the state). The claim could be for specific goods such as essential materials for survival or against other people to allow the claimant to engage in certain actions (i.e. non-interference in the rights-holder's affairs). Thus a claim right has a number of elements: the *rights-holder* (the moral agent who makes the claim), the assertion of a *claim*, the *object* of the claim (for example, free speech or liberty), the *recipient* of the claim (the duty-bearer), and the *grounds* for the claim. Rights in this sense are viewed as entitlements to non-interference from others in the affairs of the agent or to the provision of specific human goods that are seen as being owed to the person concerned. Rights necessarily involve duties or obligation; the recipient of the claim therefore has a duty to provide the claimant with the object in question. It is clear that a right is a robust moral concept and is thought to typically trump other moral considerations (Gewirth 1981; Orend 2002; Talbott 2005). It is a particularly powerful claim against other individuals obliging them to act in certain ways and/or to allow the rights-holder to pursue the goals that they desire as long as the rights of other people are not infringed. Because of their overriding moral status, rights are considered to be underpinned by additional moral concepts such as the dignity of persons and their significant interests.

A right can be moral (based on a moral theory or principle), legal (prescribed by particular laws), or social (guaranteed by a social institution, such as the right to speak for a group organization). Human rights are typically viewed as moral rights that are often legally instantiated as well. As noted by Orend (2002, p.24), 'A right is an entitlement that endures even when the right holder is not actually making a verbal claim'. In the absence of being asserted it still remains a justified claim and the rights-holder is entitled to receive certain actions, services or goods depending on the right concerned.

Rights theorists typically make a distinction between negative and positive rights (Churchill 2006; Freeden 1991; Orend 2002; Rasmussen and Den Uyl 2005). A *negative right* is one that imposes a duty of inaction on the duty-bearer and simply requires that the entity concerned (a person or institution) refrains from acting. A good example is the duty to respect an individual's right to free speech; the claim is for the duty-bearer to desist from suppressing the rights-holder's expression of his or her views. A *positive right* is one that imposes an obligation on the duty-bearer to act in certain ways in order to provide the rights-holder with a specific good. An example is a claim against the state to provide unemployed individuals with financial support or prisoners with recreational activities.

## Definition of human rights

What then are human rights? A human right is a *claim right* held by individuals by virtue of the fact that they are human beings. Human rights are not tied to a particular social class, professional group, cultural collective, racial group, gender, or any other exclusive category. Individuals hold human rights simply because they are members of the human race and as such are considered to be moral agents or have the status of moral agents if unable to exercise agency (e.g. infants). Moral agents are individuals who are capable of initiating their own personal projects and seeking ways of realizing them in their day-to-day lives. That is, agents are able to deliberate about what is in their own best interests and act accordingly to secure it.

The relationship between human rights and the attributes required for agency is well described by Michael Freeden (1991, p.7) who argues:

> a human right is a conceptual device, expressed in linguistic form, that assigns priority to certain human or social attributes regarded as essential to the adequate functioning of a human being; that is intended to serve as a protective capsule for those attributes; and that appeals for deliberate action to ensure such protection.

Freeden's definition usefully points to the fact that human rights are intended to function as a *protective capsule* – to provide a kind of defensive zone around each individual so that they can get on with the business of leading a worthwhile life. This means a life that is chosen by them and that involves the unfolding of personal projects embodying their particular goals in life (for an interesting discussion of the relationship between personal projects and human rights see Lomasky 1987). Theorists argue that human rights defend what are considered to be essential attributes of human beings: needs, capacities and interests that if met or safeguarded will ensure that their dignity as persons is respected, but if unmet or violated will result in lives of desperation and diminishment. The violation of human rights occurs when individuals are treated as objects, simply as means to other people's ends rather than as ends in themselves (Banks 2006; Churchill 2006; Freeden 1991; Freeman 2002; Gearty 2006; Gewirth 1981, 1996, 1998; Lomasky 1987; Nussbaum 2006; Orend 2002; Talbott 2005; United Nations 1948). In brief, human rights create a protective space within which individuals can lead at least minimally worthwhile lives that allow them to maintain a basic sense of human dignity.

Rights and human rights have a relatively recent history although it is possible to trace their conceptual precursors back to ancient civilizations such as the Greek and Indian (Ishay 2004). Donnelly argues that the concept of individual rights was only formulated in a recognizably modern form in the seventeenth and eighteenth centuries by thinkers such as Hobbes, Locke, and other natural law theorists. These theorists attempted to justify the ascription of natural rights to all people by appeals to universal features of human nature such as rationality or prosocial sentiments. In other words, the presence of a certain universal attribute was hypothesized to justify all humans being afforded specific kinds of entitlements irrespective of the actual customs, norms or laws prevailing in a given society. Donnelly argues that elements of the contemporary conceptualization of human rights are evident in early rights documents such as the American Bill of Rights and the French Declaration of the Rights of Man and Citizen (Donnelly 2003).

The affirmation of the rights of individuals to liberty, property, equality and protection is apparent in the rights discourse of these periods and served to justify massive social and cultural changes in a number of European countries. However, the notion of natural rights was not without its critics and became the subject of withering attacks from thinkers such as Marx and Bentham in the eighteenth and nineteenth centuries and was really only revived to any significant degree following World War II (Freeman 2002; Ishay 2004). The horrors of World War II and the atrocities committed by the Nazis motivated Allied governments to enshrine human rights and ensure that such catastrophic events never occurred again. It focused the attention of the United Nations on the idea of human rights of individuals and resulted in the publication of the Universal Declaration of Human Rights in 1948 (United Nations 1948). In the UN document the concept of natural rights was effectively transformed into that of human rights, a key difference being that the latter was grounded in the dignity of human beings rather than human nature (Donnelly 2003; Orend 2002). Furthermore, contemporary views of human rights were less individualistic, more concerned with social, cultural, and economic benefits, more internationally oriented, and egalitarian in nature (Nickel 2007). Effectively this meant including positive as well as negative rights and the stipulation that governments were required to provide services and goods to their citizens as opposed to simply ensuring they were not subject to arbitrary violence or unjustified restrictions of liberty.

The Universal Declaration of Human Rights consists of a preamble asserting the dignity of human beings followed by 30 articles outlining specific rights to objects such as freedom from torture, security of the person, a fair trial and due process, property ownership, freedom to and from discrimination, freedom to marry, access to work, religious freedom, and so on. The first 21 articles of the UDHR are concerned primarily with civil and political rights and in this respect resemble bills of rights developed during the Enlightenment and even earlier periods of history. Examples of this type of rights include the right to own property (article 17.1), freedom from discrimination (articles 2, 7), opportunities to vote in periodic elections (article 21.3), freedom of assembly and association (article 20), freedom of movement and residence (article 13), and freedom of thought, religion and conscience (article 18). In contrast, articles 22 to 27 outline entitlements to social, cultural and economic benefits, such as an adequate standard of living (article 25), reasonable health care (article 25), social security (article 22), a just wage for workers (article 23.3), special care for children and mothers (article 25.1), rest and leisure (article 24), and at least an elementary education (article 26).

The UDHR was followed by two international covenants in 1966 (the International Covenant on Civil and Political Rights and the International Covenant on Economic, Social and Cultural Rights) that provided more detail on the various articles outlined in the original UN declaration (Freeman 2002; Nickel 2007). Since the ratification of the UDHR and its associated covenants by nearly all states several other UN treaties have been developed. These include the Convention on the Elimination of All Forms of Discrimination against Women, the Convention on the Rights of the Child (UNCROC), and the International Convention on the Elimination of All Forms of Racial Discrimination. For more detailed discussion of these see Donnelly (2003), Freeman (2002), Nickel (2007), Orend (2002).

## Values underlying human rights

The objects of human rights are linked to values and as such reflect judgments concerning the experiences, activities, and situations that benefit human beings and make their lives more positive. A value judgment assigns a value, either positive or negative, to specific qualities that characterize aspects of people or the world (Kekes 1993; Rescher 1993). For example caring relationships are positively valued and corporal punishment negatively valued. Value judgments reveal what the individual in question considers to be of worth (and beneficial to self or others), or of disvalue (and therefore harmful to self or others). In essence, value judgments reflect what overarching ends are considered good and worth seeking, all things being equal. We propose that values have an objective dimension in the sense that individuals can be mistaken about what experiences and situations *actually do* benefit or harm them. That is, sometimes people behave in ways that they believe will improve their lives but that in fact diminish their level of well-being (e.g. extreme sexual risk-taking). Human nature is such that we all require certain kinds of goods in order for our lives to go well. We are biologically embodied beings and therefore require goods such as adequate nutrition, water, physical comfort, good health, security and intimate relationships. These goods, that enhance the quality of our lives, are linked to the core values that human rights function to protect, values that if violated result in undignified and wretched lives (see below).

A number of theorists have articulated what they consider to be the core values that underlie the UDHR, and its justification. For example, Nickel (2007) argues that freedom from suffering, pain and death, autonomy and dignity are core values that can be used to justify human rights and also to account for the various articles of the UDHR. He proposes that these core values can be incorporated into four principles or grounds of human rights:

- the secure claim to have a life – protection against unjustified infliction of violence resulting in death, and having one's physical needs met
- the secure claim to lead one's own life – defending the autonomy of human beings and their entitlement to 'evaluate, choose, deliberate, and plan' aspects of their life (p.63)
- the secure claim against severely cruel or degrading treatment – the right not to be tortured, enslaved or raped
- the secure claim against severely unfair treatment – the right not to be discriminated against and treated in an unjust way.

Nickel asserts that 'all four principles can be thought of as requirements of human dignity' (p.66) and represent an interpretation of the basic ideas underpinning the UDHR.

While we like the way Nickel has attempted to derive core values and principles from the UDHR and think his argument is plausible, we prefer the analysis of Orend (2002) because of its greater breadth and tighter linkage to the themes contained in the UDHR (but we note that the two lists of core values overlap somewhat). Following Orend we suggest that it is possible to group the various rights contained in the UDHR into five clusters, each cluster associated with a basic object (i.e. activity, experience, situation, etc.):

- personal freedom
- material subsistence
- physical security
- elemental equality
- social recognition.

The object *personal freedom* refers to a subset of objects such as freedom of speech, assembly, movement, association, conscience, religion, and is associated with a number of specific rights contained in the UDHR. Furthermore, it is directly linked to the right of individuals to rely on their own judgment when deciding how to live their lives.

The object *material subsistence* refers to a subset of objects including rights to basic levels of physical health, food, water and education.

The object *physical security* concerns the physical safety and welfare of individuals and includes more fine-grained objects such as freedom from torture, violence, due process rights in law, and the right to seek asylum.

The object *elemental equality* denotes goods such as equality before the law, and freedom from discrimination on the grounds of religion, gender, disability, age, or some other feature considered to be irrelevant for the holding of human rights.

Finally, the object *social recognition* is essentially concerned with acknowledging the rights of individuals to direct the course of their own lives and to be treated in a dignified and respectful manner in accordance with their status as autonomous agents. The goods of self-respect and self-esteem are aspects of this category of goods and point to the importance of enabling individuals to possess positive attitudes toward themselves and their own lives (in a sense, this is the internal component of human dignity).

Thus, according to the UDHR and the two associated covenants, human rights are universal entitlements to certain goods that if obtained will result in at least minimally decent and dignified human lives.

Orend argues that the five core objects evident in the UDHR correspond to basic human needs and interests and that:

> Not having any one of these five core elements does real damage – verifiable harm – to one's functioning as a human being. This is perhaps clearest with physical security and material subsistence, but it does not take much imagination to realize that lacking the other elements also harms human functioning: why else, for example, would we make the deprivation of liberty, the core ingredient in human punishment? Similarly, it is clear that there are no acceptable substitutes for any one of these five core elements of vital human need… Such goods are beyond price and measure…all five elements together appear necessary for living a minimally good life in the modern world (pp.64–65).

We suggest that human rights are arguably in the first instance *moral rights* and can be utilized to evaluate critically existing laws and customs. If a law or policy denies individuals the entitlements stipulated by human rights then they are immoral and should be modified. In fact, it is the duty of moral agents within these situations to assert pressure on the relevant authorities to change the law or policies in question. However, human rights are frequently also legal rights and those states which have signed declarations such as the UNDR are legally bound by the articles contained within them to act as prescribed. Even in the absence of a legal commitment, however, theorists have argued that states and citizens are still morally obligated to act in accordance with human rights and if they fail to do so ought to be held morally accountable (e.g. Freeman 2002; Gewirth 1996; Li 2006; Lippke 2002; Nickel 2007; Orend 2002; Talbott 2005).

## Justification of human rights

Theorists such as Freeden (1991), Orend (2002) and Nickel (2007) have attempted to justify human rights in part by referring to the relevance of human rights for establishing basic human dignity and living a minimally worthwhile life. While we accept the general tenor of these arguments, we consider it important to provide a more rigorous justification of human rights and explanation of their link to human dignity. In particular, it is incumbent upon defenders of human rights to provide a justification that would prove acceptable to individuals with varying political, philosophical and cultural commitments. Human rights are accepted as having universal scope and therefore apply to individuals from different cultures, ethnic origins, social classes, genders and so on. Quite simply, human rights apply to everyone who qualifies by virtue of being human, but this immediately raises problems concerning the validity of the concept of human rights when applied to certain cultures (Li 2006). The argument has been raised by a number of thinkers that human rights are a Western invention protecting Western ideas and therefore distort values of other societies, such as Asian values (Donnelly 2003; Li 2006). In particular, the concept of human rights and their implementation in various covenants and treaties have been criticized for placing far too much emphasis on the value of individuals and not enough on the rights of communities. While there is an element of truth in this criticism, Ishay (2004) has convincingly shown that the ideas and values contained in human rights treaties and documents can be found in the religious and ethical writings of numerous cultures, sometimes going back several thousand years.

Two questions need to be answered when considering the issue of the justification of universal human rights. First, what kind of features must the holders of rights possess? Second, why does the possession of those features justify holding those rights?

The answer to the first question concerning the necessary and sufficient features that qualify individuals to be rights-holders needs to be suitably inclusive to apply to all individuals whom people intuitively believe are examples of rights-holders – such as the mentally disabled, healthy adults, offenders, children including infants, as well as the old and infirm (see Orend 2002; Talbott 2005; Warren 1997). In other words, what are the necessary attributes that a bearer of human rights must possess? This is not necessarily an easy question to answer but theorists have formulated a range of criteria that can help us to identify rights-holders (Donnelly 2003; Gewirth 1981; Orend 2002; Warren 1997). Relevant attributes include rational agency, sentience, emotional responsiveness, having an interest in living a good life, belonging to a human community, and being biologically human. We do not have the space here to examine the arguments for and against each of these proposed attributes but we agree with Warren (1997) that no single feature can serve as the single criterion that determines the moral status necessary to be a human rights-holder. (The issue of whether offenders forfeit some or all of their human rights or have them simply curtailed will be discussed in Chapter 5.) Therefore, we think that Orend's formulation (2002, p.65) serves our purposes as an approximate set of criteria:

> To hold human rights, one must be biologically human, one must avoid violating another's rights, and one must have fundamental interests in, or vital needs for, living a life of minimal value.

This formulation is pretty much in keeping with our earlier discussion of moral status and stresses the important link between human rights and basic human needs and interests. Moral status refers to the moral standing an individual has and covers all moral obligations, entitlements and so on, while human rights serve to identify only those internal and external conditions required to function in the world as a purposive agent. In other words, these are the conditions necessary to be able to promote one's fundamental concerns in such a way as to bestow a sense of human dignity (i.e. a life of at least minimal value) upon the individual.

The second question that needs to be addressed concerns the justification of human rights: given that a rights-holder is biologically human and has fundamental interests that need to be met, why *should* we respect those rights? What reasons can be given for the duty to guarantee individuals' rights to personal freedom, material subsistence, physical security, elemental equality and social recognition? Why should the state and citizens have a duty either to provide goods to rights-holders or not to interfere in their activities? The justificatory task is to elucidate the premises or core principle(s) that support the claim that individuals who meet Orend's criteria should be accorded human rights and enjoy the benefits of their elevated moral status.

The justifications for human rights have ranged from appeals to human nature, the common conditions in which all human beings live, social contracts that provide each individual with the goods necessary for a worthwhile life, and human dignity (see Churchill 2006; Donnelly 2003; Freeden 1991; Freeman 2002; Gearty 2006; Gewirth 1996; Li 2006; Nickel 2007; Orend 2002; Rescher 1993; Talbott 2005; Warren 1997). The reasoning used to justify human rights basically involves two distinct approaches, a consequential and a deontological (intrinsic) justification.

The *consequential* justification appeals to the benefits (i.e. utility) to individuals and society of respecting human rights, such as increased human well-being, reduced suffering, fewer wars, less crime and so on. One problem noted with this approach to the justification of human rights is that on its own it appears to sanction the suspension of human rights of individuals if the utility calculations indicate that this move will result in a greater amount of the value in question (happiness, well-being, peace, security, etc.). For example, a utilitarian could well argue that denying people the right to vote in some situations will result in higher levels of personal security and greater levels of happiness overall. In this situation, basic civil liberties have been traded off for the maximization of utility.

The *deontological* justification appeals to the intrinsic dignity of human beings and argues that it is never appropriate to violate human rights, that is, the state and citizens have a duty to recognize the intrinsic value and worth of rights-holders. From this perspective people are moral agents with intrinsic value and should always be allowed to decide for themselves what kind of life they wish to pursue, providing their actions do not violate the human rights of others. The basic ability to formulate goals and act upon the basis of personal judgment is what gives human beings their sense of dignity and ultimately grounds the deontological perspective. Thus, individuals are regarded as having their own ends and cannot be simply instruments or means through which others seek their own goals.

While it is inevitably debatable which of these two approaches is likely to yield the best defence of human rights, we are inclined to think that both are required. Fortunately for us, the moral philosopher Alan Gewirth has provided a powerful analysis of human rights based on the requirements of human agency (ability to act) and human dignity that utilizes both consequential and deontological methods. We will now briefly summarize his sophisticated and complex agency theory of human rights, and recommend interested readers to view Gewirth's original sources (1981, 1996, 1998) for a more detailed description of the theory.

There are two steps in Gewirth's theoretical justification of human rights. First he seeks to establish that every agent has to accept that as an individual they have rights to well-being and freedom (Churchill 2006). Second, once this is accepted then it follows as a matter of logic that every agent must accept that other people have the same rights to freedom and well-being. This second step means that every agent must accept the existence of *human* rights and the fact that they apply to all prospective agents.

Gewirth argues that the concept of human agency provides a culturally neutral essential foundation for any moral or political theory concerned with specifying and justifying individual entitlements and duties. This is because ultimately the aim of such theories is to identify correct and incorrect, right and wrong, *actions*. Ethics is fundamentally about establishing principles for coordinating human interests and resolving conflicts between people with incompatible aims. In other words, rights and duties are ethical concepts designed to help regulate the way people pursue their personal projects in the world. In fact, according to Gewirth, the *dignity* of human beings resides in their capacity as prospective agents to formulate and pursue their own interests in the world by virtue of their own judgment and actions.

Gewirth asks prospective agents to consider the value of the goals of their potential actions. On reflection it is clear that any ends a person intentionally aims to achieve must have value for them or otherwise they would not bother to seek them. Furthermore, it follows that a prospective agent must also accept that any conditions that are required to accomplish their goals will be viewed as *necessary* goods. That is, the conditions needed to attain the agent's goals will also be viewed as having value because of the necessary relationship to their ends. Gewirth argues that an agent has rights to whatever is necessary to achieve the purposes of their actions because without such guarantees they may not be able to function effectively and it may become impossible to realize their goals successfully. In light of these considerations, Gewirth asserts that *freedom* and *well-being* are necessary conditions for the attainment of aims and therefore an agent has rights to these goods. This follows because if these conditions were denied to individuals concerned they would be unable to achieve their valued objectives; if freedom and well-being are necessary conditions then it follows they must be protected and should be considered to constitute entitlements. Gewirth concludes that an agent's prudential (focused on own interests) actions are necessarily linked to prudential rights.

Freedom involves the ability to act upon the basis of a person's particular intentions. This means being able to have access to the relevant information needed to make a decision, consider the possible options, formulate a plan and then to implement the plan without interference from other people.

Well-being is constituted by three types of goods: *basic, non-subtractive*, and *additive*. Basic goods are those essential for a person to act and include those necessary for life, physical integrity, mental equilibrium, and the capacity to think and formulate plans. Without access to basic goods people would not be able to function in the world at all. Non-subtractive goods are those that maintain a person's current way of living and the various projects engaged in (e.g. income, relationships). Additive goods are those required to implement and develop new projects and include access to information, work, medical care, education and self-esteem (Churchill 2006; Gewirth 1998). In a nutshell, basic goods enable people to act, non-subtractive goods sustain their current level of achievements, and additive goods are necessary to increase well-being and advance various interests. These categories of goods can be considered to constitute a hierarchy with the most fundamental being basic goods, then non-subtractive goods, and finally additive goods (see Figure 1.1).

When there are competing rights claims this hierarchy can be utilized to decide how best to act: priority must be given to basic goods, then non-subtractive goods, and finally to additive goods. If a person is starving then they have a right to be provided with food by the state or fellow citizens, even if this means others are taxed more and therefore are not able to use their additional income to pursue valued recreational interests (additive goods). Individuals have the right to be provided with the goods necessary to pursue their purposes and to have the freedom to be able to do so. Both sets of rights have positive and negative aspects to them.

The second step in Gewirth's argument represents the transition from prudential to moral (human) rights (Orend 2002). Once the prudential argument has been accepted, Gewirth asserts that if you grant these rights to yourself, then because of the principle of universality you must also grant them to other prospective agents. Other people share your need for freedom and well-being if they are to attain their desired objectives. They are also prospective agents who value their own goals and require the goods of freedom and well-being to be able to act in pursuit of those ends. The denial of the rights to freedom and well-being to other people amounts to a denial of their dignity and worth as agents. The dignity of human beings resides in their capacity to act in accordance with their conception of a good life. The various life projects that people engage in reflect their significant values and express their identity and sense of purpose. It is also *irrational* to deny the rights of others: if a person claims that the successful pursuit of their own goals requires the conditions of freedom and well-being, then they cannot consistently deny other people the same rights. For example, if someone claims that in order to pursue his goals he requires a minimal wage, he cannot consistently deny other people access to same level of income. This is because other people are in exactly the same position and as prospective agents require identical necessary conditions if they are able to act effectively in pursuit of their goals. The common feature shared by nearly all human beings is the attribute of agency. Therefore, all agents have the rights to freedom and well-being in order to be able to accomplish their purposes in life; as such they constitute *human rights* and ground the dignity of human beings because of their necessary connection to agency.

The respect for human agency and (thus) dignity is a deontological justification (relating to intrinsic moral worth). It is simply the case that we should respect a human being's capacity to act in accordance with their favoured conception of a good life. We value our own goals – this is simply a basic feature of human action – and all things being equal, we should accept other people's desire to act in the service of their own goals as well. Furthermore, denial of human rights to freedom and well-being is irrational because it effectively says that on the one hand people value their goals and necessarily require certain conditions to achieve them, but on the other hand states that these conditions are not necessary (they can be suppressed). That is, the (irrational) claim is that they are both necessary (required for personal effective action) and yet unnecessary because they can be removed from or not provided for others. The only rational alternative, according to Gewirth, is to accept the claim that individuals should act in accordance with the human rights of others and also their own (Gewirth 1981).

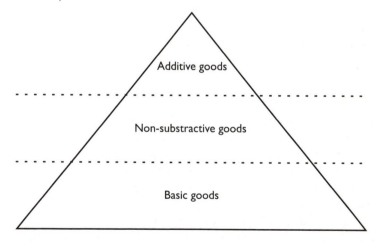

*Figure 1.1 Hierarchy of types of human rights goods*

Thus we should respect each individual's judgment of what is in their best interests even though we might think they are morally wrong. For example, political and religious beliefs can legitimately vary, although opponents may regard each other as seriously misguided in their choice of commitments. Of course, when people lack freedom or have diminished levels of well-being it may be that they lack the basic goods required to function as agents at all. In these situations we are obligated to intervene in order to ensure their welfare (e.g. in the case of mental illness). This may mean supplying them with specific goods required to function effectively as an independent agent, for example, food, shelter, education, income and so on. Gewirth stipulates that children, mentally disabled individuals and infirm adults possess human rights to the *degree* they have the requirements for agency. This can only be ascertained by considering the nature of the decision task in question and should not be decided in an a priori or all-or-nothing manner. We have an obligation to provide the resources that will enable them either to function as purposive agents on their own (following a period of training, etc.) or else to continually scaffold their agency attempts. For example, with intellectually disabled people the state and other adults are obligated to supply the degree of supports necessary for those individuals to live the most independent lives they are capable of. The support may need to be provided on a permanent basis (e.g. sheltered living) or on a temporary basis (sustained and intensive education and skills training). One caveat is that other citizens are only expected to provide the goods they can realistically manage without unduly lowering their own level of well-being. In other words, it is unethical to require people to enhance the well-being of others by reducing their own level of well-being to a point lower than that of those they are trying to help. The consequential method is apparent in Gewirth's identification of the requisite levels of well-being required to act in certain contexts. The relevant thresholds required for the provision of different goods are established by various types of empirical research and social consensus. Later in this book we will directly consider the human rights issues associated with children (Chapters 4 and 7) and intellectually disabled individuals (Chapter 6).

## Structure of human rights

In this chapter we have used somewhat abstract notions as we have sought to define and justify human rights. We would now like to consider more explicitly the structure of human rights and unpack the abstract notions of agency and freedom in a more concrete way, thereby clarifying their relevance to practitioners. To help us in this process we will be drawing directly upon the work of Rescher (1993), Orend (2002) and Li (2006).

In our view it is useful to distinguish between the core values protected by humans rights and their ultimate articulation in the more specific rights evident in documents such as the Universal Declaration of Human Rights (see Figure

1.2). The movement from core values to specific ones is one of decreasing abstraction, from extremely abstract values and rights to quite specific rights, such as the entitlement to paid holidays. In our model there are three layers to human rights: the core values of freedom and well-being, which are protected by rights and validated by a justificatory theory (Gewirth, 1981, 1996, 1998), their unpacking into a number of basic objects or goods, and finally the elaboration of those objects into human rights policies as outlined in documents such as the UDHR. The critical issue is to make sure that the rights specified in covenants and declarations are always approached in the light of those core values and basic goods. Failure to do so will make the various lists of human rights appear to be arbitrary and overly specific and prescriptive. It goes without saying that corresponding to each of the three layers of the concentric human rights 'circles' are corresponding duties that we all have to respect the stated rights of others. Interestingly, advancement outward from abstract to more specific human rights is likely to be associated with legal enforcement (alongside moral and social legitimacy) with the inner circles tending to reflect primarily moral legitimacy. This is due to the essential nature of the core values and their corresponding vagueness. That is, abstract values can be interpreted in a number of ways, a fact not lost on cultural critics of the UDHR (see Li 2006). An additional point is that the less the degree of human rights specification, the more it is necessary to reflect on the relevant contexts and circumstances of the individuals concerned.

The inner circle of the human rights model represents the core values. In our analysis we have agreed with Gewirth that freedom and well-being constitute the two core values required for individuals to be able to function as purposive agents and therefore to have human dignity. These are complex values and on closer inspection can be broken down into a number of components. Freedom will involve situations in which coercion is absent as well as involving internal capabilities such as the capacity to formulate intentions, to imagine possible actions, and to form and implement personal valued projects (Lomasky 1987). As noted above, well-being can be further broken down into the various types of basic, non-subtractive and additive goods. The state and citizens who are the recipients of human rights claims have a duty to provide the necessary goods associated with these rights and to refrain from interfering with the enjoyment of these rights by individuals, assuming of course that the rights-holders in question are not currently violating the rights of others.

The middle circle of our human rights model involves the elaboration of the two primary core values of freedom and well-being. In our view these two values are able to be unpacked into the five basic human rights objects formulated by Orend (2002) in the following way. The objects of personal security, material subsistence, and elemental equality unfold out of the core value of well-being, while social recognition and personal freedom unfold out of the core value of freedom. This matching process is not exact and we are not wedded to the allocation sketched out above, but at the very least, we propose that all five basic human rights objects can easily be derived from the two abstract core values. According to our analysis there are rights associated with all five objects and corresponding duties by others to ensure these rights are able to be exercised.

The outer circle of the human rights model encompasses human rights policies. This involves the codification of the more abstract rights objects into specific lists of human rights. Declarations of human rights such as the UDHR are excellent examples of such lists and provide normative guidance to the state, agencies and individuals concerning their duties to human beings within their country and in other parts of the world. This will include the specific rights and goods requirements of groups such as the intellectually or physically disabled, the mentally ill, children, refugees, members of minority groups, the elderly, offenders and ordinary citizens. For example, the human rights relevant to offenders as stated in the *Charter of Human Rights and Responsibilities Act* 2006 (Vic) provide concrete examples of areas requiring policy responses.

A key insight of our human rights model is that the moral justification and basis for the ascription of human rights resides in the core values and their justifying theory. In our case, this is Alan Gewirth's agency theory and the attendant notion of human dignity. Another important implication of our approach is that there are rights and duties associated with each of the three levels but they become increasingly prescribed as you move outwards from the inner circle. That is, there is less room for individual judgment and interpretation of the specific rights and their concomitant duties at the more concrete level – the level of declarations, conventions, government policies and so on. It must be noted, however, that this is not entirely the case and arguably it is possible to meet one's obligations legitimately to human rights declarations in more than one way (Li 2006). We suspect this is especially pertinent when applying lists

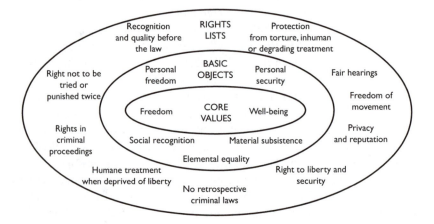

*Figure 1.2 A model of the structure of human rights*

of human rights such as the UDHR and its associated covenants to different cultural and ethnic groups (see Chapter 2).

Once it has been ascertained that a practice matter does indeed involve a human rights issue, then our model can be used to guide the assessment and intervention components of practice. The first step is to decide whether or not the case is covered by an existing treaty or protocol, and if so, whether the relevant article is specific enough to give clear guidance. If this is not the case then the next step is to fall back on the basic objects in the middle circle of our model and use them to decide what are the relevant obligations of practitioners, the state/institution, and the individuals involved. In addition, Gewirth's theory can be used if a clinician is required to provide a theoretical justification of his or her intervention plan.

It is clear that the use of judgment is crucial to the success of our human rights approach and we are deeply sceptical of any moves to make ethical decision-making entirely dependent upon lists of rights or duties. In our view, the complexities of practice and the rather general language used to formulate human rights mean that it is always incumbent on individuals to use their own judgment to decide (a) what the problem or issue at stake is, (b) whether or not it is a human rights matter, and (c) if so, what is the optimal way to proceed. Judgment resides at the heart of practice and cannot be eradicated; it functions to identify both values and facts, the twin strands of effective practice plans.

## Practice implications

The application of human rights ideas to the practice domain needs to occur at all three levels of abstraction outlined earlier. Starting from the outer concrete level, countries legally bound by the UDHR, the two associated covenants, and other treaties concerning the rights of clients should ensure that the management or treatment of individuals complies with these requirements. In the case of children and their rights this is likely to be reflected in the incorporation of UNCROC (the Convention on the Rights of the Child) principles within child welfare legislation, policy and practice frameworks. In the case of offenders this is likely to be reflected in specific polices regulating the running of correctional agencies and community correctional services, such as disciplinary procedures, home leave entitlements, access to medical care, work opportunities, adequate living conditions, educational resources and so on.

We propose that a human rights perspective constitutes a valuable ethical and therapeutic resource for practitioners in that it facilitates the process of rehabilitation/treatment and directs attention to the conditions required for individuals to live socially acceptable and personally meaningful lives. The key point is that by focusing on the requirements of effective agency (freedom and well-being) practitioners are able to integrate the values and skills aspects of therapy. The aim is to ensure clients acquire the capabilities to identify important personal values and projects, to implement them in the environments they are likely to be living in, and in the process, grasp the necessity of respecting the rights of others. In a nutshell, a human rights perspective provides an ethical core for the delivery of skills-oriented human service programmes. It connects values and skills in a useful and simple way.

In this book we will provide a range of examples of the ways in which a human rights perspective is relevant to practice. To illustrate briefly the way in which our model of the structure of human rights (see Figure 1.2) relates to practice, however, we will use the illuminating example of practice with sexual offenders.

A key aspect of applying a human rights perspective to work with sexual offenders is to comprehend that they are both rights-holders and duty-bearers. From the point of view of being rights-holders, the history of sex offenders often includes severe neglect, abuse and inadequate socialization, which means they are ill-equipped to achieve important goals in socially acceptable ways. This lack of the fundamental capabilities needed to function adequately in the community essentially hinders individuals and makes it more likely that they will experience a range of psychological and social problems. Thus arguably the state and correctional practitioners have a duty to provide offenders with specific goods related to well-being and freedom that are necessary for them to function as purposive agents who can make their own decisions about their lives. The skills aspects of treatment can do this.

Because sex offenders are also *duty-bearers* (i.e. they are obliged to respect others' rights), this means ensuring that treatment focuses on providing them with the learning experiences and resources to develop a regard for the interests and rights of others. Practitioners need to concentrate on increasing offenders' empathy skills, improving their ability to problem solve, locating them in supportive social networks, and enhancing their intimacy skills. We hypothesize that equipping sex offenders with the capabilities necessary both to secure their own rights and to acknowledge those of others will also reduce their criminogenic needs (i.e. dynamic risk factors) and hence risk of re-offending.

In our view the concept of human rights is particularly useful for clinical practice with sex offenders because of its dual focus on (a) the values that ought to guide treatment and (b) the capability building aspect of therapy. It beautifully combines values (what *ought* to be the case, e.g. empathy) and facts (what *is* the case, e.g. egocentrism). How does this work? The inner circles of our model are concerned with the core values underpinning human rights and their elaboration into the five basic objects or goods. The outer circle concerns the codification of these fundamental values and objects into specific norms, for example those contained in the UDHR. The assessment and treatment process should therefore respect these values and the status of sex offenders as human rights-holders. Furthermore, the actual content of a treatment plan should take into account the core values associated with human rights and ensure that the training required to engage with them is built into it or at least, if already present, reinforces them. In addition, we have found it useful explicitly to teach offenders – as part of social skills modules – their rights and worth as individuals, as well as the rights of other individuals in the community.

Thus human rights can serve a dual purpose when working with service users. First, they can be used as a guiding framework for examining our own interactions and responses to the people we work with. Second, they can be used as a clinical tool to increase service-user awareness and help with the design and delivery of therapy and practice.

## Conclusions

In this chapter we have analyzed the concept of human rights and attempted to justify such rights in terms of the essential conditions for human agency. In our view Gewirth's theory is useful because it does not beg any important theoretical questions concerning the nature of human beings and thereby run the risk of alienating people who do not share such commitments. Rather, it works from a generic conception of agency that should in principle be acceptable to practitioners with diverse theoretical commitments. In the next chapter we will explore the relationship between human rights and culture and discover that the universal nature of human rights discourse provides a powerful antidote to strong relativistic concepts of morality while still allowing for differences in the way human rights norms are interpreted and practised.

## Chapter 2

# Human Rights and Culture

The concept of human rights is a universal one and the Universal Declaration of Human Rights and the various conventions it has inspired have been endorsed by a majority of countries around the world (Nickel 2007). However, despite broad agreement at an abstract level about the relevance of human rights for all cultures, there have been a number of criticisms about its cross-cultural applicability (Ife 2001; Kymlicka 1996; Li 2006; Nickel 2007; Parehk 2006; Wong 2006). A common concern has been that the fleshing out of the broad values enshrined in the human rights declaration and covenants necessarily requires attention to the nuances of individual cultures. More radical critiques include the assertion that comparisons across cultures and critiques of other cultures are meaningless and that it is simply not possible to evaluate the practices of one culture objectively from the perspective of another (Li 2006).

The determination to protect core human interests across different cultures is evident in what are called second and third generation human rights (Ife 2001; Nickel 2007). In brief, *first generation rights* are concerned with the protection of civil and political rights such as the right to vote, freedom of speech, and the right to a fair trial. *Second generation rights* refer to the economic, social and cultural entitlements of individuals, such as rights to employment, a fair wage, education, health care, and participation in the cultural life of the community. Finally, *third generation rights* involve rights at a collective or group level and reflect group entitlements to goods such as economic development, an unpolluted environment, and self-determination for colonized peoples. Group rights are held by indigenous people, ethnic groups, women, the disabled and children rather than individuals, and are intended to supplement rather than replace the rights held by individuals. The basic idea is that considerations of equality or historical agreements mean that it is important to modify social and state institutions to allow certain groups greater access to resources such as education or special representation on decision-making bodies.

In this chapter we will focus on the implications of multiculturalism for human rights and will consider the mediating role of culture when determining the entitlements of individuals from minority ethnic groups (or groups such as the Amish in the USA who arguably have their own culture). First, we will briefly examine the concept of culture and the various ways in which it impacts on human rights issues. Second, the major culturally based objections to the idea of human rights will be outlined and responded to. Third, we will outline procedures for utilizing human rights ideas in a culturally sensitive and rationally defensible manner that will help practitioners address possible human rights violations in different ethnic groups. Our analysis will be based on the model of human rights outlined in Chapter 1, supplemented by some extremely useful suggestions from Li (2006), Parekh (2006) and Wong (2006).

## What is culture?

A key issue when examining the implications of cultural diversity is to ascertain the particular level at which it is evident within a country as well as contemplating differences between cultures located in different countries. It is typically the cultural challenges within a given society that are likely to prove most taxing for practitioners in the course of their day-to-day duties. With respect to intra-community diversity, Parekh (2006) argues that there are three common ways in which the influence of culture is experienced within a society. First, there is *sub-cultural diversity* where different groups within a society share a set of common values and practices but differ with respect to certain lifestyle choices. For example, groups such as gays or lesbians may have quite distinct sexual, political, personal and relationship preferences that manifest themselves in relatively unique ways of living. Second, *perspectival diversity* is evident when certain groups within a society are deeply critical of the values of the dominant culture and agitate to reform it along alternate lines. A good example of this is the complaint by strongly religious groups that society is materialistic and overly secular in its orientation to important moral and social issues. Third, *communal diversity* is apparent when societies 'include several self-conscious and more or less well-organized communities entertaining and living by their own different systems of beliefs and practices' (Parekh 2006, p.3). The kind of groups Parekh has in mind are newly arrived immigrants, established religious communities such as the Amish in the United States, and indigenous people, for example, Maori in Aotearoa New Zealand or Native American Indians. Parekh persuasively argues that it is the third kind of diversity that is most appropriately referred to by the term 'multiculturalism'. He further states that contemporary multicultural societies are characterized by the fact that ethnic minorities actively seek to have their voices heard and resist any suggestion of inferior status. Moreover, culture is increasingly accepted as a politically relevant category in liberal democracies and can provide a focus for intense debate over fundamental moral and social values. The widespread penetration of diverse cultural ideas within modern societies also means that frequently there are multiple perspectives on important social issues and subsequently fierce debates over issues such as education, health and gender relationships. The pluralist nature of modern societies points to a need to look more deeply at the cultural underpinnings of social institutions and to consider carefully the viewpoints of minority groups. Additionally, it is wise to look beyond simplistic nature-versus-nurture dichotomies when evaluating diverse social practices and forms of human flourishing. Parekh makes this point nicely when he says:

> Neither naturalism nor culturalism gives a coherent account of human life and helps us theorise multicultural societies. One stresses the undeniable fact of shared humanity, but ignores the equally obvious fact that human nature is culturally mediated and reconstituted and cannot by itself provide a transcendental basis for a cross-culturally valid vision of the good life; the other makes the opposite mistake…human beings are at once both natural and cultural (Parekh 2006, p.11)

All cultures are comprised of individuals with common psychological, social and physical needs but cultures provide diverse ways of realizing these needs. Furthermore, human beings are inevitably confronted with living conditions that place constraints on the kinds of cultural solutions and meanings that can be constructed. The presence of factors such as changing climatic conditions, diseases and ill health, political and social change and so on all present challenges to human survival and demand creative responses. Thus we argue that the goods protected by human rights reflect universal requirements as well as some inherited needs and capacities. This conclusion leads us into a consideration of the nature of culture.

## The nature of culture

Culture has been usefully defined as 'a socially transmitted or socially constructed constellation consisting of such things as practices, competencies, ideas, schemas, symbols, values, norms, institutions, goals, constitutive rules, artefacts, and modifications of the physical environment' (Fiske 2002, p.85). Fiske argues that these components are causally related to each other and, in some cases, mutually constitutive in that the presence of one factor is entirely due to the existence of another (Fiske, 2002). Additionally, Kitayama (2002) states that culture is a dynamic system that exists 'not just in the head' but also 'out there in the form of external realities and collective patterns of behaviour' (p.92). Kitayama and Markus (1999) offer the following thoughtful description of culture:

> Everyone is born into a culture consisting of a set of practices and meanings, which have been laid out by generations of people who have created, carried, maintained, and altered them. To engage in culturally patterned relationships and practices and to become mature, well-functioning adults in the society, new members of the culture must come to coordinate their responses to their particular social milieu. That is, people must come to think, feel, and act with reference to local practices, relationships, institutions and artefacts; to do so they must use the local cultural models, which consequently become an integral part of their psychological systems. Each person actively seeks to behave adaptively in the attendant cultural context, and in the process different persons develop their own unique set of response tendencies, cognitive

orientations, emotional preparedness, and structures of goals and values. (pp.250–251)

The central message communicated by these definitions is that culture is a dynamic system consisting of a combination of interrelated components that develop to work coherently together. In sum, culture is something that greatly influences what we do and how we do it. Culture is distinct from social structures, as well as political and economic institutions, and is essentially concerned with the creation of *meaning* and prioritizing the range of values existing in a society. The kinds of priorities and meanings settled on will be evident in cultural practices such as ways of eating, types of religious rituals and services, relationship norms, marriage rituals, preferred occupations, ethical systems, and the type of apparel worn. In a real sense, the ability to formulate and pursue a conception of a good life is shaped by the possibilities and resources made available to an individual by their culture (Kymlicka 1996).

We favour the more recent conceptualization of culture by anthropologists as an open and dynamic entity rather than a closed, homogeneous monolithic structure that is relatively impervious to change (Li 2006). A problem with the idea that cultures are self-contained and impervious to change is its inconsistency with empirical research. Li (2006) captures this well when she states that 'culture may consist of ancient, local, as well as new and globally portable norms, ideals, perspectives and views. Culture need not be predominantly associated with "roots", with the past' (p.11). In other words, culture appears to be a collection of diverse beliefs and practices derived from a variety of sources. The fact is that today very few people live in isolated environments and the combination of globalization and rapid development has resulted in the exposure of individuals to an array of ethnic and cultural influences. While certain groups have managed to minimize the influence of external cultural ideas and live a relatively self-contained life (e.g. the Amish) even they are unable to insulate themselves completely from some degree of exposure. There has been a 'creolization of diverse views and practices' (Li 2006, p.11). By 'creolization' Li refers to the incorporation of diverse, sometimes conflicting, cultural beliefs and practices from other cultures into a particular culture. For example, western ethical and political values promoting the idea of equality between genders or amongst different social classes have been relatively recently integrated into Indian culture alongside traditional beliefs concerning the perceived superiority of some castes over others and men over women (Nussbaum 2000).

A major implication of a dynamic, 'creole' view of culture is that a particular cultural group may be comprised of multiple, somewhat paradoxical elements. That is, despite the presence of dominant views on issues such as gender relationships and education, there will also be dissenting voices. In authoritarian societies these voices might be relatively mute, but they exist all the same and are likely to be evident in some form (e.g. underground religious rituals, subversive newspapers, etc.). An example of an internally complex society is the Yanomami, a South American tribe, whose glorification of violence is not shared by some members of the tribe, particularly the females who are frequently the victims of rape and other forms of violence (Li 2006).

The paradoxes or internal tensions in a culture can be usefully categorized in the following way (Li 2006): (a) uniqueness versus similarity with other cultures, (b) common heritage and uniformity versus internal heterogeneity, and (c) continuity and identity conservation versus a focus on renewal and self-critique. Li's point is that all cultures contain these paradoxes in some form, and collectively they create a dynamic tension that enables them to adapt to new challenges. From the perspective of human rights, a view of cultures as being internally complex and dynamic entities means that simple culturally based criticisms such as the incompatibility of western and Asian values are likely to be mistaken (see below). In fact, the existence of overlapping values and beliefs opens up the possibility of inter-cultural communication over some controversial practices (e.g. female circumcision).

In summary, following Li (2006) we define culture in the following manner:

> A culture is a body of informal knowledge that is historically inherited and transformed, embodied and contested in traditions, incorporated and inno-vated in practices, and transmitted and altered through social learning in a community of evolving and porous boundaries. (p.18)

On a final note, in our view cultural explanations of individual actions can only be weakly predictive and on their own will not be able to illuminate the reasons why people behave in certain ways. The reason for this is that first of all cultures are internally complex and therefore individuals will be subject to a number of, possibly conflicting, influences. Second, while certain character traits may be culturally mediated, the complexity of the relationship between individuals and cultural influences, and the fact that culture is not the only causal factor that impacts on behaviour, means that any satisfactory account of human behaviour will need to consider biological, social, circumstantial as well as cultural vari-ables. Third, the ability of human agents to reflect critically on their basic values and their associated practices further complicates matters and indicates that to some degree human nature is plastic and formed through a process which involves individual judgment and social facilitation (i.e. subject to the con-straints of agency).

## Cultural critiques of human rights

In this section we will briefly consider some of the major cultural challenges to the concept of human rights. We will first outline each criticism and then briefly indicate a plausible response for practitioners to consider. Following this we will apply our model of human rights to cultural issues and, drawing upon some of the excellent work by human rights theorists, formulate a number of strategies that practitioners can utilise when addressing human rights disputes between cultures. The four major criticisms of the applicability of human rights in different cultures that are typically made include: (a) the assertion that it is wrong to evaluate the beliefs and practices of a culture from the perspective of another; (b) a related complaint is that the western concept of human rights is too individualistic and precludes a group or community focus; (c) human rights are too abstract to be practically useful; and (d) human rights ignore the rights of minority groups.

## Cultural relativism

The criticism that it is wrong to evaluate the practices and beliefs of a culture from the perspective of another is frequently tied to the thesis of normative cultural relativism (Li 2006; Wong 2006). While it is clearly the case that cultures have diverse ways of acting and possess different sets of beliefs this does not of itself exclude the possibility of intercultural debate. However, the strong relativist thesis maintains that because cultures are independent, capsulated systems of meaning they resist entry from outsiders. The only way it is possible to understand and criticize a culture, the argument runs, is from the inside. It is claimed that people from one culture cannot understand the meanings of the views or practices of those from another; it is as if they speak different languages without the possibility of an easy translation. That is, it is asserted that distinct cultures are incommensurable – unable mutually to understand each other. Thus, it is thought to be presumptuous for feminists from a western culture to criticize the practice of female circumcision found in middle eastern and African countries (Parekh 2006), or indeed for westerners to criticize the male/female power dynamics across differing cultural experiences. While critics may think they grasp the meaning of the practices and what rests behind them, they are simply mistaken. It is argued by proponents of this view that these practices serve a valuable cultural function and if banned would undermine the cultural integrity of the group in question.

An initial response would be to contest the assumption that cultures are homogeneous and inaccessible to individuals from other cultures. First, cultures are constructed by human beings and partially represent systems of meaning designed to meet common human needs and interests. Human nature is shared by all human beings and therefore there will be common elements in all cultures. Second, the human condition is such that all cultures are faced with similar problems of reproduction, survival, and overcoming disease and environmental challenges. The fact that all cultures are confronted by these problems also points to a degree of commonality. Third, anthropological research indicates that cultures are dynamic and internally complex, and contain points of tension around which different groups within the society conduct debates. Cultures are not homogeneous and tend to overlap with others by virtue of shared ethnicity, religion or simply due to the rapid development and globalization of the modern world. All these responses undermine the claim that differences between cultures prevent meaningful dialogue over human rights issues. Finally, unless we are capable of understanding the attractiveness of the way of life provided by another culture it seems unlikely that we would consider it to be a rival to our own (see Wong 2006).

## Collectivism versus individualism

Human rights are frequently criticized for being excessively individualistic and neglecting the interests of the community in favour of those of individuals. A related complaint is that the emphasis of human rights and their accompanying treaties and theoretical justifications is on the value of *autonomy* at the expense of *relatedness*. One form this criticism has taken is that Asian values are said to be incompatible with human rights because of their strong inclination to stress the good of the community and family and to downplay the specific needs and interests of individuals. The major target of this critique has been first generation political and civic human rights.

A first response to the complaint that human rights are too individualistic and contrast with non-western values is to point to the internal complexity of rights-supporting cultures. For example, Wong (2006) has persuasively argued that the presence of 'the value of community is nevertheless real' (p.22) in the United States and has served as a counterpoint to that of autonomy for many years. He points out that the strength of the family and the greater good of the community is evident in western cultures although they have been underemphasized at times. The critical point is that a morality centred on the good of individuals need not exclude that of the community, but rather points to a need to attend to the value of both.

Second, it can be argued that certain liberty and civic rights are necessary preconditions for the enjoyment of cultural rights (Li 2006). Thus, the rights to freedom of association, expression, assembly, conscience and religion are arguably necessary for the exercise and enjoyment of a minority group's cultural practices. Failure to guarantee these rights may result in the oppression of the minority group and/or its valued practices and traditions. Therefore, the presence of individual human rights can protect the collective interests of cultural groups rather than necessarily undermine them.

Third, according to Gewirth, individuals require two sets of conditions for them to be able to advance their personal conception of a good life: freedom and well-being goods. Well-being goods necessarily involve the provision of social and community services such as education, health, a sense of belonging and so on. Furthermore, the argument for protecting the interests of individuals also necessarily applies to other agents and their interests. Thus, from the perspective of our conception of human rights, what results from the application of human rights is a community of rights-holders rather than a collection of selfish individuals jostling for supremacy.

## Abstractness of human rights

There are two strands to the general criticism that human rights are overly abstract in nature. One is that the values protected by human rights are simply too abstract and, while inspiring at a general level, cannot be easily applied in concrete situations. They are theoretically *thin* concepts and have relatively little content to them. For example, equality, justice, liberty and well-being are all core values associated with human rights but on their own are relatively uninformative. Just what counts as *equality* arguably depends on the context and also a specification of whether the term is referring to outcomes, procedures or status (as in equal moral status). Second, a related point is that the failure to incorporate the contextual features of moral situations means that the application of human rights to other cultures can sometimes seem dogmatic and intolerant. For example, the decision not to allow Muslim girls to wear head scarves (hijabs) to school in France was based on the secular nature of French society and a reluctance to allow the display of religious symbols (Parekh 2006). Additional reasons given for the ban were that the wearing of head scarves signified the (alleged) inferior status of females in Muslim society and also that the girls were under pressure by parents to take the stance they did. The abstract human rights values of equality, freedom and autonomy were arguably interpreted in a culturally insensitive way that only served to alienate individuals who may have otherwise been receptive to the notion of human rights – appropriately interpreted. Indeed, the whole issue of the proper interpretation of human rights by non-western cultures continues to be a thorny problem for the United Nations and western countries.

A first response for practitioners is simply to acknowledge that the core values protected by human rights (well-being, freedom, equality, social recognition and so on) are abstract and rather thin concepts. However, it is arguably this very abstractness that gives human rights the immense moral significance they possess as they provide a common focus for cultures with markedly different political traditions and ethical systems. In Chapter 1 we developed a three-layered model of human rights that linked core abstract values with the more specific rights contained in various rights treaties and covenants. Furthermore, we argued that even greater specification was required in the day-to-day practice of individuals because lists of rights are unlikely to cover every possible contingency. Thus our argument was really a reminder that in order to apply human rights it is necessary to take relevant *contextual* factors into account. For example, in the case of the ban on head scarves in French schools, there is a need to understand exactly what was at stake for the Muslim school girls, their families and culture, and for the French educational authorities. A closer analysis of the contextual factors may have revealed important similarities between religious symbols such as the Christian cross and the hijab and, given the permissibility of wearing the former, may have persuaded the government to allow the girls to wear the latter. As long as the girls did not attempt to convert their fellow students or make a great show of religious zeal during school hours then it is hard to see what harm was being perpetrated by wearing the hijab in schools.

A second response is to agree that a failure to engage in a dialogue like the one sketched out above is arrogant and runs the risk of failing to appreciate the different perspectives and values of members of minority cultures. But the recommendation that individuals should be willing to examine diverse cultural viewpoints does not necessarily mean that permission should automatically be given for cultural-based differences in behaviour (Parekh 2006). A first step is to ascertain the significance of the practice in question for a particular group, and the social and psychological implications of it being banned. If it turns out that the impact of banning it would be significant for the members of a minority group, and it is clear that no harm is being perpetrated (to the wider community and to the members of the minority culture itself) by allowing it to persist then we would argue its allowance. This kind of procedure may allow practices such as Sikhs wearing turbans instead of motorcycle helmets, or Moslem women wearing the hijab in public institutions, but is unlikely to permit female circumcision or forced marriages – an issue we will come back to later in the chapter. Sometimes, therefore, it is appropriate to be intolerant of certain things in our society because of their threat to the fundamental human rights of particular individuals while still embracing an ethnically diverse pluralistic society (Kymlicka 1996).

## Minority group rights

A relatively common criticism of the concept of human rights and its application to non-western cultures is that it fails to promote group rights adequately and therefore does not address some fundamental problems faced by minority groups such as indigenous people and the disabled community (Donnelly 2003; Freeden 1991; Kymlicka 1996; Li 2007; Nickel 2007; Orend 2002; Parekh 2006). It makes sense to claim that colonized indigenous peoples require additional rights if they are to retain their language and customs and not be swamped by a dominant culture. The danger is that without additional resources such as language schools, guaranteed political representation, provision for working different days, etc., then members of those minority groups may be unable to keep their culture alive. Positive examples of this type of special treatment is the funding of Te Reo Maori schools for young Maori children and the existence of designated seats in the national parliament for Maori in New Zealand (Kymlicka 1996). The existence of reserved lands for indigenous people is another example evident in many countries throughout the world where there has been colonization (Li 2006).

Despite the existence of these provisions the concept of group rights has seemed to some theorists to violate the very idea of human rights and the equality of all human beings. It has been argued that the specific entitlements of some minority groups amounts to the provision of unwarranted benefits and that this clearly cuts across the idea of the fundamental equality of all individuals. Furthermore, conservative liberals have argued that it is nonsense to say that a *group* can have rights. Given that rights function to protect the agency requirements of individuals, and given that individuals within a group act on behalf of the group, a group cannot be a rights-holder.

A quick response to the second criticism is first of all to agree that it is indeed individuals that hold rights. But individuals are members of a group and they share important features in common with other members of the group, such as language, beliefs and cultural practices. Thus to say a group has rights is simply a short-hand way of stating that some individuals' fundamental interests as members of a culture are protected by granting group rights. That is, their human rights as individuals are facilitated by virtue of their group membership and its privileges.

With respect to the claim that group rights violate the equality assumption of human rights, our response is to emphasize the issue of redress. The purpose of granting additional entitlements to specific groups is to ensure that they find themselves on a level playing field in which to advance their own interests within a country and to pursue their conception of a good life. In view of the important role played by culture in providing individuals with opportunities to pursue valued activities it makes sense to invest the resources needed to keep the culture viable and alive, especially if it is subject to demonstrable threats. Failure to do so may leave people feeling socially alienated and without a sense of purpose or meaning to their lives. Of course, this does not mean that every minority group is entitled to special treatment – only those that can present an argument on the basis of achieving equality or by appealing to an historical agreement of some kind, for example, a pre-existing treaty such as the Treaty of Waitangi in New Zealand. The equality argument needs to demonstrate that failure to grant additional entitlements or special rights may result in members of the culture experiencing significant difficulty in exercising their human rights (Li 2006; Parekh 2006). This may occur because of gross deprivation, lack of education, social exclusion, or extreme alienation. Li (2006) captures the role of special rights in promoting equality nicely when she states that 'unequal and partial rights (privileges and exemptions) for disadvantageously situated, unequally treated, persons can level the playing field so they could equally exercise impartial and universally granted equal rights' (p.84).

Therefore we conclude that human rights are not necessarily inconsistent with the notion of culturally based group rights and that their existence is justified in some situations, and functions to redress problems of inequality and disadvantage experienced by minority nations or ethnic minorities. Cultural membership rights differ from other types of social group rights, such as those relating to sexuality or gender, and function to protect things such as language and traditional ways of life (Li 2006). Ensuring equality involves taking into account relevant personal, social, financial and cultural deficits when allocating resources.

## Validating human rights

In the last section we examined a number of criticisms revolving around the claim that the concept of human rights was inapplicable to non-western cultures. In addition we also debated the charge that the notion of cultural membership rights was incoherent and unjustified. Rather than being a western notion we concluded that it was possible in principle to assert the essential human rights of all human beings in every country of the world. While human beings are profoundly shaped by their culture, the combination of biologically based needs and shared living conditions entails that all human beings have certain interests in common. The function of human rights is to protect the necessary conditions universally required for a minimally worthwhile life, and this means ensuring that each person (as a prospective agent) has the capabilities and freedom to realise their beliefs concerning the kind of life they would like to live, and also possesses the necessary well-being goods (e.g. education, health care, adequate living conditions, freedom from physical pain, etc.).

Human rights spell out the basic conditions of a life of minimal dignity, a life that is recognizably human. The basic rights to freedom, security, equality, recognition and subsistence should enable individuals to acquire the basic goods necessary to advance their own conception of a good life. It is through the advancement of personal projects that people obtain a sense of meaning and identity, and stamp their individuality upon the fabric of the world. The model of human rights presented in Chapter 1 is sensitive to social and cultural differences. The very notions of well-being and the various goods that constitute it will vary according to local conceptions and norms (Wong 2006). For example, in one culture education may involve a secular scientific education while in another it may also involve instruction in traditional cultural beliefs and practices. In other words, the meanings of core values of freedom and well-being are shaped somewhat by local interpretations of the component goods. Of course, as stated earlier, common human needs and interests derived from a shared human nature should also be taken into account when considering individuals' claims for well-being goods (Buss 1999). The capabilities necessary to realize the two conditions of freedom and well-being are wide ranging and depend on the availability of social and cultural resources of one kind or another.

We would now like to offer some concrete suggestions for incorporating cultural differences into practitioners' decision-making concerning human rights: working with the internal dynamics of a culture, uncovering core functions, ruling out corrupt judgments, and building cultural capital. In our view human rights are universal and apply to all people around the world. However, their application requires careful attention to local values and practices and to the various priorities of a given culture. In the majority of cases the different groups will coexist within a mainstream culture and will share a number of values in common with members of the dominant culture.

## Internal dynamics of a culture

We have argued that in the modern world cultures tend to be multi-textured and dynamic. They typically contain different, sometimes conflicting views on sensitive issues and have traditions of debate. This is apparent in the topic of female circumcision where it seems that there are a variety of positions within societies that practise it, from conservative religious figures claiming that it is consistent with the Koran to dissenters arguing that it represents an outdated and offensive practice (Li 2006; Parekh 2006). Furthermore, advocates of female circumcision claim that it promotes important community values such as self-discipline, control of sexuality and hygiene (Parkeh 2006). In reply, those opposed to the removal of female genitalia rebut these arguments stating that individuals' rights to control their own sexuality and not have their bodies unnecessarily mutilated is of paramount importance and overrides the views of a conservative clergy.

In situations where a cultural practice is clearly in conflict with basic human rights it is important that practitioners obtain detailed knowledge of the ethnic group and/or culture concerned. They need to ascertain the history of the practice, its relationship to the culture's other social and moral beliefs and practices, the justifications offered and their location in revered texts or author-ities, whether or not there are opposing viewpoints, and if so what kind, and so on. It may then be possible to work with opponents of the objectionable practice in question to persuade other members of the group to change their attitudes.

Of course, in some instances there may, in fact, be no clash with human rights protocols or values at all. An examination of the relevant facts and the benefits and harms associated with the practice could reveal that on balance it is the dominant culture that should change rather than the minority group. A good example of this is the recent case in the UK of Sikhs finally being allowed to wear their turbans instead of motorcycle helmets or protective headgear in potentially dangerous situations such as building sites (Parekh 2006). In these situations the laws were changed to allow what was considered to be a legiti-mate alternative – one that was consistent with deeply help cultural beliefs.

## Uncovering core functions

In the second strategy practitioners are encouraged to look beneath the surface of the practice in question and try to identity its core function. For example, with female circumcision the core function of the practice could be to 'protect' the integrity of women and/or to ensure that they can be satisfactorily married. If a careful analysis of a disputed practice (e.g. female circumcision, forced marriage under duress, polygamy) indicates that it does violate human rights norms then the aim should be to explore alternative ways of protecting the values in question, that is, working out a more acceptable means of carrying out the core function of the practice. In brief – see Li (2006) for more detail – the suggested steps are: (1) identify the perceived core function of the practice, (2) compare the function with human rights values and note any discrepancies, (3) evaluate whether the practices in question are still necessary and whether they are able to achieve the core function, and (4) identify any practical alternative practices that might achieve the core function in ways that are consistent with human rights and their underlying values.

## Ruling out corrupt judgments

The claim that certain practices which violate human rights norms are culturally necessary, and if outlawed would seriously compromise the integrity of a way of life, should be subjected to close scrutiny. We argued above that sometimes there are acceptable alternative ways of accomplishing the core functions of such practices and on other occasions the apparent conflict may not actually exist. Furthermore, sometimes it is the dominant culture that needs to reorientate itself and allow for culturally based behaviours that conflict with its accepted norms. However, as with any moral action, at times the problem may reside not in the cultural elements of the behaviour but in the judgment of the actors concerned. Moral actions depend on the judgment of individuals, and these judgments are themselves underpinned by clusters of capabilities: evidence evaluation and decision-making skills, the ability to detect correct values, a lack of vested interests, and intact moral sentiments or emotions (Li 2006; Wong 2006). If there are deficiencies in any of the components of judgment then the resulting beliefs may be flawed and can be dismissed without further evaluation of the practices concerned. For example, the claim that women are naturally inferior to men can be refuted on the basis of the research evidence (clearly false) and the presence of vested interests of individuals who are likely to benefit from the subjugation of women. The provision of accurate information can immediately expose certain assertions as mistaken and therefore rule out some cultural practices based on erroneous assumptions.

The situation gets more complicated when it seems that the victims of discriminatory or abusive cultural norms appear to be supportive of them – for example, women who assert that they welcome circumcision or are happy to be sequestered away from the outside world in order to please their husbands. In these situations it is important to ascertain whether or not the women's judgments have been compromised by social pressure, impoverished emotional awareness, lack of knowledge of alternatives, or poor self-esteem. If this is shown to be the case then it may be appropriate to disregard such affirmations when human rights violations are at issue. According to Gewirth, freedom and well-being are the essential prerequisites of agency and this entails access to relevant information and knowledge of the crucial phases of effective decision-making. The ability to make informed decisions and to advance one's own freely adopted conception of a good life crucially depends on an array of psychological, social and cultural resources.

## Building cultural capital

An important resource for dealing with cross-cultural disagreements over human rights is the development of cultural capital (Li 2006). Cultural capital accumulates by cultivating a body of informal knowledge of a culture and its customs and symbols, which results in the acquisition of attitudes and dispositions that respect other cultures and the dignity of human beings (Li 2006; Parekh 2006; Wong 2006). The significance of this term is well captured by Li (2006) who states that, 'The cultural capital of human rights can facilitate (1) forming the motivation to act in compliance with, (2) efforts to implement, and (3) public support for, human rights' (p.214).

At an institutional level, ensuring that representatives from different ethnic and cultural groups are represented on relevant institutions will help to incorporate varying perspectives on matters of public interest. The institutions in question are those that revolve around public and civic life and include governmental agencies, local councils, education and health boards, community groups, advisory groups and professional bodies. The participation of members from minority groups is likely to help members of the dominant culture appreciate the vibrancy of different cultures. In these situations moral disagreements can reveal alternative but real values and provide an opportunity to acquire a richer understanding of the contested social phenomena (e.g. wearing of head scarves, initiation ceremonies, funeral rituals, educational practices, collective decision-making, gender relationships, upbringing of children, etc.).

At a public level, exposing the children and adult members of a dominant culture to the beliefs, norms and customs of minority cultures will facilitate greater understanding and willingness to engage in dialogue when serious moral disagreements do occur. In such situations, it is important that the issue of human rights does not become a blunt instrument used to coerce individuals simply to abandon traditional practices. What is needed is a serious attempt to grasp the meaning of a practice and its broader links to the identity of the persons concerned and their way of life. This does not mean that marked divergences from the values underlying human rights should be tolerated; merely that serious analysis of the origins of the differences and an attempt to find mutually agreeable solutions should be a primary aim of intercultural discussion. Appreciating the internal complexity of a culture and using the strategies identified above will also help people to reach agreement on basic human rights and their application to different ethnic groups.

From an individual practitioner perspective, becoming educated in the history, social structure, languages and cultural practices of the various minority groups that comprise the society they live in is likely to enrich one's moral imagination, and intellectual and emotional capacities. In addition, an advantage of being introduced to differences in cultural beliefs and lifestyles is that practitioners will be better able to understand the meaning of potentially problematic child-rearing or interpersonal problems and therefore respond in a more sensitive and appropriate way. It is easy to lose sight of the fact that for members of a dominant social group cultural norms are often invisible, taken for granted features of their lives. Social regularities such as public holidays, the structure of the working week (and weekend), social and gender norms, dress codes and safety rules in fact reflect deeply entrenched cultural norms. All humans are cultural beings and derive their values and conceptions of the good life from the wide array of cultural resources available to them: parenting practices, education, literature, film and popular culture. The foundations of personal identity are socially and culturally constructed and constrain the choices people make about the quality of their own lives and the significance of other people's. Adopting a pluralist perspective on what constitutes acceptable social behaviour will help practitioners understand that human rights are devices designed to protect the minimal conditions required for worthwhile lives, and that there are multiple ways of living such lives, all equally valuable.

## Conclusions

In this chapter we examined the relationship between human rights and culture and in particular evaluated the claim that it is not possible to apply human rights ideas to different cultural and ethnic groups. We have argued that human rights are based on abstract values that can be meaningfully translated into local norms that protect the conditions required for people to live minimally worthwhile lives. To underline the value of adopting a pluralistic viewpoint in the application of human rights, we cannot think of a better way to end this chapter than to quote from Parekh's (2006, p.338) excellent book on multiculturalism.

> What I might call a multicultural perspective is composed of the creative interplay of these three complementary insights, namely the cultural embeddedness of human beings, the inescapability and desirability of cultural diversity and intercultural dialogue, and the internal plurality of each culture. When we view the world from its vantage point, our attitudes to ourselves and others undergo profound changes.

## Chapter 3

# *Values, Rights and the State*

The impact of religious beliefs and values on the delivery of human services has been significant throughout history. In the context of discussing religious/spiritual values, many writers have noted the charitable origins of human services, the impact of religion, and the ways in which attitudes towards those values have shifted over time (Bowpitt 1998; Daly 2006; Healy 2005; Melville and McDonald 2006; Modood 2005; Tangenberg 2005). Any consideration of the influence of religious beliefs and values on practice requires that we also examine the ways in which differing world views influence the helping systems that have developed, the work they do and how they do it. In general it requires that we consider the ways in which service relationships are imbued by values, and how this fits with a human rights perspective. In the context of religious values it requires that we look particularly at the ambiguities within the relationship between the secular state and religious organizations and at what happens to the value base of each entity when collaboration and partnership are considered. We will look at how rights fit within this context – in particular the service provider's right to embed religious values and beliefs in their service delivery, and the right of service users not to have those values or beliefs imposed upon them (Leveratt and Pargeter 2001).

As we explore these issues, we will initially look at the nature of the secular state and the public–private partnerships that have characterized the development of human services. We will then consider the rights of service users within the context of faith-related service delivery and will discuss the need for principled practice by those working within those services. Influenced by Smith and Sosin (2001), in this chapter we will use the term 'faith-related' rather than 'faith-based', as we feel it better reflects the diverse range of systems of service delivery and the varying levels of faith commitment within them. We will then finish the chapter by considering issues related to the impact of service users' belief and value systems upon the provision of services. In this context we will look particularly at the development of the consumer rights movement in the fields of health and welfare. First, though, we will consider the nature of secularization and the secular state.

## Secularization and the secular state

The debate over secularization has kept sociologists busy for decades. A radical shift in perspective has occurred from accepting the standard account of the process of secularization to discarding it as unsupportable myth (Casanova 1994). Put simply, secularization relates to the separation of the secular sphere from the influence of religious institutions, the decline of religious beliefs and practices, and the marginalization and privatization of religion and its services. We will not spend time here arguing whether or not all or some of these putative elements of the process hold up to scrutiny – the issues are complex and would not be served well by a brief analysis. But we will consider each of the three elements of secularization as they are helpful in illuminating the issues involved in the relationship between religious organizations and the state as it has developed over time.

Exploring the history of secularization from a British perspective, Bowpitt (1998) notes three factors that have contributed to the differentiation of the state from religious institutions. First, in the public perception societies were becoming 'rationalized' and therefore more controllable. Science could explain things that had previously been the purview of God. Second, during the nineteenth century the growing 'new urban proletariat' moved increasingly beyond the reach of the influence of the church. Third, what Bowpitt argues was the most powerful factor, the very basis of Christian beliefs, was undermined:

> The result was a dilution of the power of the Christian concept of charity as a motive for social concern amongst precisely those middle classes who had felt its force most strongly. For them, there was a general crisis of meaning which inspired a search for a world-view that was both intellectually satisfying, and carried prescriptive implications. (Bowpitt 1998, pp.681–2)

By the end of the nineteenth century, religious participation across dominations had declined significantly (Fulcher and Scott 1999). While there was a dramatic expansion of secular state welfare services during the twentieth century and a decrease in the number of religiously inspired 'social workers' employed, Christian services within the voluntary sector have nevertheless survived, and now contribute strongly to the landscape of welfare services in Britain. Between editions of the *UK Christian Handbook* (1983–1998/9), the number of Christian human service agencies had more than doubled (Brierley 2000).

Perhaps not surprisingly, state systems across international boundaries have developed differently, both with respect to the nature of state welfare provision and their relationships with religious bodies. Founded as British colonies, Australia and New Zealand both have a history of the state encouraging the establishment of British-styled benevolent societies (Melville and McDonald 2006). Inevitably, moral convictions and religious beliefs that supported the state's controlling functions permeated 'welfare practices', for example, saving souls, reforming character, getting the poor to work, and delineating between the 'deserving' and 'non-deserving' poor. Nineteenth-century welfare in the colonies therefore:

> constituted a clear example of governing through 'pastoral care'... in which religion informed practices undertaken by charities and, in doing so, promoted the interests of the state. (Melville and McDonald 2006, p.74)

The role that religion played in the delivery of welfare services was accepted as the usual state of affairs, and indeed, it was not unusual for leading church workers also to be servants of the Crown.

As Australia and New Zealand became increasingly secularized during the twentieth century there was a developing expectation by communities that church-based institutions would deliver services in a similar way to the state. Not being a member of the church would not prevent a person from receiving the service.

By comparison, the United States has been exceptional in its religiosity, in its general commitment both to religious practice and to religious involvement in the welfare state (Daly 2006). American churches have played an important role throughout history, with religion and the state working together to address human need (Yancey *et al.* 2004). As a consequence of fleeing religious persecution, many of the earliest settlers in the United States brought with them strongly held religious belief systems and a robust commitment to formalized church attendance still evident today, at least by comparison with other western nations (Melville and McDonald 2006). Volunteers from religious communities were instrumental in the development of care activities in early American history, and during the nineteenth century this became progressively more formal as population growth, greater urbanization and rising economic disparity became increasingly problematical (Tangenberg 2005).

Throughout the twentieth century, like their counterparts in the UK, many social workers in the United States began to distance themselves from religious affiliation. New thinking about the importance of research methodologies and the establishment of training opportunities for social workers contributed to this distancing:

> Publication of Mary Richmond's *Social Diagnosis* (1917) coincided with the growing bureaucratization of social services and the belief that scientific methods of inquiry could help resolve social problems. The emergence of university social work programs in the early 20th century also suggested the need for a professional foundation of scientific knowledge and methods. (Tangenberg 2005, p.2)

In general, recent years have witnessed something of a resurgent interest in religion and spirituality in professional human services. There has also been renewed interest in the question of whether the state can be secular in the sense of being religiously neutral, and the nature of the public and private spheres.

In modern Britain, for example, issues relating to multiculturalism and the division between public and private spheres have become increasingly relevant as a consequence of migration:

> The increase of ethnic minority religions in the UK has resulted in a new set of demands and problems for the social services. The importance of immigrant assimilation in modern secular cultures has been replaced by immigrants now retaining their religious affiliations and cultural identities. (Furman *et al.* 2004)

Migration inevitably brings a diversity of religious beliefs that are likely to create a set of expectations as different religious groups assert their right to practice according to their belief systems.

Originally, the notion of 'public and private spheres', often referred to as a dichotomy, developed out of the state emancipating itself from church control. Over time religion increasingly became a private reserve, withdrawn from the modern secular state. In reality, however, the separation is more complex:

> the modern walls of separation between church and the state keep developing all kinds of cracks through which both are able to penetrate each other; that religious institutions often refuse to accept their assigned marginal place in the private sphere, managing to assume prominent public roles; that religion and politics keep forming all kinds of symbiotic relations, to such an extent that it is not easy to ascertain whether one is witnessing political movements which don religious garb or religious movements which assume political forms. (Casanova 1994, p.41)

According to Modood (2005) the public and private spheres mutually shape each other as interdependency pushes each to alter within the exchange. In this context, Modood questions the neutrality of the state. If this is accepted, then it is easy to see why immigrant groups would also want the state to recognize them, acknowledge their world views, and ways of living. Asserting this as a right is likely to be particularly powerful for them if they have been denied rights of participation in their country of origin. For Modood (2005, p.147) this means:

> The goal of democratic multiculturalism cannot and should not be cultural neutrality but rather inclusion of marginal and disadvantaged groups, including religious communities in public life.

He goes on to argue the need for compromise. Moderate secularism, as reflected in the relationships between the state and the church in Western Europe, provides the basis from which the state can adopt a more diverse set of relationships with religious groups including, for example, Muslim communities. Such inclusivity, Modood argues, would do much to avoid the polarization of marginal groups, and the negative consequences of that polarization.

The interdependency of the public and private spheres is also very evident within the modern United States political environment, but here the state's engagement has been largely along Christian lines. The history of Christian involvement in welfare in the United States was further strengthened throughout the 1980s by scholars in evangelical circles who articulated the ideas that have now been integrated into modern faith-based initiatives. For example, Daly (2006), exploring the debate around whether or not religious character is impaired when taking the step toward partnership with the state, quoted one such scholar (original emphasis):

> The solution I am advocating...is *the disestablishment of secularism* in the mediating structures on the part of every level of government and the *equal protection of the free exercise of religion* in those structures. (Daly 2006, p.67, quoting Bernard Zylstra)

Subsequently these ideas have become embedded in initiatives that have explicitly involved faith-based organizations in all areas of social policy (Melville and McDonald 2006).

Having looked briefly at the evolution of the secularization we will now consider the complexities of state–religion partnerships and whether compromise is an essential characteristic of the relationship between faith-related services and the state.

## Religious agencies and the state: partnership and compromise

Writers have questioned whether the autonomy of religious agencies is compromised by the funding dependency they may have upon the state (Healy 2005; Yancey *et al.* 2004). Funding criteria can become the driver for programme development rather than the needs of service users shaping the nature and type of the service. In this regard Healy notes the potential for the core mission of an agency to be compromised if, for example, their service contract restricts them from advocating publicly on issues of concern.

While research is generally underdeveloped in this area, Yancey and her colleagues' research with 15 faith-based service programmes indicates that they carefully consider issues of compromise when applying for state funding:

> If we seek funds it will be because we're convinced that those funds will not, in any substantive way, change our mission or restrict our ability to service those children. (Yancey *et al.* 2004, p.9)

Some also have found the developing relationship with the state to be positive:

> I have not seen [church–state interaction] affect us in any way but positive. I am finding that we are working together because there is a common goal to help other individuals to get back on their feet again and or take that next step in their life. (Yancey *et al.* p.10)

Perhaps not surprisingly, Yancey and colleagues found a range of experiences and perspectives on church–state service partnerships. Relationships themselves also varied. For some, the nature of the relationship was purely financial; for others it represented referral partnerships. Most of the services within the study, however, presented as being open to cultivating their relationships with the state.

While the notion of compromise is often considered more of a problem for agencies than for the state, reciprocal relationships are by nature two-way and the increasing involvement of groups with deeply held religious or spiritual beliefs in the provision of human services will also impact upon state systems. This is sharply illustrated in the context of indigenous spiritual concerns.

In Aotearoa New Zealand, the privileging of traditional indigenous religious practices that support Maori culture has provided challenges for the secular liberal state (Ahdar 2003). For example, the inclusion of elements of Maori protocol during the formal opening of state-funded service initiatives has proved problematic at times, as seating and speaking arrangements that reflect Maori spiritual beliefs about the different status of men and women can come into conflict with the government's secular commitment to gender equality.

Criticisms pertaining to spiritual beliefs in the context of state developments have also characterized indigenous peoples' disputes with secular states internationally (Ahdar 2003; Winthrop 2002). Ahdar raises the question: does sensitivity to indigenous spiritual values violate liberal principles and is it possible to reconcile such divergent views?

A positive example of the state embracing indigenous spiritual values can also be identified in Aotearoa when the government introduced the *Children, Young Persons and Their Families Act* in 1989. The legislation enshrined a model of whanau (extended family) decision-making and empowerment that was partly based on traditional Maori beliefs about the spiritual connectedness of whanau members (see Chapter 10). It also enabled Maori families to choose to hold the decision-making meetings at traditional venues (marae) where Maori protocol is required, including karakia (prayer). This then became an expected part of the legal process of decision-making in which representatives of the state fully participate. Indeed, it is now not uncommon in New Zealand for official occasions to also begin with a karakia. Hence, while government institutions and policy domains remain secular, exceptions will be made to provide official endorsement of Maori spiritual beliefs and practices.

Another example of the integration of indigenous spiritual and western secular approaches can be found in the youth justice area in New Zealand. The restorative justice model used in practice with young offenders (see Chapter 4) has partly been based on Maori notions of responsibility and restoration:

> In Maori custom and law, *tikanga o nga hara*, the law of wrongdoing, was based on notions that responsibility was collective rather than individual and that redress was due not just to any victim but also to the victim's family. Understanding why an individual had offended was also linked to this notion of collective responsibility. (Maxwell 2005, p.210)

The New Zealand youth justice model is not an indigenous model as such. Rather it is a model that has been developed by the state and incorporates features of Maori spiritual values and decision-making protocols within a more culturally responsive state system.

Having tentatively explored some of the issues relating to secularization and the tensions between the sacred and secular spheres, we will now consider the renewed professional interest in religion and spirituality and how the rights of service users can be protected in the context of these developments.

## Religious belief systems and practice

Interest in the role of spirituality and religion in professional practice has strengthened in recent years, and some writers have argued the need to better integrate religious understandings with professional skills and values (Cnaan, Bodie and Danzig 2005; Hodge, Baughman and Cummings 2006). Research that has been undertaken to explore the focus on religion and spirituality in social work training and practice suggests that levels of knowledge about religious and spiritual helping practices are low, and that some settings may not be conducive to these practices (Furman et al. 2004). In the study undertaken by Furman and her colleagues, the majority of respondents felt that spirituality was 'a fundamental aspect of being human' and strongly approved of raising it in particular areas of practice (p.767). Almost half of the respondents considered that the inclusion of religion and spirituality in practice was 'compatible with social work's mission' (Furman et al. 2004). That said, many of the respondents noted that service users were entitled to exercise their right to self-determination with regard to any discussion of religion or spirituality, the worker's role being limited to offering an opportunity for discussion. A small number of respondents expressed strongly held negative views with regard to the integration of religion and spirituality discussions into practice, noting the potential for proselytizing and 'religious abuse'. While the sample group in this study was a large one (n=789), it represented a modest 20 per cent response rate, and the researchers acknowledge that the sample may represent practitioners who have greater interest in the subject than a more representative sample might have produced.

While some studies have illustrated a degree of ambivalence toward discussing religious/spiritual elements in practice (Joseph 1988), many indicated a receptiveness to the idea. For example, one randomly selected study (n=328) looking at professional responses indicates that:

> As a whole, respondents were found to value the religious or spiritual dimension in their own lives, to respect the function it serves for people in general, and to address, to some extent, religious or spiritual issues in their work with clients. (Sheridan and Amato-von Hermert 1999, p.127)

While it is not clear how extensive professional interest is in strengthening the content of religious and/or spiritual discussions in practice, it is apparent that for some workers these discussions are important, and are introduced into their work with service users. This then raises the question of the rights of service users to accept freely or reject the inclusion of religious/spiritual elements in the services provided.

## Service-user rights and faith-related services

There have been a number of critiques concerning the provision of faith-related services. Healy (2005) raises the issue of the role that religious institutions have had in the historical oppression of some service users, particularly indigenous peoples. (We discuss this in more detail in the context of law, policy and practice in Chapter 10.) Other writers have also noted the abuses that have been perpetrated on individuals receiving services from religiously based institutions (Weber and Lacey 2005). Healy notes that people may therefore be reluctant to accept services from groups with this historical legacy. Healy also comments that people who do not hold religious beliefs may not wish to seek services from religiously based organizations, and indeed the service may not have a good fit with the kind of help they require. For example, some faith-related services may struggle to provide the kind of balanced advice needed to explore issues related to pregnancy termination or safe sexual practices. Hence religious values and beliefs may present a barrier to the delivery of effective services or represent an imposition of unwanted religious ideology. An important right in this context is the freedom to access all of the information needed to make an informed decision about matters of personal significance. Lack of reliable and valid information may well result in poor judgment and ultimately ineffective action

Article 18 of the *Universal Declaration of Human Rights* confirms the right to freedom of thought, conscience and religion. Article 14 of the *Convention on the Rights of the Child* also states this right. Furthermore, according to our model of human rights (see Chapter 1) freedom, along with well-being, constitute the two essential conditions for successful agency. Within the context of human rights, therefore, it is clearly important to support the provision of social services that acknowledge the spiritual well-being needs of service users. It is equally important, however, to protect the service users' freedom right to decide whether or not a religious or spiritual dimension is included within the service they receive. In this context the need to respect fully the agency of service users, and to ensure that access to services occurs in the full knowledge of the institution's moral or religious commitment and/or intent, is important.

In the US context, the Working Group on Human Needs and Faith-Based and Community Initiatives (2003) has introduced recommendations to protect the religious freedom of people accessing services from faith-related organizations. Recommendation 7 provides for the religious freedom for individuals by requiring that government departments ensure that all potential service users:

- have an accessible alternative that is secular or otherwise without objectionable religious messages

- have that accessible alternative reasonably equal in quality to funded faith-based programs

- be allowed to exercise their constitutionally protected right to choose such an alternative if they do not wish to participate in a program with religious messages

- receive sufficient information about the available programs in order to be informed, in advance, about the extent to which any program is (or is not) religious

- be allowed to exercise their constitutionally protected right to participate or not participate as they choose in any separate, privately funded religious activity conducted by the same or related organizations

- have notice of, and access to, a practical way of informing public officials and receive appropriate assistance if...the program...is in conflict with his/her values or beliefs.

(Working Group on Human Needs and Faith-Based and Community Initiatives 2003, p.18)

Recommendation 18 also requires that faith-based service providers respect the religious beliefs of all potential service users, and outlines what service users can expect from the service, in particular: that the provider has a responsibility to assist them to understand the agency's religious nature; that the agency allow them avenues to express any concerns they may have regarding religious content or lack of it and to facilitate alternative services if necessary; and to seek honest evaluation regarding the service.

These recommendations are in response to concerns about the potential for faith-related services to influence inappropriately service users, and they highlight the need for principled practice – practice informed by an appreciation of the ethical obligations generated by a commitment to human rights when working for a faith-related service provider. Ethical practice includes the need to ensure that any provision of religious/spiritual counselling or services follows the free expression of interest by the service user, and is not imposed by the practitioner. Such services must also be compatible with the user's own belief system. After Canda and Furman (1999), Tangenberg summarizes a number of questions that practitioners can use to test the appropriateness of the faith-based service provided (2005, p.7):

- Is there potential for discrimination – might the practitioner's efforts trivialize or attempt to change the service user's belief system?

- Does the service user have the agency and capacity to resist the religious dimensions of the service if he or she objects to them?

- Are there processes of the organization that are likely to conflict with the service user's beliefs or values?

- Does the institution have the necessary skills and resources required to meet the service user's needs?
- Is it possible for the institution to engage in effective collaborations with secular providers, particularly when monitoring service-user satisfaction and progress?

Professional responses to such values-based services requires a consideration of the complex relationship between services influenced by beliefs and values and service-user self-determination. In the final section of this chapter we will briefly examine, in the context of the consumer rights movement, how the beliefs and values of service users can impact upon service delivery from a human rights perspective.

## Consumer rights and the delivery of services

According to Healy (2005), the consumer rights movement presents service users as:

> rights-bearing citizens who have the right and the capacities to fully partici-
> pate in determining their health and welfare needs. (pp.70–71)

This contrasts with the traditional view of service users as passive recipients of services, who are viewed as 'abnormal' and 'different' because of their needs. Within the world of consumer rights, also referred to as 'patients' rights' and 'citizens' rights' movements (Healy 2005), issues such as disability, mental illness and other areas of service need have become politicized and argued for on the basis of civil rights. In this context disability, for example, is reconceptualized as a strength, in which disadvantage is considered a product of discrimination rather than stemming from the disability itself (Levy 2002). This has been particularly strongly expressed by deaf communities which have perceived deafness as a rich cultural experience rather than a deficit state representative of damaged people. As Bauman (2005, pp.311–312) puts it, such a community forms 'a minority whose views run counter to a larger, wealthier worldview and morality founded on institutionalized notions of normalcy'.

In reconceptualizing the nature of disability or need, members of the consumer rights movement become the experts, promoting the value of service-user knowledge and mutual support models in response to service need:

> In the process of developing collective support, consumer groups often partic-
> ipate in developing new understandings of themselves, to, in effect, reinvent
> themselves not as victims or service users but as survivors and rights-bearing
> citizens. (Healy 2005, p.72)

Human rights are particularly important to consumer rights advocates. Take, for example, the issue of sterilization as a method of menstrual management for young women with intellectual disability. Sterilization has been a popular method of menstrual management for decades, persisting well into the modern era, as this quote from the superintendent of a large Australian residential institution attests (Davies 2005, p. 4, quoting Goldhar 1991).

> I am intrigued by the fact that vast numbers of operations are continually being performed on adult retarded people on the consent of their parents or next of kin (this includes many sterilization operations and also includes hysterectomies, sometimes on pre-pubertal children).

From a consumer rights' perspective, this would represent an oppressive contravention of the human rights of individuals – a practice based on moral judgments about personal pathology that excludes recognition of the moral status of the young women and their human agency. According to Davies (2005, p.13):

> Such ideas have played an important role in rendering those least well-positioned in society vulnerable to professional and state intervention, abuse and exploitation.

Self-determination is a key construct within the consumer rights movement. So too is the importance of people coming together with a shared purpose and commitment to reducing negative stereotyping and disadvantage. According to Smith (2005, p.101):

> The contrast between rights and needs is particularly highlighted, because it represents the difference between a person's own definition of the 'problem', and a definition imposed from outside, based on limited understanding.

Built on notions of social justice, the consumer rights movement provides practical ways of furthering service-user rights, and of ensuring that individuals fully participate in both the assessment of need and the identification of the kind of services that will be of greatest help. This creates opportunities for practitioners to support service users on their own terms, so that they can realize their own conception of a good life (Healy 2005).

Notwithstanding the many positive aspects of the consumer rights movement, Healy notes that there has been critical debate within the movement itself. Aggressive action by consumer rights advocates when there is a lack of consensus over developments, such as medical advances within their area of interest, has done little to promote positive alliances with important stakeholders. Healy also raises the question about the possible negative impact that calls for reduced professional services would have on the social service funding in general.

It is, however, the goods of identity and self-determination, and how they impact on each other in the context of competing interests, that create the most complex human rights issues. Healy argues that a potential challenge for groups that develop fixed identities, for example, 'Deaf identity' or 'Deaf culture', is that it may also limit potential. Fixed identities can become the dominating feature of the group's existence, closing down opportunities for alternative choices and permeable experience.

An example of this can be found in the controversial debates over cochlear implants (hearing implants) and 'designer babies', both recent issues for deaf communities. The issues are complex, but essentially relate to the rights of deaf parents to control the future hearing capacity of their children. In the context of cochlear implants, this could mean a decision by the parents to deny their child a hearing implant and therefore the possibility of being able to hear. In the case of 'designer babies' this involves deaf parents seeking to increase their chances of conceiving a deaf baby by selective reproductive technology. In both situations, the issue comes down to what could be either a potential violation of the child's right to an open future (i.e. a hearing future), or the parents' right to ensure their child's access to a rich deaf culture (Levy 2002, p.284):

> Deaf activists often argue that deafness is not a disability. Instead, it is the constitutive condition of access to a rich and valuable culture.

Reworking the argument from a medical construct to a social one, as some writers have argued, enables the consideration of alternative worldviews with respect to the institutionalization of normalcy:

> By laying claim to disability, the defense of designing deaf babies has the potential to contribute to the larger reworking of a moral perspective that allows for alternative and equally valid standards of normalcy. (Bauman 2005, p.312)

Clearly these issues are complex. However, given the likelihood that medical advances will continue to create new opportunities such as these, it is equally likely that they will push the boundaries of discussion in years to come.

## Conclusions

We have traversed examples of the kinds of issues that reside at the moral and ethical heart of rights-based practice. Whether the parents of an intellectually disabled young woman have the right to resolve the issue of menstrual management by sterilization, whether a deaf parent has the right to choose against a hearing future for their child or, as we considered in Chapter 2, whether a cultural group has the right to impose practices that impact on the future health and/or well-being of their people, are all issues in which human rights discourses play a critical part. They are not issues that can be easily or straightforwardly resolved. They are issues that require us to understand the impact of values and beliefs, the nature of moral status, the significance of agency, the capacity for consent, the core values underlying human rights, and the ways in which these interact within a cultural milieu. In practice, they are issues that we have to navigate carefully and work within the difficult interpersonal dimensions of decisions-making (Healy 2005). It is this navigation of rights and practice that we now explore in Part Two of this book.

# Part Two
# Navigating Rights and Practice

## Chapter 4

# *Navigating Rights across the Life Course*

Although human rights seek to protect the necessary conditions that individuals require in order to exercise agency and realize their conception of a good life, exploring how changing human needs across the life span impacts upon human rights has received minimal attention within the human science literature. Nevertheless, the ways in which a rights perspective interacts with human needs, interdependencies, responsibilities and obligations are of considerable importance as we consider how the capabilities required for agency unfold in a developmental way as individuals acquire the capacity to live a good life. In this chapter we will consider both moral claims and human rights that are salient at various stages and transitions across the human life course, particularly those that relate to developmental issues which impact on human relationships within the social environment. We will consider individuals as adaptive persons interacting within an ecological frame, and focus on ways in which rights are negotiated through processes of reciprocal development. One of our critical assumptions will be that the essential well-being goods required for a minimally worthwhile life include community networks as well as familial and intimate relationships.

Adopting a family life-course perspective, we will look at Germain's (1991) notion of tandem development – the reciprocal influence of family members on each other's development. Essentially, Germain's approach to the life course is ecological, a perspective that focuses on the interaction of people within the context of their environment. From a rights perspective this is a particularly useful approach as the negotiation of moral claims and human rights is influenced by interactive processes, both within and outside the family context, as humans develop. Human service work has also been strongly influenced, both in theory and practice, by the ecological perspective, which means that the rights-based ideas are more likely to resonate with practitioners working with children and families on a day-to-day basis. Using the ecological approach, practitioners view human behaviour from a holistic perspective, emerging from a complex interplay of biological, psychological, social, economic, political and physical forces. Human beings adapt and develop through transactions with their environment. For example, with respect to tandem development, the behaviour of a child is influenced by parenting behaviour, but the parenting behaviour is invariably reciprocally influenced by the child's behaviour. Development therefore occurs through these reciprocal exchanges as people influence each other.

Germain also writes about families having unique family paradigms or patterns of development which define shared beliefs about themselves in the context of their social world. Paradigms shape a family's basic patterns, taking us away from the traditional developmental concept of sequential family stages to a more family-responsive notion in which individuals and families develop according to their own experiences, pressures and opportunities over time. This allows us to consider moral claims and human rights in the context of particular family experience. For example, within this conceptualization a family that has a disabled child will develop differently from other families with respect to the ways in which they meet their own needs and give effect to interdependencies, responsibilities and obligations. Cultural belief systems also influence development, whether they are related to ethnicity, gender or class. Parenting practices across boundaries of class will impact on our understanding of moral claims and human rights, and so, too, across ethnic cultures.

Using a family life-course framework we will now explore the ways in which negotiating rights occurs in the context of individuals developing adaptive relationships within their social and physical ecology. While we will be focusing on specific life-course periods and transitions in this chapter, our purpose is not to provide a comprehensive analysis of human development. Rather, we will use these examples as a mechanism for illuminating issues related to moral claims and human rights. As such, we have identified four aspects of the life course which lend themselves particularly well to the exploration of moral rights: family formation, childhood, adolescent development in the context of youth offending, and grand-parenting rights.

## Family formation: rights and responsibilities

Becoming a parent brings with it an intricate set of responsibilities, expectations and commitments. According to Saleebey (2001, p.297), the needs and developmental requirements of children 'both challenge and strengthen the relational and structural sinew of family life'. While the state of parenthood is not always realized by deliberate choice, many adults now have choices with respect to parenthood, for example, having a child now or later, building a family through new birth technology or remaining childless. We will look at some rights issues related to becoming a parent, in particular antenatal rights and responsibilities, and contestable rights in the complex area of new birth technology.

Conceiving a child results in a major life transition. It initiates a new set of relationships: the mother–foetus relationship as the pregnancy develops, followed by other relationships after birth (mother–child, father–child, sibling–sibling, etc.). As the nurturer of the foetus, the mother is already charged with responsibilities. A foetus's rapid development requires adequate conditions for growth and makes heavy demands on the mother's body to provide the necessary nutrients for healthy development (Germain 1991). Adverse uterine environments, such as parental drug and alcohol addiction or poor nutrition, have been recognized as highly risky with respect to foetal development. For example, children born with foetal alcohol syndrome can suffer significant long-term health consequences, and children born to drug-addicted mothers can suffer severe withdrawal symptoms and ongoing disorders. These conditions clearly present obstacles to optimal foetal development. For the foetus, both adverse and favourable conditions are entirely dependent upon another to provide.

Who has rights within this situation, and upon whom do responsibilities lie? As a potential human agent the unborn child has moral status and its safety and nurturing matters. While it could be argued that the responsibility for this nurturing rests primarily with the mother, issues of poverty, abusive environments, and poor access to knowledge and information are social-structural obstacles (Berger, McBreen and Rifkin 1996). Basic life-sustaining resources, income, food and shelter are required to protect the interests of both mother and unborn child. The state and its constituent agencies arguably have human rights obligations to ensure that the mother has the well-being goods necessary to function as a nurturing agent so that the unborn child will develop capacities that will help it to function as a purposive agent in its future life. This means that the state has a duty to ensure that the mother has necessary well-being goods, such as adequate nutrition, medical care, income, and protection from physical and significant emotional harm, as well as freedom goods, such as freedom from alcohol or drug addiction. As a consequence of poverty some women have limited access to basic human rights goods. Poor access to resources can have direct implications with respect to both the health of the mother and unborn child, for example, the mother's capacity to access adequate nutrition and health care during pregnancy.

While a straightforward solution to overcoming such obstacles may be the provision of state care and/or financial resources as of right, some writers have argued that such provision can also 'promote a sense of dependence which only perpetuates inequality' (Smith 2005, p.100) and further oppresses certain groups:

> Services should promote independence, rather than maintaining people in dependent states, enable users to exercise choice and autonomy, and promote social inclusion as opposed to specialist provision which stigmatizes and isolates participants (Smith 2005, p.101).

How then can we reconcile meeting human needs and ensuring human rights in ways that promote well-being and freedom goods rather than reinforce oppression? Ife (2001) suggests that that rights-based practice requires a professional exploration of the right that rests behind the statement of need. So, in the context of becoming a mother, a pregnant woman *needs* a healthy antenatal environment in order to nurture her growing foetus, and therefore has a *right* to basic life-sustaining resources that would enable her to do so. Beyond this, the *way* in which support, if required, is provided, either within a context that promotes social inclusion or via potentially stigmatizing specialist provision that could increase dependency, becomes important.

Beresford (cited in Smith 2005, p.102) argues the importance of reconciling rights and needs from the perspective of the user by focusing on autonomy, participation and inclusion (essentially Gewirth's freedom condition):

> This gives equal priority to: establishing and securing people's common and shared civil and human rights and meeting their different self-defined needs in the way they, ensured full knowledge, support and choice, prefer.

Hence the facilitation of self-defined need becomes essential to rights-based practice (Ife 2001).

Parental choice in forming a family and, in particular, becoming a parent through the application of new reproductive technologies, provides us with a different set of complexities with respect to reconciling the rights and needs of different individuals. Recent years have seen an increase in the number of children conceived with the assistance of reproductive technology. The issues related to human rights within the context of these medical advances have produced significant debate within the literature and, indeed, the popular press. Issues arise most frequently in situations involving third-party assisted conception, for example donor insemination (in which the child is genetically related only to the mother) and egg donation (in which the child is genetically related only to the father). Blyth and Landau (2005, p.11) capture nicely the issues relating to anonymity and secrecy:

> The legal status and the practice regarding the relationship between the donor and the recipient individual or family and between the donor and child vary from country to country …Secrecy is usually seen as a means of protecting an infertile man from the embarrassing disclosure of his infertility, the child from feeling that he/she does not fully belong to both parents, and the donor from any legal or moral responsibility for any resultant offspring.

It is perhaps in these areas in particular that the tension between the rights of the adults and those of the child become most acutely contested. A number of questions then become relevant when considering the rights of the parties involved in the conception of these children. Do children conceived with the assistance of reproductive technologies have a right to their identity and information about their genetic family lineage? Related to this, do parents have sole discretion regarding whether or not the child will be told of their conceptive history? And do donors have any rights or responsibilities beyond the birth of the child?

Focusing on the issues of identity and information, Blyth and Landau note that while secrecy around third-party assisted conception is well meant, it nevertheless has the potential to impact negatively on the physical and mental health of the child:

> Without knowledge of one or both of their genetic parents, donor-conceived people are deprived of the information they need to develop a full sense of their identity (Blyth and Landau 2005, p.11).

Questions about identity, while culturally influenced, can be answered through life narratives – knowledge contributions from our present and our past (Saleebey 2001). Identity issues can become critical for some adolescents as they piece together where they fit in the world, where they come from, and where they are going. While not all individuals will want to know their biological origins, many will. The problem is: it is not possible to know in advance who will and who will not.

The United Nations Convention on the Rights of the Child (UNCROC 1989) provides some guidance with respect to identity issues and the rights of the child:

> State Parties undertake to respect the right of the child to preserve his or her identity... Where a child is illegally deprived of some or all of the elements of his or her identity, States Parties shall provide appropriate assistance and protection, with a view to re-establishing speedily his or her identity (Article 8).

However, while there may be a moral right to lineage information (based on UNCROC requirements and need), no legal rights are being violated when information is withheld because of the donor's right to anonymity. As Archard (2007) notes, moral rights are not necessarily legal rights, nor are legal rights necessarily always viewed as moral rights. In this regard, UNCROC does not necessarily help us to untangle whether children should have lineage information as of right, either when they are children or when have they reached a certain age. Indeed, Blyth and Farrand (2004) note that while the Convention provides a good framework for challenging donor anonymity, it has been ineffective as a mechanism for facilitating policy change.

Many writers are, however, keen to explore the issues of donor anonymity versus the right of children to know their genetic history (see, for example, Tobin 2004; Wallbank 2004). Wallbank's analysis of private family disputes indicates that while the child's right to know about their biological lineage is generally a consideration in the dispute, it is not consistently accommodated in law. More frequently, she suggests, the child's right to know is subordinate to wider interests, including the protection of the nurturing family. Supporting the right of children to know about their genetic origins, she calls on governments to 'take the "bull by the horns" and institute that right' in legislation (Wallbank 2004, p.262).

With respect to legislative change in this area, perceptions about moral rights tend to drive demands for legal rights provision (Archard 2007).

Frequently this is also driven by self-defined need, and the issues are complex, particularly in the context of conflicting needs. Moral status claims of the unborn child further complicate the debate. Once the child is born, moral status, moral rights and legal rights begin to clarify, but issues related to competing interests and rights remain. From our perspective, individuals possess rights to the *degree* that they have the capacity for agency, that is the degree to which an individual is capable of acting on their own conception of a good life. It is also the case that *human* rights are those rights necessary to protect the conditions required for us to function as agents, and as such are fundamental (see Chapter 1). In the case of a child conceived using donated sperm, there are two sets of claims to consider. On the one hand, the biological father has been assured of anonymity and only donated his sperm on the basis that his privacy would be preserved. To violate this agreement would be to compromise his desire for privacy and ultimately override one of his freedom rights (to privacy). On the other hand, the child has a legitimate moral claim to know where they 'come from'. In seeking to weigh up these competing interests/rights the question to be decided is whether denying a child this knowledge would be significantly harmful and compromise their ability to function as a prospective agent. Thus, the key issue is whether keeping this information from a child would violate any of their fundamental well-being rights as opposed to simply overriding other moral claims. If the child concerned is able to develop normally despite their evident disappointment at being denied information, then from a human rights perspective the genetic father's freedom right of privacy would outweigh the child's moral claims to lineage and identity information. If the child's development, however, is being compromised because of the lack of critical information (e.g. medical history, identity dislocation), then the dispute over 'rights' becomes more contestable. Nordic countries have been at the forefront of legislative change that affords donor-conceived people the right to learn the identity of their donor (Blyth and Spiers 2004). In this regard, perceptions about moral rights may well become increasingly important drivers of demand for legal rights provision in this area.

## Childhood: competing interests and/or rights

By virtue of being human, children have both moral status and human rights. Nevertheless, the overlapping needs and interests of children and parents create tensions that are evident when we explore the issues surrounding familial rights and responsibilities. These tensions, played out primarily within the family, are also evident in human rights discourses, family social policy, service and practice systems.

It is certainly clear that issues related to children's rights have increasingly moved to the forefront of public concern in recent years. Identified as an historic milestone (Verhellen 2004), UNCROC was a huge step forward in providing a comprehensive legal statement about the rights of children (Freeman

2004). Countries responded with alacrity in ratifying the Convention, with only two countries now having failed to ratify: Somalia and the United States of America. Despite this overwhelming support, Freeman argues that there remains a chasm between the stated expectations of the Convention and the way in which countries support children's rights in practice. One aspect of what Freeman identifies as a backlash against children's rights has been the perceived clash between parental and children's rights.

As its title dictates, the Convention is primarily concerned with children's rights. Nevertheless, it is also centrally concerned about the rights and responsibilities of parents and families (Henricson and Bainham 2005). For example, the Convention acknowledges parents' rights and duties in Article 5, and then requires that these be respected:

> State Parties shall respect the rights and duties of the parents…to provide direction to the child in the exercise of his or her right in a manner consistent with the evolving capacities of the child. (Article 14)

Parental responsibility is then located within the context of the child's best interests:

> Parents…have the primary responsibility for the upbringing and development of the child. The best interests of the child will be their basic concern. (Article 18)

Reinforcing the family as fundamental to the child's interests and welfare, the Convention makes it clear that, if required, the state should ensure that the family has the necessary protections and provisions that would enable it to fully exercise its familial functions. It is apparent, therefore, that the Convention sees the family as essential both for securing the child's best interests and for nurturing the child's capacity to exercise their rights.

Given the inextricability of parental and children's rights in the context of family life, the need to move away from a binary analysis of familial rights (i.e. parental versus children's rights) towards a more integrated approach involving concepts such as interdependency and stewardship would seem like a useful way forward. In Chapter 1 we discussed Freeden's (1991) notion of rights functioning as a kind of defensive zone (or *protective capsule*) around individuals so that they can get on with the business of leading their lives. This encourages us to consider parents as the primary supporters of their children's protective capsules. A child's protective capsule facilitates the acquisition of an increasing, developmentally driven, capacity for agency and ability to exercise their own rights. The maturing of a child's capacity for agency, and the associated need for increased autonomy, are part of an important developmental process, and given that a crucial role for parents is to nurture their child's development, it is incumbent on them therefore also to support the child's enabling protective capsule – to become the champions of their children's rights. That role entails providing 'in a manner consistent with the evolving capacities of the child, appropriate direction and guidance in the exercise by the child of those rights...' (Article 5, UNCROC), and educating children about the responsibilities and obligations that their rights give rise to.

This leads us to consider the notion of parental rights as *stewardship rights* (Brennan and Noggle 1997). A stewardship right 'is the right a person has by virtue of being the steward – as opposed to an owner – of someone or something' (p.11). In arriving at the concept of stewardship rights, Brennan and Noggle first develop a theory of moral status that with respect to children is compatible with three claims: 'that children deserve the same moral consideration as adults, that they can nevertheless be treated differently from adults, and that parents have limited authority to direct their upbringing' (p.2). First, they argue that children, because they are persons, are entitled to the same moral consideration as any other person (the Equal Consideration Thesis). Few would argue with this – to do so you would have to try to explain why a child is not a person when it is obvious that children, even at a very young age, possess 'enough features of personhood that they must be counted as persons' (p.23). They then argue that persons can receive equal moral consideration, but nevertheless have differing packages of moral rights and duties (The Unequal Treatment Thesis). 'Children, at least at certain ages, can be legitimately prevented from doing certain things that it would be illegitimate to prevent adults from doing.' (p.3). They base this on strong practical reasoning – that whatever moral status the child has, there are some freedom rights that should not be available to the child because of their limited capacity to act in their own (and other's) best interest:

> No matter what we decide about children's moral status, as a practical matter, few of us are ready to endorse letting children – especially young children – vote, sign important contracts, or have an unrestricted access to firearms, alcohol, tobacco, automobiles, and so on. (Brennan and Noggle 1997, p.4)

According to Gewirth's analysis of human rights (see Chapter 1), children have equal moral status but require active support and scaffolding to develop their capacities to function as fully fledged agents. That is, they require the acquisition of specific sets of cognitive, affective, and behavioural skills and resources to enable them to possess the required freedom and well-being goods, and ultimately participate fully in civic and community life. In order to acquire the necessary capabilities to function as mature agents they need considerable input throughout their childhood and adolescence from parents, teachers, and the community in general.

From a developmental perspective, securely attached infants more confidently explore their environment because they know that their parents will be available if necessary to provide comfort and security. Being able to safely explore the environment the child develops an increasing sense of competence, self-esteem, self-direction (Germain 1991), which contributes to their emerging agency. The family provides the 'emotional cradle' for the child (Berger *et al.* 1996) and the boundaries necessary for the child to grow up safely and eventually make their way in the world. This leads us to Brennan and Noggle's final claim: that parents have limited but significant discretion in the raising of their children (the Limited Parental Rights Thesis).

Parents have the responsibility to care for and nurture their children on a daily basis, and have the right to exercise their own judgment about what is in their children's best interests. This is also difficult to argue against, given the reality that the immaturity of a child requires the presence of a protective adult. Within this context, however, parental rights do have limits:

> A parent's right to make choices involving the child generally gives out at the point at which the child's right not to be harmed is violated ... The fact that parents do have rights means that so long as the child is not being harmed, parental rights are generally not to be infringed merely to provide some marginal benefit for the child. (Brennan and Noggle 1997, p.9)

When a child's human right to personal safety is significantly compromised by parental maltreatment, the parents' moral right to raise the child as they see fit will have to give way because of laws that place limits on those moral rights. An extreme expression of the conflict between familial needs, rights and obligations occurs when parental rights are involuntarily terminated (Haugaard and Avery 2002). The involuntary termination of parental rights is petitioned through the court, and is generally initiated by representatives of the state under child welfare law. However, there have been situations in which the child has sought to terminate its parents' rights when care decisions have been made against the child's wishes. For example, Haugaard and Avery describe a situation in which a social services department returned a 12-year-old boy to his parents care against his wishes. The boy then petitioned the court to have his parents' rights terminated:

> The initial legal issues was whether Gregory, as a minor, had standing to bring a termination petition to court. The trial judge ruled that Gregory did have standing, and the rights of Gregory's birth parents were terminated at trial. However, an appellate court overruled the trial court, stating that Gregory did not have standing to initiate court proceedings... however, the appellate court let stand the ruling terminating Gregory's parents' rights. (Haugaard and Avery 2002, pp.139–140)

These situations are rare, but nevertheless reflect an increasing awareness of children's rights and their capacity to exercise them. Once children begin to take legal action against adults, children will inevitably be seen in a different light: rather than being helpless and dependent, they will be seen as autonomous agents claiming their own rights (Archard 2007).

For the most part, however, negotiating parental and children's rights becomes a question of balance. It is important that the state intervenes in family affairs only when parents are not providing for the basic needs of their children, and even then in graduated and appropriate ways. For example, inappropriate removal of a child from family care could represent a violation of both parental rights and the child's basic human right to goods such as continuity of connection with family and culture. Parents have the right to exercise their discretion in providing for the best interests of their children, but they too must strike a balance between their duty to nurture their children and their obligation to respect their children's rights. The issues in question become human rights issues only when they pertain to the essential freedom and well-being conditions required for agency, or in the case of children, their emerging agency. The United Nations Convention on the Rights of the Child is helpful in identifying specific rights of the child but requires interpretation in particular contexts and may not be readily applied in some situations. As we have seen, in situations where there is a conflict between parental and children's rights/interests/needs, an analysis that involves a consideration of the core values underpinning human rights (freedom and well-being) along with their constituent goods (freedom, subsistence, security, equality and recognition) can be utilized to help practitioners decide upon the correct course of action.

## Adolescent development: 'needs' versus 'deeds' responses to delinquency

During adolescence significant transitions occur as young people complete a long process of maturation and finally acquire autonomy and the capabilities required for fully fledged agency. Existing in between childhood and adulthood, adolescents are often given conflicting messages about what is expected of them. On the one hand they are exhorted to 'grow up and behave like adults' but on the other hand adults often restrict their choices and limit their autonomy. Youth offending can be viewed as one response to this ambiguity. As such it provides a fertile example of a life-course transition which illuminates issues related to moral claims and human rights.

Supporting the best interests of the young offender, protecting their rights, and ensuring accountability for offending provides a tricky mix of imperatives. Historically, state responses to young people who offended against the law assumed their needs were best served by placements in care 'for their own good' (Muncie 2002). Welfare responses such as this, however, were not universally accepted as being the best way to respond to young offenders and, following an English lead, infrastructures for deterrent custodial options were established in most jurisdictions:

> A pattern developed of using boys' and girls' homes to offer training for younger offenders until they reached the minimum school-leaving age. Borstals were developed for the older group of young offenders. (Maxwell, Lo and Wong 2005, p.4)

By the end of the twentieth century, however, it was becoming clear that this mix of welfare and punitive responses was struggling to produce positive results for young people. Institutionalization effectively removed them from the kinds of normal experiences that fostered positive development, and at the same time exposed the young person to the influences of delinquent peers, creating what Maxwell and her colleagues termed 'schools for crime' (p.5). Hence a shift toward more effective solutions saw systems developing a greater emphasis on diversion and deinstitutionalization. In contrast to the welfare approach, the emphasis of the new justice approach was on 'deeds' not just 'needs'.

From a developmental perspective, keeping young people out of the court system for as long as possible can provide them with the time they need to move through transient phases of offending behaviour. According to Butts, Mayer and Ruth (2005) many young people move through difficult developmental transitions and over time acquire adult capacities for reasoning, taking responsibility and making a commitment. They further argue that society has a duty to ensure that young people have access to necessary developmental assets: skills and experiences across the physical, intellectual, emotional and social spectrum.

While countries have generally adopted approaches that are characterized by either a welfare or a justice orientation, in reality, most approaches include elements of both (Archard 2007). It could be argued that a purist welfare response that focuses only on a offender's needs has the potential to undermine the young person's progress towards fully fledged agency and violates their right to due process. In this regard, rights-based discourses have influenced thinking about adolescent accountability and agency:

> the shift to a criminal justice model may also be attributable to a changing perception of children as agents, a change that can be explained in part by the increasing use of a participatory rights discourse in respect of children. (Archard 2007, p.259)

From a developmental perspective it is important that young people who offend are able to engage in increasingly adult-like processes that reinforce accountability and restoration, while at the same time being protected from the full force of the law in recognition of their special status under UNCROC as young offenders with special rights (Article 37, UNCROC). Rights-based youth justice solutions have the capacity to provide social-structural resources that can accommodate a young person's maturing capacity for agency and its concomitant attribute – responsibility, while at the same time recognizing that young people, by virtue of their relative immaturity, have special needs that must also be considered. Reconciling welfare and justice approaches, Archard proposes not only their integration, but also introduces the notion that they are, by necessity, inextricably connected:

> Justice is not sacrificed to welfare. Rather attending to the needs of the child may be what justice requires. It is entirely consistent with the approach that recognizes the child's right to protection, her right to participation in matters that affect her, her welfare and the rights of other parties. (Archard 2007, p.261)

Archard's emphasis here on the rights of other parties brings us to a further consideration with respect to rights in the area of youth justice: the rights of the victims of adolescent crime. This is captured most strongly in the emergence of restorative justice approaches to youth crime.

Roche (2006, p.217) identifies the dimensions of restorative justice as being:

> a particular method for dealing with crime that brings together an offender, his or her victims, and their respective families and friends to discuss the aftermath of an incident, and the steps that can be taken to repair the harm an offender has done.

Community-based strategies combining elements of restorative justice and family decision-making have developed most strongly in Australia and New Zealand. In New Zealand, in particular, a youth justice practice framework has been developed to capture this more holistic response to offending, incorporating elements of restorative justice, the rights of a young person, as well as their needs. We will use this framework to further our discussion of human rights issues related to young offenders and how these interact with practice.

The youth justice framework draws on the research and best practice literature to develop a model based on four strands or perspectives. These strands respectively involve practitioners in responding to issues of justice and accountability, taking a young person focus, being family-led and culturally responsive, and being strengths- and evidence-based. The cultural metaphor used to illustrate the weaving of these perspectives through the phases of the work is that of the 'kete' – a woven basket, representing, in this context, a basket of knowledge about what works best in the complex area of practice.

The *justice and accountability* strand of the framework is focused on the principle of holding young people to account for offending behaviour. It recognizes that youth justice is concerned with the rights and needs of a wide group of stakeholders, including but not restricted to the young people themselves (Connolly 2007b). Restorative justice processes rest at the heart of the justice and accountability perspective, such practices being seen to offer opportunities for offenders to gain an understanding of the harm caused by their offending, and for reaching agreement on how best to make amends (Walgrave 2004). The involvement of the victim(s) is the key to this process and research indicates the need to ensure that the victim is well prepared for the meeting and is responded to respectfully throughout the process (Maxwell *et al.* 2004).

The second strand of the framework, the *young person focused* perspective, resonates with a human rights-based orientation as it is respectful of the young person's agency and human dignity. UNCROC is central to this, and in particular its underpinning theme relating to the right of young people to special care and the right to provision, protection and participation. The 'Beijing Rules' further dictate that young people who offend should also have their own needs met, that age and vulnerability should be mitigating factors, and that attention

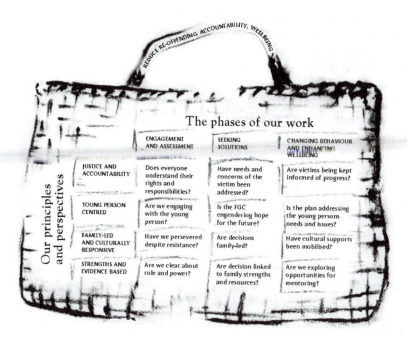

*Figure 4.1 The New Zealand Youth Justice Practice Framework (Connolly 2007, p.20). Reproduced with kind permission of Social Work Now*

should be paid to the rights of the young person (Office of the High Commissioner for Human Rights 1985).

Youth justice systems that respond to the young person's specific needs, including their developmental needs, are more likely to have positive outcomes in the longer term. As noted above, diverting young people from court systems is more likely to result in them growing out of their offending, rather than growing into it (Doolan 1988). Enhancing well-being for young offenders includes promoting reintegrative and rehabilitative options for young people, including the provision of appropriate mental health services and making arrangements for education, training or employment (Maxwell *et al.* 2004).

The third strand of the framework reinforces the need for practice to be *family-led and culturally responsive*. Emphasis on collective responsibility for young people and the centrality of the family, a view which is fully supported in the preamble of UNCROC, is a key practice principle in New Zealand. Youth accountability is fostered in the context of family support and the strengthening of the family. In this regard New Zealand's youth justice legislation, through the mechanism of the Family Group Conference, encourages family-centred practice where family, including extended family and kin networks, are seen as practice partners (for an extended discussion of New Zealand's youth justice system including the practice of Family Group Conferencing see Morris and Maxwell 2001).

The final strand of the framework focuses on the importance of *strengths-and evidence-based* practice. In this strand the framework draws together the research that supports good outcomes for young people and then weaves it, together with the other three strands, through the phases of the youth justice process (for an extended discussion of the mechanisms used to accomplish this, see Connolly 2007b).

New Zealand's approach to youth justice uses the mechanism of its youth justice practice framework to integrate needs and rights-based approaches within the context of restorative justice practice. Other countries use similar models and approaches which aim to bridge the gap between welfare and justice orientations. We believe that holistic approaches that respond to both the developmental needs of the young person and their rights, as well as the rights of victims of offending, are more likely to result in good outcomes in the longer term.

We now turn to our final example of a family life-course transition that illuminates issues of moral claims, responsibilities and human rights: grandparents who become 'parents' to their grandchildren.

## Grandparents parenting: continued obligations versus the right to relax

From a life-course perspective the middle years, from 45 to 65, are marked by a number of transitions, variously individual and familial. For many individuals in this age bracket, children have grown up and they now enjoy freedom from the responsibilities associated with child rearing. For those more fortunate, financial security can strengthen this sense of freedom to enjoy grandparenthood, strengthen familial relationships, and start thinking about their own personal goals and interests. There is a sense in which they may rightly feel they have a moral right, at least, to relax a little.

It is true, however, that the changing demographics of aging populations in developed countries have introduced changes in kinship structures and, indeed, the nature of familial relationships within those structures (Grundy and Henretta 2006). Research has noted that in the UK, 80 per cent of 20-year-old people have living grandparents, and that most adults are part of family groups consisting of three living generations (Grundy, Murphy and Shelton 1999).

This is particularly significant when juxtaposed with the emergence of state-supported kinship care, and in particular, grandparents assuming the care of their grandchildren. Although practised in some societies for centuries, kinship care is a relatively new phenomenon within systems of child welfare. In the past two decades kinship care – and in this context we are referring to the practice of extended family members looking after children in state care – has become an internationally favoured system for children who are unable to be looked after by their parents. Not only has kinship care emerged as a significant contributor to the range of family foster care services, but there has also been a palpable shift in state preference toward kinship care as the first option when an alternative to parental care is needed (Geen 2000; Gleeson 1999; McFadden 1998). Kinship care is generally seen as being in the child's best interest, and while international comparisons suffer from definitional issues, there would nevertheless appear to be strong support for the practice – between 30 and 40 per cent in most English-speaking countries (Connolly 2007a).

According to the research, however, children coming into kinship care are more likely to have experienced personal health challenges, exhibit higher levels of behavioural or emotional problems, and face their own personal challenges following a history of child abuse and/or neglect. At the same time they are more likely to live with family members who may themselves be experiencing health and mental health challenges, and live in situations of low income and/or poverty (Ehrle and Geen 2002). In a review of the research, Scannapieco (1999) found that women are the most frequent kinship caregivers, with grandmothers providing more than 50 per cent of the care, and aunts providing a further 30 per cent of the kinship placements. More recent research reports similar findings (Broad, Hayes and Rushforth 2001). Most research suggests that kinship carers are more likely to be older than foster caregivers, and more likely to be single parents.

How, then, does the phenomenon of kinship care relate to issues of rights and the responsibilities that may accompany them? Looked at from a life-course perspective, it is clear that there are many kinship caregivers who are meeting the expectations of parenting, as opposed to meeting traditional grandparenting expectations. There are at least two ways of looking at this. First, grandparents may consider it a moral right to be able to look after their grandchildren if they so wish. This constitutes part of their familial rights and responsibilities as a contributing member of their kinship group. This may be more or less reinforced from a cross-cultural perspective (see Chapter 2). Conversely, they may consider that their own needs and, indeed, the contribution that they have already made both to their kinship group and to society more generally, provide them with a moral claim to enjoy the last period of their lives free of the obligations of raising grandchildren as if they were their own children.

In a sense, this brings us back to Beresford's notion of 'meeting their different self-defined needs in the way they, ensured full knowledge, support and choice, prefer' (cited in Smith 2005, p.102). An adult has a right to exercise choice in the restructuring of family relationships, as long as this does not undermine the rights of other family members, particularly children, to basic goods such as care and safety. If an extended family member chooses not to provide care for a child within the family group, it is important that this decision be respected. At the same time, in the context of state-supported kinship care, when a family member partners with the state, it is incumbent on the state to ensure that kinship placements are not disadvantaged by a lack of the three key resources that are provided with non-kinship care placements:

support, training and remuneration. Kinship care reflects a partnership relationship between the family and the state. The kinship carer is providing a placement for a child who would otherwise require a foster placement. The state is reliant on kinship carers to support the state's systems of care for children at risk, and carers have a right to expect to be supported in doing so.

## Conclusions

At the beginning of this chapter we noted that thinking about human development has remained largely separate from discussions about human rights. We have argued, nevertheless, that a rights perspective interacts with human needs, interdependencies, responsibilities and obligations across the life-course in important ways. We think it is important to bring together human development concepts and rights-based ideas at a theoretical level, which then lays a platform for rights-based practice. Influenced by Marks (2005) we have done this by looking at the commonality between the two. Essentially, we have argued that human rights, as protective capsules, provide the environment within which individuals can develop their full potential as effective agents in the world as they traverse various phases of the life course.

We have teased out issues of rights and responsibilities that arise during the life course, and have argued the importance of using a rights perspective when working through these complex human transitions. We will now look at the ways in which the rights of marginalized people have been undermined over time.

*Chapter 5*

# *Losing Rights:*
# *Offenders on the Margins*

The topic of offender rehabilitation is likely to generate intense and sometimes acrimonious debate amongst politicians, researchers, practitioners and members of the public. In our experience such exchanges revolve around two fundamental attitudes toward crime and the individuals who commit crimes: offenders are dismissed as *alien* others, or accepted as *fellow* human beings. According to the first view, offenders are 'moral strangers' who do not merit consideration and therefore their interests are of peripheral concern when imprisoning them. By way of contrast, according to the second position, offenders are still valued human beings and as such deserve the chance to redeem themselves and to live worthwhile and better lives. While they may have inflicted significant harm on other people and deserve punishment for their actions, they do not forfeit their basic dignity as persons. Both sets of attitudes are evident in the various arenas of the correctional system, penetrating to the core of containment and rehabilitation policies (Andrews, Bonta and Wormith 2006; Garland 2001; Ward and Maruna 2007).

Academic interest in this field has been limited, and what work has been undertaken is generally disconnected from traditional human rights scholarship and is theoretically unsophisticated (Finkel and Moghaddam 2005). It appears that the topic of human rights has held little fascination for psychologists. Puzzling, however, is the relative lack of research and theoretical attention paid to *offenders'* rights – moral, social, or legal – despite rapid developments in the field of forensic psychology (Coyle 2003; Lazarus 2006; Lippke 2002). Indeed it could be argued that while rights have been secured for offenders in the area of prison conditions, in the core areas of personal freedoms and social well-being there is a danger that rights are being clawed back by governments concerned with their public image on law and order matters (Hudson 2001; Schone 2001). The fear of being seen as being soft on crime has arguably resulted in the neglect and even violation of offenders' basic moral and human rights. Furthermore, virtually no attention has been paid to the application of a human rights perspective to *practice* with offenders (although see Lewis 2005; McNeill 2006) – that is, the assessment, treatment and monitoring of individuals who have committed crimes. The majority of the work on human rights (or the closely associated construct of values) within the criminal justice system has been undertaken by lawyers, psychiatrists, philosophers, criminologists and policy analysts but not practitioners (e.g. Abramowitz 2005; Carrabine 2006; Hayden 2001; Lazarus 2006; Lewis 2005; Liebling 2004; Morris 2006; Nussbaum 2000, 2006; Valette 2002). This is indeed worrying. We argue that given the enormous amount of attention rightly given to the topic of human rights, and the appreciation of how adherence to human rights and the values they embody should regulate the actions of the state and its citizens, it is time for correctional practitioners to catch up. In our view human rights pervade multiple practice contexts and can potentially provide a fertile moral and therapeutic resource for practitioners working with offenders.

## Human rights and forensic practice

We have seen that human rights are possessed by all human beings, although the degree to which they are held is proportional to each individual's capacity for agency. Therefore it is clear that if offenders have the capacity for agency they ought to be treated with the respect afforded to all agents. It is obvious that offenders' freedom rights are typically curtailed in some respects and their movements, rights to privacy and association are restricted. Incarceration, parole conditions and community-based orders severely limit the realization of some of their rights. However, from a human rights perspective, offenders still possess rights to the well-being goods and some of the freedom goods necessary for their functioning as purposive agents. This would mean that offenders should either be able to access for themselves, or have the state provide, goods such as basic educational resources, medical care, self-esteem, adequate nutrition, leisure activities, healthy living conditions, work opportunities, and psychological and psychiatric services. It is also important to provide as much choice over rehabilitation options and activities as possible within security requirements, as well as just and fair disciplinary procedures with due process. That is, physical, social and psychological human needs must still be met. The state is only justified in restricting certain freedoms in so far as this is necessary for the implementation of offenders' punishment (loss of certain liberties). The five human rights objects identified by Orend (2002) should be guaranteed as a matter of right: personal freedom but with some significant restrictions, material subsistence, personal security, elemental equality and social recognition. In fact, restriction of freedom arguably constitutes the punishment, and the failure to provide the minimum level of well-being goods and residual freedom goods constitutes a violation of offenders' human rights (see Lippke 2002). In a nutshell, offenders retain their human rights despite the fact they have been convicted of crimes, although the ability to exercise some of these rights may be restricted during the period of their correctional sentence. In our view the logic is straightforward: if human rights are those held by all human beings (all things being equal) then offenders by virtue of this fact also possess human rights. As we will see, the implications of this conclusion are significant. But one thing seems painfully obvious: the human rights of offenders are typically not respected and their access to the five classes of human rights objects not secured. The puzzle is why is this so?

In our view the answer to this question is that members of the community, correctional officials and political figures believe that offenders *forfeit* their human rights because of the crimes they have committed (Lippke 2002). That is, through their unlawful actions offenders have placed themselves outside the protection zone of human rights declarations and polices. However, the forfeiture approach is subject to a number of problems. First, if offenders' actions merit the forfeiture of rights then there should be a specified relationship between the type of crimes committed and the rights they forfeit. This is typically not the case with proponents of the forfeiture approach advocating wholesale removal of offenders' human rights (Lippke 2002). This appears to be a rather arbitrary and less than convincing reason to justify such a radical move. Second, even if it is decreed that offenders do forfeit specific rights according to the type of crime they have committed, the thorny issue remains of establishing relevant criteria for guiding the forfeiture process. This is indeed a complex and confusing issue and it is not clear just how long rights should be forfeited, exactly what kinds of rights should be removed, and when it comes to extremely aggressive offences, whether the state should attempt to inflict crippling losses of rights on offenders.

Other positions include the views that: (a) offenders retain their human rights but that they may be overridden if the claims of non-offenders dictate this – even if these claims are less pressing; (b) offenders retain their rights but the state has no obligation to facilitate their exercise; and (c) the process of rehabilitation demands that the rights of offenders must be secondary to the rights of society to, for example, make treatment compulsory. Some authors argue that risk management concerns should always override the promotion of the human rights goods of offenders (e.g. Andrews and Bonta 2003). We agree with Lippke (2002) that all of these positions are vulnerable to strong objections and that human rights are such that curtailment should only occur when necessary for legitimate security reasons or for the humane and efficient running of prisons and community correctional services. It is apparent that this would only justify restricting the exercise of certain freedom rights and very few (if any) well-being rights. In other words, the state should make provision for offenders to access the same goods necessary for a life of dignity even when their liberty rights have been curtailed. Being able to exercise one's rights to freedom and well-being goods is necessary for agency attempts and without them offenders will be unable to advance their conception of a good life or to exercise their judgment concerning what is in their interests and what is not. It goes without saying that they must also respect the rights of others in the process.

The issue of offenders' rights is closely linked to the aims and justification of punishment (Lippke 2002; Matravers 2000). If the aim of punishment is to *deter* individuals from committing further offences then it seems obvious that depriving them of their human rights is only likely to result in feelings of resentment. Human rights function to protect the dignity and self-esteem of human beings, and a life without dignity is arguably barely a human life at all. If the aim is to encourage offenders to appreciate the rights and interests of their victims, then it seems counterproductive to violate their own rights and interests in order to achieve this goal. In fact, we argue that there are dangers in this as the release of disaffected individuals into the community whose criminal dispositions have not altered at all, and may even have been strengthened, is likely to pose a greater threat. If the aim of punishment is *retribution*, to correct the moral balance of the community, stripping offenders of their human rights is somewhat contradictory. This is because the point of retribution is to encourage individuals to appreciate the harm they have done and this presupposes that they are moral agents. An individual without human rights is someone without moral status, and therefore beyond the reach of retributive policies (Lippke 2002). Finally, if the aim of punishment is to *rehabilitate* offenders, then as stated above, subjecting them to lives without dignity and moral status will probably only increase their tendency to reoffend rather than reintegrate into the community.

## Human rights, offenders, and the criminal justice system

The application of the concept of human rights to the criminal justice system needs to occur at all three levels outlined in Chapter 1. Starting from the most concrete level, countries legally bound by the UDHR, the two associated covenants, and other treaties concerning the rights of prisoners should ensure that the management of offenders complies with their requirements (see Coyle 2002). This is likely to be reflected in specific polices regulating the running of prisons and community correctional services, such as disciplinary procedures, home leave entitlements, access to medical care, work opportunities, adequate living conditions, educational resources and so on. For example, the International Covenant on Civil and Political Rights, Article 10, states that 'All persons deprived of their liberty shall be treated with humanity and with respect for the inherent dignity of the human person' (cited in Coyle 2002).

With respect to the core human rights values of freedom and well-being, and their elaboration into the five component objects of freedom, subsistence, security, equality, and social recognition, it is clear that the responsibilities here are moral rather then legal. What we mean by this claim is that the core values, the component objects, and their justifying theory provide practitioners with a rich resource for reflecting on ethical aspects of their practice. The problem with lists such as the UDHR is that they tend to be quite narrow and therefore are hard to apply in day-to-day therapeutic work with offenders. Understanding that human rights function to protect the agency of individuals, and therefore their dignity, helps practitioners evaluate all aspects of their work and to consider the ethical implications of rehabilitation programmes. Therefore, in our view, the two core values of freedom and well-being and their component objects ought to be a primary focus of practice decision-making. We will discuss the implications of applying a human rights perspective in some detail later in the chapter.

Despite the fact that many countries have committed themselves to upholding offenders' human rights they do not appear high up in the lists of policy priorities of many states. For example, Schone (2001) has recently argued that the impact of the European Convention on Human Rights on prisoners has been quite limited and there are signs that earlier gains in areas such as the right to open communication with lawyers have been clawed back. In addition, the right to work and the right to due process with regard to disciplinary matters while in prison are often restricted in the interests of prison security. Indeed, according to Hudson (2001) and Lippke (2002) current discourse in criminal justice and crime prevention has excessively privileged risk considerations over offenders' rights (see below). Certainly the excellent work by theorists, researchers, and policy makers such as Andrew Coyle (2002, 2003) has seen strong initiatives to ensure that prisons comply with human rights conventions. In particular, Coyle argues that having a human rights orientation to prison administration is simply good management and will result in more efficient as well as more ethical institutions. However, we suggest that unpacking the notion of human rights in terms of the core values, as applied to corrections, is required to justify rationally and convincingly the stipulations outlined in human rights documents. Furthermore, understanding the nature of human rights and their justification will assist practitioners in making ethical decisions in situations not covered by treaties and in constructing and implementing new assessment procedures and treatment programmes.

A final general point is that it is important to grasp that offenders can be human rights-violators, duty-bearers, and also human rights-holders all at the same time. The fact that offenders have often violated the human rights of their victims is reflected in their punishment and loss of liberty. It is possible to see rehabilitation as centrally concerned with all three rights issues. Providing individuals with the core capabilities ('virtues' in moral language) that undergird agency, freedom and well-being should both promote their capacity to achieve good lives and also reduce their risk of damaging the good lives of others (Ward and Gannon 2006; Ward and Maruna 2007; Ward and Stewart 2003). Furthermore, modules such as empathy training, cognitive skills, understanding the offence process, social skills, intimacy training, and emotional regulation are directly concerned with facilitating offenders' abilities to infer accurately, respond to, and appreciate the experiences and needs of others. The acquisition of the general skills to improve the quality of their own lives will necessarily involve recognition of the freedom and well-being rights of other people.

## General practice implications

In terms of forensic psychology practice, Perlin (2005) indicates that the literature is 'strangely silent' on whether it meets human rights standards even though forensic psychologists have at least 60 discrete opportunities to come in contact with the criminal justice system (from testifying in court about the defendant's cognitive capacity to providing rehabilitation in correction facilities). Perlin argues that there is a significant 'disconnect' between forensic psychology practice and human rights norms, and the lack of attention to this is disturbing. Human rights violations arise in the context of abusive power dynamics, the vulnerability of the offender, blurred role boundaries, and a lack of respect for the offending individual's rights and dignity.

What are the general practice implications of the above analysis of human rights for correctional practitioners such as psychologists, social workers and other workers? We propose that the implications are diverse and span the whole range of practice tasks from assessment to treatment to monitoring. In addition, the types of duties that practitioners have will vary depending upon the level of analysis undertaken. At the most general level the duty of care is essentially a moral or ethical one of ensuring that the activities undertaken with offenders respect their rights to freedom and well-being. In some contexts this will mean providing basic or core goods (e.g. information) while in others it may be listening carefully to what individuals want from their contact with the service provided. At the more specific level it is making sure that the policies applied to and the procedures undertaken with individuals do not violate the relevant human rights treaties and the human rights legislation of the state. In the absence of such legal requirements we argue that all workers are morally obliged to act to ensure that their clients' basic human rights to freedom and well-being are respected. Moreover, we assert that it is of paramount importance that practitioners facilitate the provision of basic human rights goods for offenders. In this chapter our focus is on offenders sentenced to corrections (to prison, parole, or a community order). We will spell out in reasonable detail below the various obligations that the concept of human rights imposes upon practitioners.

In terms of offender rehabilitation, a human rights framework resonates strongly with strengths-based approaches to offender rehabilitation such as the Good Lives Model (Ward and Brown 2004; Ward and Gannon 2006; Ward and Maruna 2007). The Good Lives Model (GLM) is a theory of rehabilitation that endorses the viewpoint that offenders are essentially human beings with similar needs and aspirations to non-offending members of the community and as such should be treated with the basic respect that such status implies. The model is based around two core therapeutic goals: to promote human rights goods (for example, satisfactory relationships or meaningful employment) and to reduce risk. The model aims to: (a) focus on utilizing the individual offender's primary goods (e.g. mastery or relatedness goods) and cherished values in the design of intervention programmes, and (b) equip an offender with the capabilities necessary to implement a better life plan founded on these values. The model is an approach based on the pursuit of a better life – a way of living that is constructed around important values, and concrete means of realizing one's goals in a certain environment (Maruna 2001; Ward and Maruna 2007). A human rights perspective can be conceptualized as the ethical heart of a strengths-based approach such as the GLM, and by virtue of its emphasis on rights and duties can deal with the risk management aspect of rehabilitation alongside the promotion of offenders' personal (and socially acceptable) goals.

In terms of offenders and the criminal justice system, the impact of the legal system also needs to be considered within a human rights framework. If the law is psychologically orientated, as it ought to be, then it will promote well-being, 'do good' and assist the state to give practical meaning to the aspirations of the community (Melton 1992). Therapeutic Jurisprudence is a legal theory that uses psychological knowledge to determine ways in which the law can enhance well-being for those individuals who experience it (including both victims and offenders). Therapeutic Jurisprudence has a particular focus on human rights.[1] Furthermore, Therapeutic Jurisprudence allows an intersection between forensic psychology and human rights (Perlin 2005). In this context, psycholegal soft spots are anticipated areas where legal procedures may be anti-therapeutic and so will result in reduced well-being (Stolle *et al.* 2000). For example, Birgden and Ward (2003) consider denial of parole to treated sex offenders as a potential psycholegal soft spot – treated offenders detained unnecessarily in prison will lose the motivation to sustain changes in their lives. In particular, Therapeutic Jurisprudence considers the impact of substantive law, legal procedures, and the role of legal actors (Wexler 1990). For the purposes of this chapter, Therapeutic Jurisprudence is particularly useful when considering the therapeutic role of correctional practitioners in the assessment, treatment, and monitoring of offenders (Birgden 2004). Practices that do not align with human rights standards are potential psycholegal soft spots that can result in reduced well-being.

A human rights perspective has significant implications for offender rehabilitation, and a crucial task is to ensure that the assessment, treatment and monitoring models underpinning practice are consistent with the core human rights values of freedom and well-being. An ethical problem with some treatment models is that their primary concern is with reducing risk rather than offender welfare (Ward and Maruna 2007). While it is true that risk

1    See www.therapeuticjurisprudence.com.

management models stipulate that interventions should be implemented in an ethical and humane way, the interests of offenders are typically overridden in principle by the concern for community protection. This tendency to disregard the well-being of offenders can result in a rather cavalier dismissal of their needs and aspirations. Therapeutic initiatives need to be based on respect for offenders' agency and human dignity.

## Human rights and assessment

There are three major assessment issues that warrant commenting on in our discussion.[2] These are: (a) ensuring that the assessment is conducted in a respectful, transparent and competent manner; (b) being clear about the intrusion of our own social and moral values into the assessment process; and (c) ensuring that the rights of the offender are not automatically assumed to carry less weight than those of other members of the community. We will briefly discuss each of these issues in turn.

First, it is evident that respecting human rights imposes significant duties on practitioners concerning the way they go about the assessment process with offenders. The implications of forensic assessment procedures in general, and risk assessment in particular, are such that care must be taken when gathering information about an individual's criminogenic needs (offender attributes that contribute to criminal behaviour) and other problems. If practitioners are using tools, they have an obligation always to use them appropriately, ensure they are trained in their administration, and most importantly, ensure that the assessment process culminates in a formulation that is based around the individual's unique features alongside those they share with other similar offenders. This is particularly salient in risk assessment when the absence of data unique to an offender's personal circumstances can result in poor estimates of risk level (Vess 2005). Drawing upon the concept of human rights (core values and objects) can help practitioners to make sure that the information they have gathered is of the highest quality possible and that any decision that might restrict the offender's freedom, and possibly well-being, is rationally justified. The trouble with existing codes of ethics is that because they are essentially collections of rules and specific duties little attention is paid to a justifying theory, and therefore they lack an appreciation of how values such as freedom and well-being are related to human dignity. Approaching assessment through a human rights lens facilitates a respectful and transparent assessment process and restricts the degree to which practitioners might engage in sloppy practice (by viewing offenders as agents of harm rather than as rights-holders). A positive spin-off from approaching offenders in a respectful manner is that there is likely to be an

---

2    See Ward and Vess (2006) for an extensive treatment of the ethical issues associated with assessment.

improvement in the quality of the assessment data and therefore better formulated decisions will result. For example, a collaborative approach involves a genuine commitment by the practitioner to work transparently and respectfully with the offender, and to emphasize that the offender's best interests are to be served by the assessment process. Potential issues of risk and need are transparently presented to the client as areas for collaborative investigation. Results of risk assessment procedures and psychometric testing are discussed and the client is invited to collaborate in drawing conclusions from them. When the collaborative risk assessment process is introduced as a conscious strategy the early research indicators are that the relationship between practitioner and offender is greatly improved, with a subsequent positive effect on motivation and retention in treatment (Mann and Shingler 2006).

Second, it is clear that some of the concepts utilized in assessment, particularly risk assessment, are strongly influenced by the anxieties and interests of the community. For example, with respect to risk assessment, it is acknowledged that the construction of risk categories reflects non-scientific concerns such as the community's perceived degree of tolerance for reoffending (Denny 2005; Monahan and Steadman 1996). The issue at stake here is that decisions concerning how many risk categories there are and what criminal justice interventions they entail depends in part on the balance communities draw between offender freedoms and risks to its citizens. The interface between the science and social meaning of risk assessment is nicely expressed by John Monahan and Henry Steadman (1996, p.935):

> The political issue of who decides the number of risk categories and the category labels and the prescriptions for information-gathering and risk management that accompany each category must also be confronted. In light of legitimate concerns…that categorical risk assessment conflates scientific questions (i.e. probability estimates) with questions of social values (i.e. the choice of cut-off scores distinguishing categories), we believe that it is essential that the ultimate users of risk communications about violence (e.g. judges and other policymakers) be centrally involved from the beginning in developing any categorical risk communication scheme.

There is no agreed meaning of categories such as 'low', 'medium', or 'high' risk and it is likely that political and social agendas strongly influence the process of risk assessment and the construction of the measures themselves, at least to some degree. Furthermore, Miller and Morris (1988) argue that unacceptable levels of risk are social, political or policy determinations rather than psychological, empirical or statistical ones; the practitioner offers a clinical opinion about the *probability* of risk and the court decides on the *unacceptability* of risk. This means that practitioners should be cognizant of the ethical issues associated with assessment and the relevance of human rights. The various positions and assumptions should be explicitly stated and publicly debated, not smuggled in under the auspices of science.

Third, a related point is that the human rights of offenders should not be *automatically* assumed to carry less weight than those of other members of the community. This is a sensitive and complex matter that is not easy to discuss or to factor into the assessment, treatment and monitoring of offenders. The powerful nature of human rights discourse, and the fact that all human beings are assumed to be both rights-holders and duty-bearers, places practitioners in the eye of a perfect ethical storm. There are potent political, ethical and professional forces pressing upon the integrity of individuals working with offenders, forces that frequently push in opposing directions. The pressure is to discount the rights of offenders and to think of them as risk-bearers rather than human beings with inherent dignity and basic rights to freedom and well-being that all individuals possess. If the community is risk averse in nature it may be reluctant to place any importance on the rights of offenders. In this situation all that may matter is whether the streets are safe and the offenders are securely quarantined away from other people (Ward and Maruna 2007). A good example of the tendency to override offender rights can be found in American sexually violent predator laws (Petrunik 2003; Vess 2005). According to Vess (2005, p.360), the social environment associated with such laws is strongly oriented toward community protection:

> In contrast to the justice model, the community protection approach is less concerned about due process, the proportionality of punishment to the crime, and the protection of offenders' liberty or privacy rights. In contrast to the forensic–clinical model, it is less concerned about treatment or rehabilitation of offenders intended to reduce recidivism or facilitate community reintegration. The primary goal of the community protection model is the incapacitation of sexual offenders for the sake of public safety.

We are proposing that the rights of offenders should always be acknowledged and weighted equally in the assessment process. The aim should be to formulate an intervention plan that respects the offender's agency and their personal preferences in relation to their significant projects and plans. It is important to stress that this does not mean that whatever an offender wants will trump the interests of others; the human rights of an offender entails an obligation by the state as long as the holder does not infringe the rights of others. Thus any intervention plan has to respect the human rights of other people without losing sight of the fact that it is the offender's life that is of concern. We would also like to note that it may be perfectly legitimate to place onerous parole conditions on some individuals because of the extreme level of risk they pose to the community. However, such determinations should always proceed from a thorough and ethical assessment process in which the human rights of offenders are carefully considered and balanced against their propensity to harm others.

# Human rights and treatment

What are the human rights implications for offender rehabilitation? As a first comment, we propose that all three layers noted earlier in the description of the Good Life Model are applicable. To start with, practitioners need to ensure that the selection, implementation and assessment phases of intervention are in accord with the relevant human rights declarations, covenants and state laws (Churchill 2006; Donnelly 2003; Li 2006; Orend 2002). Compliance with human rights treaties requires ensuring that there are no discriminatory practices evident in the rehabilitation process, for example, excluding individuals from programmes on the basis of race, class, age or gender. In addition, offenders should be treated with dignity and their agency respected. They should only suffer restrictions of freedom that are rationally justified, and they should have access to the basic goods of well-being such as education, self-esteem, support, mental and medical resources, and so on. We argue that such an approach is a minimum standard in correctional service delivery.

Looking at the treatment process more directly, we suggest that human rights should be factored in two major ways: (a) in the programme delivery and (b) in the programme design and content.

First, a human rights perspective makes its easier for practitioners to develop strong collaborative relationships with offenders, therefore supporting the likelihood of better outcomes. As we noted in Chapter 1, human rights can be understood as protective capsules that defend vital aspects of human functioning such as freedom and well-being. Human rights represent entitlements to the necessary conditions of effective action so that individuals can successfully pursue and implement their personal projects. The dignity inherent in engaging in effective action and realizing personal projects means that offenders will respond well to practitioners who acknowledge their right to make important decisions for themselves and their value as human beings. Indeed there is evidence that working collaboratively with offenders in developing treatment goals results in a stronger therapeutic alliance (Mann and Shingler 2001). Furthermore, evidence from offender research indicates that therapist features such as displays of empathy and warmth, as well as encouragement and rewards for progress, facilitate the change process in sex offenders (Marshall *et al.* 2003). Thus, by virtue of an emphasis on the rights of individuals to freedom (qualified of course), and the degree of well-being necessary to act effectively, adherence to human rights norms is likely to facilitate the change process and to result in higher levels of cooperation and motivation on the part of offenders.

Mandatory, coerced or compulsory treatment is becoming an increasingly popular policy initiative, particularly for sex offenders. In a Therapeutic Jurisprudence analysis of sex offender treatment, Glaser (2003) states that such an approach overrides traditional ethical guidelines and so is not in the best interest of the offender. Glaser warns that 'this sort of control comes perilously close to brainwashing, with the aversive stimulus being the threat of further punishment if the offender does not comply' (p.146). While sex offenders may superficially participate, they will do so without the commitment and motivation required for successful treatment (Winick 1998). Only those individuals who require rehabilitation should be offered treatment and ideally the offender should consent to participate in rehabilitation. The key issue from a human rights perspective is to balance the rights of the offender with those of the community in an explicit and reasoned way. In considering rehabilitation options, the seriousness of the offence should be considered. The seriousness of the offence is pertinent as the legal consequences need to be morally justified. We suggest that if the individual is low risk and has committed a less serious offence, no treatment should be required. If the individual is considered low risk but has committed a serious offence, a management plan that is least intrusive of the individual's autonomy may be required to meet community's expectations. If the individual is considered moderate or high risk and has committed a less serious offence, voluntary treatment should be offered, and informed refusal to participate should be respected. If the individual is considered moderate or high risk and has committed a serious offence, voluntary treatment should be offered. If the individual provides an informed refusal to participate then his or her autonomy should be overridden in the interests of community protection and participation in rehabilitation legally required (i.e. coerced treatment), even if it has less chance of a successful outcome.

The second intervention issue relates to the design and content of the various modules offered to individuals within the criminal justice system. We propose that interventions should seek to strengthen and equip offenders with the capabilities needed to exercise their freedom and well-being rights depending upon the resources available to agencies. The state has a duty to ensure that its citizens have the levels of freedom and well-being essential to act effectively if the individuals are unable to provide these conditions for themselves. The basic components underlying freedom, such as the capacity to form and make judgments, the ability to problem solve, reasonable physical and mental heath, education and so on are the kinds of goods that are presupposed by effective action. Individuals cannot be expected to acquire these goods entirely on their own. In the case of offenders, histories of severe neglect, abuse, and inadequate socialization often mean that they are ill-equipped to achieve important goals in socially acceptable ways. The lack of the fundamental capabilities needed to function adequately in the community essentially hinders individuals and makes it more likely that they will experience a range of psychological and social problems. Correctional practitioners are employees of the state and are therefore authorized to carry out its functions and to discharge its human rights duties to offenders. It follows then that practitioners have a duty when working with offenders to make sure that their human rights are acknowledged and that any decisions taken that impact on their day-to-day lives (and their futures) are entirely consistent with the duties that practitioners bear with respect to the rights of the offenders.

The human rights objects of personal freedom, material subsistence, personal security, elemental equality and social recognition should guide both the content of specific modules and the process of intervention. The provision of human goods should enable workers to respect basic human rights and also reduce risk (i.e. respect the rights of others). This is an advantage of strengths-based approaches such as the Good Life Model (Ward and Maruna 2007).

It is arguable that the various modules currently offered to offenders can indeed help them to acquire the capabilities necessary to exercise their human rights and therefore to function as purposive agents. These modules are likely to help offenders both acknowledge the rights of others and their value as human beings, as well as enable them to pursue their own personal projects in socially acceptable ways. Thus a human rights perspective provides practitioners with an ethical framework which is both prudentially and morally grounded, that will enable them to select the therapy skills required and to deliver them in ways that are responsive to the offender's unique issues and needs. For example, the five human rights objects could be connected to general offender interventions in the following ways.

- *Personal Freedom.* In psychological terms, offenders lacking the capabilities required to achieve the good of personal freedom would be described as poor problem-solvers, lacking adequate self-regulation, and having poor insight or reflectiveness. Treatment modules such as problem-solving, emotional and self-regulation work, and cognitive skills training will enable offenders to make progress in overcoming these limitations and in general make better decisions. Furthermore, adopting a collaborative approach to treatment will aid therapists to surmount suspiciousness and distrust on the part of offenders.

- *Material Subsistence.* From a treatment perspective, the actual physical living and therapy environment of offenders is something that should be explicitly considered. Furthermore, it is obligatory for clinicians to ensure that each offender receives a competent and comprehensive psychiatric and psychological screening so that any mental health disorders are identified and appropriately treated. Undetected psychological or psychiatric disorders could corrode offenders' abilities to function in prison and in the community, handicapping their chances of meeting their basic needs. Relevant therapy modules will include those on stress management, emotional regulation, adaptive living skills or instrumental social skills, and mental health issues. In addition to this, professionals should take care to ensure that released offenders or those serving community orders are provided with humane and helpful living conditions for reintegration back into society. This will also ensure that these offenders are in the best possible environment to rebuild meaningful, offence-free lives.

- *Personal Security.* Therapy modules and aspects of treatment that are expected to help individuals achieve this human rights object are the provision of group rules, emotional skills acquisition, conflict resolution training, relapse prevention, and social skills and intimacy work. Learning how to resolve conflicts, create and maintain relationships, and reliably detect and control problematic emotional states should assist offenders to resolve interpersonal conflicts and also to detect possible risky situations.

- *Elemental Equality.* From a treatment perspective the therapeutic factors of group process, group rules, self-esteem work, empathy training, cognitive restructuring, social skills, and intimacy work should all contribute offenders' ability to secure this good. In addition, the offender's right to freedom from hostile and discriminatory practices is paramount, and practitioners need to guard against overt and covert prejudices that may disadvantage offenders while in prison and/or the subject of community corrections. Examples of such discriminatory practices would be assuming that because they are offenders they cannot be trusted, refusing to give positive reinforcement for treatment gains, denying them opportunities to discuss certain topics, ignoring their own personal and victimization issues and so on.

- *Social Recognition.* From a therapeutic point of view, treatment strategies and modules such as self-esteem interventions, mood regulation, empathy training, collaborative assessment, setting treatment goals, relapse prevention, and social skills training are expected to increase the chances that a person can achieve this human right good. In addition, adopting a humanistic, strengths-based approach throughout treatment should facilitate the sense that offenders are not alien others but fellow travellers: human beings who have committed significant wrongs but who are worthy of redemption and re-entry into the community.

## Conclusions

Human rights spell out the basic conditions required for a life of minimal dignity, a life that is recognizably human. The realization of rights to freedom, security, equality, social recognition and subsistence allows the individual the means of acquiring the basic goods necessary to advance their own conception of a good life. It is through the advancement of personal projects that people obtain a sense of meaning and identity and stamp their individuality upon the fabric of the world. Human rights are unique in that they are multifaceted and interface with multiple disciplines and their discourses: political theory and science, sociology, law, philosophy, psychology, biology, cultural studies and anthropology to name but a few. Therapeutic Jurisprudence provides a useful platform for interdisciplinary discourse on human rights matters. Another striking feature is the way the concept of human rights fuses the normative and descriptive aspects of living together: the rights human beings hold are a reflection of their intrinsic dignity and the conditions required increase their levels of well-being.

Our aim in this chapter has been to apply a human rights perspective, in association with a justifying theory and a set of goods, to the correctional arena. We are conscious of having only scratched the surface of the implications of human rights for correctional services and the criminal justice system and there is surely more work to be done in teasing out the implications for research, policy and practice. But what is stunningly clear is that as human agents and practitioners our responsibilities are both to promote the goods of offenders and to reduce risk of harm to vulnerable people. Offenders as human rights-holders and duty-bearers need our help to learn how to advance their own lives in ways that are personally meaningful and socially responsible. We need to give them the space they require to do this, to respect their human rights while demanding that they also learn to respect other people's human rights. Rights and duties can provide the ethical foundations of a liberal and flourishing community and a fairer and more humane criminal justice system.

## Chapter 6

# Claiming Rights:
# Disability and Human Rights

If there is one group which has historically been denied the dignity and value attached to the status of being human it would have to be people with intellectual disabilities (Griffiths *et al.* 2003; Herr, Gostin and Koh 2003). It seems as if the life of an individual with an intellectual disability has been viewed as less valuable than the life of a non-disabled person, lacking in fundamental equality and moral status (Stratford 1991). The tendency to downgrade the value of people with intellectual disability and subject them to gross injustices has been well captured by Griffiths *et al.* (2003):

> Historically, persons with intellectual disabilities have been denied the right to live in the community, marry, procreate, work, receive an education, and, in some cases, to receive life-saving medical treatment. They have been subjected to incarceration, sterilization, overmedication, and cruel or unusual punishment. (pp.25–26)

In this chapter we examine the application of human rights to people with intellectual disabilities. First, we will briefly consider the nature of disability in general (including physical disability), distinguishing between individually focused and social approaches to understanding disability. Second, we will define intellectual disability and then discuss different viewpoints on policy and practice revolving around needs and more recently rights. Third, we will directly apply our model of human rights to people with an intellectual disability and argue that it has the resources to bridge the perceived gap between rights and needs and to offer practitioners ethically defensible intervention guidance. We supplement this abstract analysis with two case examples. Finally we conclude with some reflections on the future of a human rights viewpoint in the arena of intellectual disability.

## The nature of intellectual disability
### What is disability?
Disability has been traditionally defined as 'an inability or limitation in performing roles and tasks expected of someone within a social environment'

(Nagi 1979). An important distinction in disability theory and research is that between the condition of *impairment* and the experience of *disability* (Shakespeare 2006). Impairment refers to dysfunction in the mechanisms comprising the psychological (e.g. cognitive, emotional, behavioural) or biological systems (e.g. sensory, motor) of human beings and it can be assessed using objective measures. Disability refers to the impact of impairment on an individual's ability to negotiate effectively the social world and it reflects the difficulties people with impairment experience in being socially accepted.

Medical approaches have traditionally tended to define disability in terms of individual impairment and focused clinical attention on helping people deal with their limitations and acquire compensatory skills to alleviate their degree of suffering. On the other hand, social approaches to disability have argued that the experience of disability is essentially a reflection of the existence of social obstacles and that if society were organized differently (e.g. adjustments made to buildings, aids provided for those with sensory impairments, etc.) then many people would be able to manage their lives quite successfully without experiencing constant frustration and discrimination. The degree to which disability is claimed to be caused by social conditions rather than being a product of psychological and/or physical impairment is well expressed in the following quote from the Union of the Physically Impaired Against Segregation:

> In our view, it is society which disables physically impaired people. Disability is something imposed on top of our impairments, by the way we are unnecessarily isolated and excluded from full participation in society. Disabled people are therefore an oppressed group in society. (UPIAS 1976, p.3)

Thus, according to the individual or medical disability perspective, to help people with disabilities it is imperative to correct the deficits by way of services provided by professionals and rehabilitation workers. Furthermore, disability is viewed as a problem that requires people to accommodate to their limitations – with additional supports and treatment provided by experts to help reduce their level of dysfunction. From the perspective of social approaches to understanding disability, effective interventions ought to 'remove barriers, create access through accommodation and universal design, promote health and wellness and health' (Brown 2001, p.157). Disability is viewed as a socio-environmental issue and disabled people are considered to be consumers or citizens who ought to be empowered to make their own decisions and be allowed to participate actively in all policy, research and practice matters that directly concern them (Brown 2001).

There is in fact a family of social approaches to disability, all sharing a common view that many of the problems that people with disabilities face are the result of social obstacles and discriminatory practices, rather than the impairments themselves (Shakespeare 2006). While sympathetic to the laudable aims of groups espousing radical social approaches to disability, Shakespeare cautions that impairments are real and cause discomfort and suffering independently of the social causes of disability-related difficulties. In order to incorporate the dynamic and complex nature of disability Shakespeare (2006) favours a more inclusive definition:

> The experience of a disabled person results from the relationship between factors intrinsic to the individual, and extrinsic factors arising from the wider context in which she finds herself. Among the intrinsic factors are issues such as: the nature and severity of her impairment, her own attitudes to it, her own personal qualities and abilities, and her personality. Among the contextual factors are: the attitudes and reactions of others, the extent to which the environment is enabling or disabling, and wider cultural, social and economic issues relevant to disability in that society. (pp.55–56)

An important policy implication following from Shakespeare's definition is that interventions designed to improve the quality of life for disabled persons will need to be multidimensional and contextual. The ability of disabled people to live according to their own conception of a 'good life' is dependent on the broader society acknowledging the social obstacles that currently exist as well as the adverse impact of personal psychological and physical impairments on day-to-day functioning. This is likely to require some degree of redistribution of economic and social resources to offset the disadvantages of both the natural and social lottery (i.e. genetic conditions, early poverty, neglect, stigmatization and so on). Thus constructing 'a level playing field is not enough: redistribution is required to promote true social inclusion' (Shakespeare 2006, p.67). From a practice viewpoint, it is imperative that workers appreciate that the needs of people with disabilities are diverse and that they can be met by the social networks and personal systems in which the individuals are embedded. The ability of individuals to exercise agency and seek to establish a lifestyle reflecting their interests is dependent upon the support of other people.

## Intellectual disability

Before we discuss the definition of intellectual disability it is important to note that there have been, and continue to be, disputes over the labels used to refer to this phenomenon. Terms such as *cretin, feeble-minded, imbecile, intellectually handicapped, mentally retarded* and *intellectually disabled* have been utilized at one time or another to denote individuals with significant developmentally acquired cognitive and adaptive limitations (Bray 2003). In this chapter we will use the terms *intellectual disability* in line with current thinking (Bray 2003; Herr *et al.* 2003; Shakespeare 2006). It is important to note that intellectual disability is a type of disability constituted by significant cognitive and adaptive deficiencies acquired during the developmental period.

As stated above, a major change in the disability arena has been a movement away from viewing intellectual disability purely in terms of individual psychological or physical dysfunction (i.e. as a pathological trait of an individual) to a more interactive conceptualization. According to this dynamic perspective, intellectual disability is an expression of the relationship between a person with impaired cognitive and adaptive skills and their social and physical environment. In addition, there is a stress on participation and social inclusiveness with activists arguing that people with an intellectual disability should be regarded as citizens rather than simply clients (Bradley 1994). As a consequence of this emphasis on the social status of persons with disability it is recommended that services are organized through a suite of supports tailored for individuals and responsive to their unique needs. A further suggestion is that networks of formal and informal supports are created so that the person with an intellectual disability is the 'subject' rather than merely an 'object' of intervention (Bradley 1994). Thus within the new, more inclusive conceptualization of intellectual disability, the focus is on the individual and their perceived need for *supports* rather than the frequently depersonalized and stereotypical views of what people with an intellectual disability are presumed to need or want. Relatedly, there is also a move away from the professional determination of individual needs. Therefore, it is argued that individual need should no longer be described in terms of what a particular service type or placement can provide 'but in terms of the types of supports that are to be addressed' (Luckasson and Spitalnik 1994, p.90). The new view of intellectual disability is evident in the 1992 American Association of Mental Retardation's (AAMR) landmark definition and associated assumptions:

> Mental retardation refers to substantial limitations in present functioning. It is characterized by significantly subaverage intellectual functioning, existing concurrently with related limitations in two or more of the following applicable adaptive skill areas: communication, self-care, home living, social skills, community use, self-direction, health and safety, functional academics, leisure, and work. Mental retardation manifests before age of 18. (Luckasson *et al.* 1992, p.1)

The AAMR has also adopted a new name that came into effect from 7 January 2007: the *American Association of Intellectual and Developmental Disabilities*. The Association has continued to stress the importance of providing intellectually disabled people with support and the need to move away from a deficit focus to one emphasizing self-determination and inclusion. The shift to a support and participation model is nicely captured in Thompson *et al.*'s assertion that 'The major focus is on the question, what supports are needed to help people participate in their community, assume valued social roles, and experience greater satisfaction and fulfilment?' (2002, p.390).

The application of the AAMR/AAIDD definition depends on five key assumptions (Bray 2003; Thompson *et al.* 2002):

- Diversity in culture, language, communication, and behaviour should all considered in a valid assessment.
- Adaptive skill deficits should always be considered within the context of the age peers and be linked to his or her specific needs for support.

- Individuals will often exhibit adaptive strengths in addition to adaptive limitations.

- An important aim in identifying limitations is to construct a profile of needed supports.

- The quality of life of a person with intellectual disability will improve significantly with appropriate supports.

Under the new conception of intellectual disability, a primary aim is to empower individuals and their families to detect their own needs, participate in society, and also to guide service planning. The goals are to shift from institutional control and coercion to individual empowerment; from a dependence on services to self-definition, personal autonomy and decision-making; and from considering people with intellectual disabilities as helpless and childlike to actively promoting (or scaffolding – see below) their transitions to adult status. The inclusion of people with intellectual disabilities is regarded as a crucial part of the decision-making process (Luckasson and Spitalnik 1994) and there is an emphasis on their interests and preferences. Self-determination is seen as a primary practice value and as such is given a high priority in the formulation of intervention plans (Bradley 1994). Thus a primary aim is to ensure that disability services work in partnership with people with intellectual disabilities and their families (Bradley 2000). Great efforts are also made to provide families and individuals with the information they need to make sound decisions.

## Rights-supportive approaches to disability practice

As stated above, there have been a number of policy and practice initiatives in the intellectual disability area that have stressed the importance of choice and agency for people with intellectual disability. The general tenor of these approaches has been to emphasize the necessity of incorporating individuals with an intellectual disability into the community and to focus practice and interventions on the unique needs of each. We will briefly consider two recent innovations that embody these values: normalization and person-centred approaches.

In effect the support paradigm for intellectually disabled people began with the *normalization* movement in Scandinavia in the late 1950s and early 1960s as a constructive alternative to caring for people with intellectual disabilities within institutions. The hope was that by 'letting the mentally retarded live an existence as close to normal as possible' (Nirje 1980) it would make their lives more satisfying and less demeaning. The mechanism by which the process of normalization was implemented was quite simple, and essentially amounted to making available to all people with intellectual disabilities 'patterns of life and conditions of everyday living which are as close as possible to the regular circumstances and ways of life of society' (Nirje 1980). In its initial formulation the theory of normalization consisted of a series of service principles based on civil rights rather than a coherent service framework (Emerson 1992).

Following the emergence of the normalization movement, approaches more directly concerned with promoting participation and social inclusion began to evolve. A particularly influential innovation was that of *person-centred approaches* which sought to promote the interests and well-being of intellectually disabled people by concentrating more on self-determination. Person-centred approaches to practice planning represent a significant philosophical and practical shift in determining how supports for families and individuals will be delivered (Becker *et al.* 2000). The guiding principles are based on the desire to be guided by:

- the individual with an intellectual disability and their advocates concerning their interests and life-style preferences
- 'bottom up' service design and the use of natural supports
- opportunities for individual choice and valued roles
- increased personal competencies
- facilitation of social connectedness and community inclusion.

(Magito-McLaughlin, Spinsoa and Marsalis 2002)

The core values evident in the normalization and person-centred approaches to working with people with intellectual disabilities revolve around the idea of participation and social inclusiveness. The principles underpinning these perspectives assume that individuals with intellectual disability ought to be treated with dignity, be provided with supports and services that will enable them to make the best of their abilities, have equal access to social goods such as work, relationships and education, have freedom of choice, and be treated fairly with respect to the delivery of social benefits and obligations. In other words, the presumption is that individuals with an intellectual disability have full human rights and ought to be given the opportunity and the resources necessary to live a life congruent with their deep commitments and interests. We will now consider more explicitly the application of human rights to the domain of intellectual disability.

## Human rights and intellectual disability

The primary emphasis in the new conceptualization of disability is on the importance of choice and empowerment for people with intellectual disabilities and their families. The accent on choice and judgment resonates strongly with a human rights orientation and is evident in the recent attention given to the area of intellectual disability by the United Nations and human rights theorists (Herr *et al.* 2006).

## United Nations and human rights

We saw in Chapter 1 that the UDHR was adopted in 1948 and since then has been supplemented with a number of human rights treaties. The original declaration was considered to apply to persons with intellectual disabilities but in the rush to defend the rights of non-disabled people, their particular interests were effectively hidden from sight. Amidst growing concern that the UDHR and the two covenants (*the International Covenant on Civil and Political Rights and the International Covenant on Economic, Social, and Cultural Rights*) did not adequately protect the rights of the disabled, the United Nations committee responsible for compliance with the Covenant on Economic, Social and Cultural Rights made an explicit statement on the matter:

> since the Covenant's provisions apply fully to all members of society, persons with disabilities are clearly entitled to the full range of rights recognized in the Covenant. In addition, in so far as special treatment is necessary, States parties are required...enable such persons to seek to overcome any disadvantages...flowing from their disability. (ICESCR 1994, para.5)

Subsequent United Nations initiatives on the matter of the human rights of persons with disabilities included the UN Standard Rules on the Equalization of Opportunities for Persons with Disabilities (1994), and more recently the adoption of the Convention on the Rights of Persons with Disabilities on 13 December 2006 (CRPD). While the former document indicates the United Nations' endorsement of the human rights of people with disabilities, it is essentially a set of guidelines that later become viewed as binding norms. However, the CRPD represents a watershed in the rights of people with disabilities and is intended to be a legally binding, authoritative statement on the matter. It consists of 50 articles that recognize the inherent dignity and value of all people, including those with disabilities, and addresses a number of areas that have proven to be problematic in the past for this group. More specifically, the CRPD establishes their rights to freedom of choice and autonomy, non-discrimination, full participation and inclusiveness in society, respect for the differences evident in persons with disabilities, equality of opportunity, accessibility to core social goods and services (i.e. to buildings, roads, outdoor facilities, information, transportation, etc.), the identification and removal of barriers, and gender equality. It also demands respect for the developing capacities of children with disabilities.

## Human rights discourses on intellectual disability

Several papers have directly examined the utility of a rights-based approach for people with intellectual disabilities and disabilities in general (Baylies 2002; Drewett 1999; Handley 2000; Hudson 1988; Rioux and Carbert 2003; Young and Quibell 2000). In brief, two general positions are evident in the literature. First, there is a claim that the concept of human rights provides a powerful language for disability advocates. Second, there are problems with using human rights arguments when agitating for equity for disabled persons. In the following section we will briefly discuss some of the key papers and argue for a view of human rights that incorporates the concept of need rather than placing it in opposition.

Rights-oriented theorists correctly point out that people with disabilities have been and continue to be frequently denied access to basic social goods and services, reproduction and work (Hudson 1988; Rioux and Carbert 2003). A legacy of the social model of disability has been the emphasis of some theorists on rights at the expense of needs when arguing for adequate services and social justice for people with intellectual disabilities (Drewitt 1999; Shakespeare 2006). An assumption has been that the concept of need provides a weak basis for equity and resourcing arguments and that utilizing the language of rights is ethically more powerful and effective. Needs are viewed as passive, indeterminate, and without the ability to create obligations on the behalf of the state and the community to meet them. While rights denote entitlements and duties, needs simply indicate a deficiency of some kind without any logical relationship to need satisfaction. Rioux and Carbert (2003, p.11) argue persuasively that:

> A human rights framework is empowering. Where a model of individual pathology marginalizes people with disabilities and forces them to conform to social contexts that do not account for their needs, a human rights approach insists that governments take measures to foster inclusive societies that anticipate and respond to variations in human characteristics that are inherent to the human condition. People with disabilities are entitled to enjoy all human rights.

In our view the sharp distinction between human rights and needs evident in the social model is mistaken and fails to appreciate the fact that *human rights* function to protect the *core interests* and *needs* of individuals. While we appreciate the pragmatic utility of relying on rights discourse to press for social services and goods for people with disabilities, it has led to conceptual confusion (Shakespeare 2006). The two conditions of well-being and freedom essential for effective agency (and thus the core objects of human rights) involve the meeting of basic needs for nutrition, safety, absence of threats, and relatedness. Human needs directly entail the conditions essential for psychological well-being and fulfilment, and individuals can only achieve satisfactory levels of well-being if these needs are met. Failure to meet our basic needs for human goods such as autonomy, relatedness and competence will inevitably cause psychological distress and will likely result in the acquisition of maladaptive defences and impaired agency (Deci and Ryan 2000). In other words, unmet basic needs result in stunted lives, psychological problems and social maladjustment. Rights and needs play distinct conceptual roles in political and social theories but they need to be considered as conceptual allies rather than rivals.

The second position evident in the disability literature claims that rights-based discourse is too impoverished to provide a satisfactory theoretical basis for effective social and political action on disability issues (Handley 2000). Young and Quibell (2000) in their important paper on rights for people with intellectual disabilities argue that rights are insufficiently engaging to motivate people to address the serious social and political injustices evident in the lives of people with an intellectual disability. They claim that the language of rights is too abstract and inaccessible to individuals with an intellectual disability and their supporters, and possessing legal citizenship rights only provides formal equality rather than material equality, and on its own is unlikely to result in effective changes (Young and Quibell 2000). Furthermore they assert that 'rights' are too individualistic in their orientation, overemphasize the importance of autonomy, and neglect the fact that individuals are interdependent beings who exist within communities. To address these problems Young and Quibell suggest that a narrative approach to social policy and social change might help to make the reality of the lives of people with intellectual disabilities more tangible to non-disabled people and hence motivate them to address the social injustices such individuals face.

While we accept Young and Quibell's point that human beings are essentially social animals and hence are strongly dependent on the good will and efforts of others for their happiness, we are concerned about their analysis. First, the focus on rights in their paper is limited to legal rather than moral rights. Second, their argument does not constitute a rebuttal of the value of a human rights approach but is more narrowly concerned with rights adherence. What we mean by this is that the major thrust of Young and Quibell's argument is that non-disabled people lack the will or motivation to meet their obligations to people with intellectual disabilities. The solution of relying on narrative methods to create a more vivid and realistic picture of the problems faced by individuals with a disability is a good idea but it is also perfectly consistent with a human rights approach. Third, the claim that human rights are individualistic and over-privilege autonomy at the expense of the community is simply mistaken (see Chapters 1 and 2). The well-being condition of our model of human rights allows for interdependency and community connectedness if such a feature is part of a culture's value system. The flexible nature of Gewirth's model means that what constitutes purposive agency in a particular context can incorporate a strong social orientation if it is directly associated with an agent's well-being goods (for example, strong filial relationships in eastern cultures may help to give a person a sense of dignity and value as a person). It is a mistake to conflate autonomy with agency; autonomy or freedom is but one of the two conditions required for agency and in itself it does not preclude a strong social orientation on the part of a particular person. Furthermore, the fact that Gewirth's model logically leads to an acceptance of a *community* of individuals with rights rather than a collection of competitive isolates also undermines the criticism that rights are narrowly individualistic.

In our view the model of human rights outlined in this book is able to bridge the gap between rights and needs, and also accommodates the fact that human beings are interdependent, not isolated social atoms. It can do this by virtue of the argument that rights are protective capsules that serve to defend and integrate the core interests (including basic needs fulfilment) of all members of the community.

## Human rights and practice

In Chapter 1 we asserted that according to Gewirth's model of human rights individuals possess rights to the *degree* that they have the capacity for agency. The requirement is not stringent and only stipulates that an individual is able to act in pursuit of their own goals after evaluating possible courses of action; that is, they are able to think about what they want and then act to bring it about. The human goods of freedom and well-being are the necessary conditions for such attempts by agents to be effective, otherwise individuals are doomed to fail to achieve their personal goals and, as a consequence of this failure, suffer a loss of human dignity. Thus being dominated and controlled by other people will result in lives of diminishment and humiliation.

Utilizing Alan Gewirth's theory we argued that human rights operate to protect the core interests and needs of people by allowing them the space to live according to their conception of a 'good life'. Effective action in the service of personal goals depends on sound judgment, and judgment in turn arises from freedom in the broad sense (i.e. not coerced, free access to information, possession of decision-making and evidence-evaluation skills, etc.) as well as satisfactory levels of well-being (i.e. physical well-being, education, social competence, being loved, etc.).

A key issue concerns those people who by virtue of intellectual impairment, illness or social discrimination lack the necessary freedom and well-being goods required to function as effective agents. Equity considerations mean that the state and citizens have an obligation either to provide the resources that will enable people with disabilities to function as purposive agents on their own (following a period of supportive learning) or else continually to scaffold their agency attempts. As we have argued, all human beings share the same degree of moral status and have intrinsic value as prospective agents. Although people with a disability may temporarily or even permanently lack the necessary capabilities to act independently in the service of their own goals, they are still capable of experiencing wants, and have fundamental interests that, if not met, are likely to result in serious harm and, if met, will lead to significantly improved well-being. In view of the fact that people with a disability have their own unique goals (desires, preferences, interests, etc.), and that action in pursuit of those goals will provide a sense of dignity, it follows that inability to act to achieve those goals will result in a lack of dignity and (feeling of) diminishment as a human being. In such circumstances what remains is a gap between the individual's aspirations and reality: they would like to achieve certain outcomes and their evaluation of their status as a person depends on it, but for a variety for reasons the individual is unable to do this. Individuals with an intellectual disability may experience discordance between their goals and their lives; unable to achieve goals they consider to be important or desirable they are left feeling powerless, without value and with a profound sense of humiliation. Their lives lack human dignity – something so fundamental to our humanity that the concept of human rights has been constructed to ensure and protect it. In our analysis of human rights, dignity is strongly related to the capacity to act to achieve one's goals and secure one's interests – to have a unique voice heard by others in the world.

In our view Gewirth's concept of *scaffolding* is extremely useful in helping to bridge the gap between aspirations, desires, wants and the unfortunately all too frequent unsatisfactory nature of the lives of people with an intellectual disability. We believe that human rights function to protect the necessary conditions for effective action and that these conditions involve freedom and well-being. Well-being goods include the resources required to meet basic human needs, such as those for nutrition, security, elemental equality, relatedness and self-esteem (see Chapter 1). Freedom goods include the ability to formulate a goal, the skills for evaluating options for action, and the capability to enact a plan intended to achieve a goal. Therefore, human rights presuppose both of the concepts of human needs and human interests, and despite the separation of the two concepts in disability discourse, they always need to be considered in tandem. Rights protect the conditions required for agency and as such stipulate that individuals with a disability are entitled to certain services and consideration from others so that they can act in accordance with their own life goals. In view of the fact that they may lack some of the necessary requirements for effective agency, they are entitled to receive assistance from the state, its agencies, and other members of the community to act in pursuit of their goals. This is not a matter of charity; it is a question of having a basic human right to a minimally satisfying level of existence – an existence where the person's preferences, desires and core interests are respected and the individual is given every opportunity to realize them in action.

The metaphor of a scaffold is helpful because it enables us to distinguish between two related but distinct dimensions of support for people with an intellectual disability: (a) the intensity of support, and (b) the duration of support. The *intensity* of support refers to the strength and extensiveness of a scaffold: just how far does it extend around a person's life and what domains of living does it cover? Thus a person with an intellectual disability who can speak but cannot function independently (e.g. is unable to address hygiene needs or deal with day-to-day living tasks) will need significant support in ensuring that their particular interests and goals are realized. This may mean having another agent function as an advocate, or belonging to a self-advocacy group as well as learning adaptive living skills. The support workers will need to consider seriously what specific goals the individual has and how best to structure their environment so that they can be achieved in a way that respects their dignity as a prospective agent and also the rights of others. Clearly the intensity of support is partly a function of the depth of the person's needs and partly of their pervasiveness (i.e. how many adaptive domains require intervention).

The *duration* of support offered by a scaffold refers to the length of time that the support will be needed in order to shore up a person's agency efforts. It may be that following a period of intensive education and skills training a person with an intellectual disability will be able to cope satisfactorily with the day-to-day demands of living and therefore only require occasional specialist service input. However, ongoing involvement in self-advocacy groups could be advisable and would help to strengthen their ability to manage their life effectively. Alternatively, a person requiring more ongoing support might need to live in a community home where live-in support staff or family members help them to translate their personal goals and interests into tangible benefits.

From a human rights viewpoint, the key point is that the level and duration of support needed by individuals ought to be based around their capacity to act in service of their own goals. The primary focus of practitioners should be on the intrinsic value of the person with an intellectual disability and the degree to which their unique interests and wishes are translated into desired outcomes. In the situation of a person with a severe to profound degree of intellectual disability it is still possible to ascertain what their favourite activities and personal goals are. It may be that close observation indicates that certain activities bring immense satisfaction or particular experiences are sought after and preferred. Despite the existence of high levels of need and the subsequent requirement for intensive support, the aim should always be to increase the degree of agency possessed by the individual with an intellectual disability and to work hard to put in place the capabilities required for them to function as a prospective agent.

## Intellectual disability case studies: human rights and practice

We would now like briefly to consider two examples of individuals with an intellectual disability where human rights issues impinge upon practice. In constructing the examples we have drawn from our experience and developed fictitious, but we hope representative, cases that illustrate two common types of problems relating to sexuality and justice. We hope to show how the application of our model of human rights, as outlined in Chapter 1, can help practitioners to identify whether there is potential for human rights to be violated, and what courses of action might be adopted to resolve the issues involved while at the same time safeguarding rights.

## Suzy and menstruation management

In the first example, a social services practitioner is called into a residential unit to help resolve a number of problems concerning Suzy, a 16-year-old young woman with a moderate intellectual disability. Suzy's parents want her to have a hysterectomy to make menstrual management easier for her carers and also to ensure that she never gets pregnant. They are concerned that she may have unprotected sex, or engage in 'immoral and irresponsible' sexual practices, or be taken advantage of by abusive predators. The staff at the residential home agree with Suzy's parents, as does her general practitioner. Essentially, there is a consensus that someone with an intellectual ability lacks the necessary cognitive skills to make appropriate decisions about sex. The adults are also concerned about the impact that hormonal changes may have on Suzy's behaviour and believe that surgery could therefore resolve a number of future problems.

The practitioner involved identified that the key human rights issues related to the right to have children and the right to exercise control over one's own sexuality and bodily integrity. At a more fundamental level the human rights objects of personal freedom, equality and social recognition were deeply implicated. The major question was whether Suzy's core interests would be best served by a hysterectomy. At the same time, Suzy was deeply cared for by her family who felt acutely protective of her and were keen to ensure that she was not troubled by future experiences that she would not be able to cope with or have the capacity to manage.

After talking with Suzy it became apparent that she was confused about what a hysterectomy was, that she was pre-menstrual, and that she was keen to have babies one day. She also said that she wanted to get married. After the practitioner carefully and appropriately explained the details of the proposed operation and how it would affect her, Suzy refused to give permission and insisted that she wanted to have children.

Applying our model of human rights as outlined in Chapter 1 it is clear that any decision to force Suzy to have a hysterectomy on the grounds of menstrual management and sexual control is likely to contravene Articles 3 (autonomy and equality of opportunity) and 17 (protecting physical integrity) of the *Convention on the Rights of Persons with Disability* (2006) and Article 16 (right to marry and have family) of the UDHR.

The structure of the human rights model then encourages the practitioner to consider the two core values of freedom and well-being and their elaboration into the five goods of freedom, subsistence, security, equality and social recognition. In the context of Suzy's experience it could be argued that the goods of personal freedom, equality and social recognition were being neglected, and that not fully involving Suzy in the discussion, and assuming that her consent was not required, would be a violation of her human rights.

Drawing from Gewirth's theory of human rights it is possible to arrive at an ethically defensible plan of action. With respect to the freedom good it is clear that contraception options and their pros and cons need to be explained to

Suzy and other less intrusive options explored. Second, with respect to sexuality, Suzy's need for a fuller understanding of her own sexuality and issues such as consent and safe sex mean that specific well-being goods need to be supplied to her. Third, adults involved with Suzy's care and support need to have both information about human rights issues in the context of disability and the opportunity to discuss these issues. They also need to be able to discuss the complex issues that they have raised with respect to her ongoing care as she enters adulthood. Fourth, if Suzy does have enduring problems with managing menstruation, this needs to be responded to sensitively and in the context of informed decision-making with the people who care about her.

## Peter and the young people at New House

In this example, New House, a semi-independent residence for young adult men and women with an intellectual disability, provides an illustration of the ways in which rights can be a complex and contested reality. New House looks after eight young adults in a semi-independent environment with staff available to provide support and assistance if required. The young adults are encouraged to manage their own allowances, to cook with staff, to look after their own rooms, and to replicate as far as possible an independent 'flatting' situation.

New House had been functioning well with residents feeling generally supported and able to develop their independent living skills in a secure and supported environment. However, this changed when a new resident arrived – Peter – whose behaviour began to impact negatively on the other people in the house. Peter was aggressive in his behaviour, always wanting his own way, and was prepared to strike out at other people if things did not go as he wanted. Over time, Peter became increasingly powerful and it was becoming clear that other residents were frightened of him. He was a large man, and one of the young women in the house expressed her fears that he would attack her, as she had seen Peter hit other males in the house. In response to this, security was increased and some of the locks on the bedroom doors were replaced as they had not been used regularly as a safety measure, and residents were instructed on how to keep themselves safe.

Nevertheless, Peter continued to act aggressively toward others and would frequently steal their possessions. The stealing caused altercations which were generally managed by the staff but there were times when staff were not around during these conflicts. After these occasions a staff member would talk to Peter and explain the inappropriateness of his behaviour. Further efforts were made to increase security in the house and educate the other residents on how to keep themselves safe. The staff felt that Peter's intellectual capability was such that he was not really responsible for his actions and reactions. Preferring to manage the problems themselves, the staff considered police or other official intervention to be heavy-handed. They were certain that Peter would not cope within a mainstream justice system and were keen to protect him from this.

After a particularly nasty attack in which one of the residents suffered a severely blackened eye, a relative of one of the other residents brought in a youth worker whom they knew from a community-based centre. The youth worker talked to staff and residents in the house and found that some of the young people were feeling terrorized by Peter and that their general well-being was being threatened. They were unhappy and scared.

Applying the model of human rights outlined in Chapter 1 it will become clear that the human rights issues are complex in this example. First, all people need to experience equal protection by the law, and in this regard people with intellectual disabilities are no different from non-disabled persons. To assume otherwise is an affront to their inherent dignity and value as agents. Yet here we have a number of people whose rights are being diminished. Second, the scaffolding role implies that practitioners and advocates should always look to see how they can further the agency attempts and core interests of people with intellectual disability, and this entails ensuring that such individuals are safe and receive adequate physical care. Thus the basic human rights goods of personal freedom, well-being, equality and social recognition are being compromised in the case of a number of residents at the house. Third, despite his behaviour Peter also has well-being needs for a secure non-threatening environment in which he can thrive, and denying him responsibility for his actions undermines his status as a moral agent which in turn subtly undermines his capacity for exercising effective agency.

The practitioner formulates a human rights intervention plan upon the basis of an analysis of the needs of all of the people within New House. In this situation the ethics of care and the need to promote human rights coexist and provide a complex set of dynamics that must be responded to by advocates and family members who care for those involved. Key to the intervention is the need to protect both Peter's interests and the interests of other members of the residence. In New House this involved bringing together professionals who were able to work with the staff and residents to create a safer living environment for all who live there. In this situation the police were called to reinforce the seriousness of the situation, and a behavioural plan was developed to support Peter to change the way he responded to others within the residence. Regular meetings were held to assess progress and to ensure that people felt safe. Failure to adhere to the safety components of the behavioural plan had consequences that everyone understood, and Peter in particular was made aware that he would be required to leave if the safety of other residents could not be assured.

## Summary: human rights and practice

What these two examples reveal is the complex nature of rights-based practice and the ways in which human rights have the potential to be undermined in the context of the care provided for intellectually disabled people. In both cases, the judgments of guardians, care givers and professionals determined what was in the best interests of the young people involved, and there is a sense in which the examples reflect an under-appreciation of the agency potential of the young people themselves. Bringing a human rights perspective into the care arena provides an additional incentive to support persons with an intellectual disability so that they can achieve their goals (i.e. satisfy desires, preferences, etc.) in ways that protect their core interests (well-being and freedom goods) and the interests of other people. Consideration of the fundamental interests of people with an intellectual disability requires close examination of the relevant contextual features of a situation and a realization that human rights extend to all individuals regardless of their perceived capacity to participate and decide on matters that concern them. Moreover, because most people are likely to suffer some degree of disability in their lives, it provides a timely reminder that human beings are interdependent and will at some point need to negotiate rights within ethical caring environments.

A marked advantage of the human rights model presented in this book as applied to the intellectual disability area is that it resonates with accepted features of best practice. First, a human rights perspective points to the importance of advocacy and self-advocacy services for people with an intellectual disability. Such service can be usefully viewed as extending the agency attempts of individuals, providing cognitive scaffolding and assisting them in the acquisition of relevant information and the implementation of problem-solving procedures. In addition, emotional and social support can be of immense help in buffering potentially disruptive influences on individual decision-making and action. Second, introducing rights-based ideas serves to clarify the relationship between rights and needs/interests in a way that focuses attention on the value of agency for the person with an intellectual disability. Human needs and interests are relevant because unmet they comprise aspects of the freedom and well-being components of effective agency. Human rights are devices that protect those core conditions and by doing so help individuals realize their unique conception of a good life (assisted in this process by their advocates). Third, our model of human rights helps to remind practitioners of the interdependency of all people and the fact that well-being goods are likely to involve community connectedness and personal relationships. It helps transcend a narrow view of rights as individualistic and adversarial: we need rights to live together in ways that are mutually rewarding and personally meaningful. Fourth, human rights are fully consistent with the principles of normalization, person-centred planning, social participation, community living, appropriate support, and inclusiveness evident in current practice initiatives. From the viewpoint of policies supporting current best practice, the aim is to embed people with an intellectual disability within normal community life and to equip them to live the best possible lives.

## Conclusions

In this chapter we have applied the model of human rights outlined in Chapter 1 to the domain of intellectual disability. In our view the existing literature on rights and disability has not provided a satisfactory justification of human rights and has also mistakenly driven a wedge between rights and needs, thereby reinforcing binary positions. The analysis of our two case examples utilizing the model of human rights revealed its ability to provide resolution of important ethical issues in ways that reaffirm the dignity and humanity of people with intellectual disabilities. In our analysis the concept of scaffolding plays a major role and reminds practitioners that their function is to facilitate the translation of the interests and goals of people with disabilities into tangible outcomes. Rights protect agency and it is through action that people form their sense of who they are and where they are going.

Chapter 7

# Contesting Rights: Cultural Values and Children's Rights

In Chapter 2 we discussed the ways in which culture influences how groups of individuals realize their conception of a good life. Culture influences what we do and how we do it, guiding our day-to-day living and shaping our understanding of what constitutes appropriate and inappropriate behaviour in any given setting (Connolly, Crichton-Hill and Ward 2006). As we noted in Chapter 4, from a rights perspective working with children and their families presents some challenging issues. How a child is reared within a family, what constitutes reasonable discipline, and how the rights of parents and children are accommodated within and across cultural groups remain at the forefront of practice concern. As such the issue of child discipline in particular provides us with a useful example to consider rights-based ideas in a practical way: what gives rise to cultural thinking about the disciplining of children, how these are realized across cultural domains, and what it might mean for practitioners working with children and families. A critical issue in considering the impact of culture on human rights is the extent to which diverse interpretations of concepts such as freedom and well-being can be responsive to cultural norms and yet still scaffold human agency.

## Child-rearing issues across cultural domains

While we have argued the universality of human rights in this book, there is little agreement that any particular set of child-rearing standards has universal applicability, particularly in the context of cross-cultural perspectives. Increasingly writers have acknowledged the importance of cultural differences in child-rearing practices (Connolly *et al.* 2006; Fontes 2005; Korbin 1991). Fontes (2005), in her important book on culture and child protection, argues that child rearing is strongly influenced by ethnicity and ethnic culture. Cultural knowledge is passed down through generations of parenting, and norms relating to appropriate disciplinary practices vary across cultures. What is considered abusive in one culture may not be considered so in another. Hence, an individual's thinking about child rearing is deeply embedded in a set of cultural values and beliefs about the world and how people should behave within it. Describing different cultural attitudes to punishment Fontes (2005, p.117) notes:

> Studies have reported that African Americans and people from the southern United States and the Caribbean are more likely to punish their children with an electric cord, belt or switch applied to the back or bottom...European (White) Americans are more likely to use a paddle or an open hand to the bottom. Recent Korean immigrants may slap a child's face and pull the child's hair. Chinese parents may pinch their youngsters more than other parents do. And Puerto Rican families may place a toddler who is having a tantrum into a bathtub of cold water.

At the same time, Fontes describes research undertaken with African American women which suggests their preference is for a light touch or tap at the moment of transgression, rather than what they consider an abusive response, screaming or cursing a child. Hence, as argued in Chapter 2, there is clearly not only diversity across cultural groupings but also *within* them. Fontes (2006, p.5) also suggests that firm discipline can be deeply rooted in family history and spiritual beliefs:

> Some African American parents feel as if they are turning their back on their ancestors and even on their race if they abandon corporal punishment.

Cultural groups who have experienced colonial victimization, she suggests, may be more likely to adopt harsher disciplinary responses and an authoritarian parenting style. Often this style of parenting expects children to be dutifully respectful of adults and to require obedience in all areas of family functioning. By comparison, a less authoritarian parenting style may see the parent–child relationship characterized by less formality and easier processes of communication.

At the same time, research has revealed little evidence that physical punishment is more acceptable within particular cultural groups (Kiro 2004, citing Marshall 2004). Indeed, some studies suggest that socio-economic status may be more relevant, with parents from lower socio-economic groups tending to engage in harsher disciplinary practices:

> Spankings may be perceived in Afro American families (where children are more often in higher levels of distress, poverty and exposed to community violence) as a protective strategy to prevent the development of further disruptive behaviour. (Maldonado 2005, p.6)

In his summary of the research, Maldonado further reports that the physical disciplining of children is regularly carried out by the majority of parents across the United States. As such it is generally seen as a normative child-rearing practice: some surveys having found that up to 90 per cent of American parents support spanking as a means of child discipline. That said, Fontes (2005) argues that while corporal punishment continues to be used widely, the practice is nevertheless decreasing in the United States, and fewer people approve of it now than in the past.

Harsh child-rearing disciplinary practices have also been associated with some religious belief systems. Proponents may claim that their practices are based on notions of 'Biblical parenting' in which the child is seen to need systematic correction to ensure that he or she develops in the context of strong limits and boundaries (Maldonado 2005). Religious and ethnic cultures have also coincided. Writing from a Samoan perspective, Pereira (2004, p.27) describes the introduction of a Christian belief system into Pacific culture:

> They brought a new God with a new set of rules encompassed in a book called the Bible, which missionaries claimed to be the ultimate sources of authority and guidance regarding every aspect of human life.

The hierarchical nature of Christianity resonated well with the hierarchical nature of traditional Samoan systems and Pereira notes the significant impact this had on Samoan child-raising practices:

> Whether implicit or not, the moral cloak of legitimacy of the Bible and its unchallenging force of authority imposed on Samoa's moral compass has had a fundamental influence on the way physical punishment has become a necessary tool for raising children. (Pereira 2004, p.28)

Pereira maintains, however, that physical punishment and harsh treatment toward children was not an aspect of Samoan culture. Indeed, pre-European contact Pacific cultures have been traditionally nurturing towards children. Familism – the strong belief in family, family duty and the obligation to support family members – is common to many traditional societies and may be associated with less coercive parenting styles. While harsh punishment is sometimes seen as being connected to religious belief systems, Maldonado (2005) also found that a strong sense of religiosity was instrumental in supporting less coercive parenting styles.

Discussing child rearing in different cultures Hindberg captures the delicate balance with respect to parental authority:

> Successful parenthood depends on the adults being rooted in a fabric of values, customs and habits which support their parental authority, and on how secure they feel in their parental role. A good parent is differently defined in every culture, and migration can threaten the parental role if the prerequisites for the maintenance of parental authority are removed in the new culture. (Hindberg 2001, pp.19–20, citing Broberg 2000)

In many respects the literature discussing child rearing from a cross-cultural perspective highlights the diversity of parenting styles, and of the research methodologies that try to make sense of them. Maldonado (2005) cautions against making an assumption that even within a culture parents necessarily endorse the same beliefs, or indeed engage in similar practices. Making cross-cultural comparisons is extremely difficult and research findings are far from equivocal – a reflection of both inherent complexity and significant methodological differences across research studies.

While child-rearing practices vary across and within cultural groups, both differing and similar attitudes to corporal punishment can be found in societies overall.

## Corporal punishment in different societies

The difference between discipline and corporal punishment has been identified as:

> Discipline is guidance of children's moral, emotional and physical development, enabling children to take responsibility for themselves when they are older…Physical or corporal punishment is the use of forces to cause pain, but not injury, for the purposes of correction or control. (Smith 2004, p.8)

How corporal punishment is labelled also varies across and within cultures (Durrant 2005). For example, such punishment may be referred to as paddling, spanking, smacking, cuffing or 'the bash' – in fact the range of terms is as broad as the range of attitudes toward it.

Durrant's analysis of 24 research studies into the prevalence of parental corporal punishment across different countries provides us with a useful international overview. We will summarize her findings here, but for a fuller discussion with citation to the studies she has examined, and her analysis of predictors and implications, we refer readers to her original chapter. Durrant looked at studies from Barbados, Canada, China, Egypt, England, Greece, Hong Kong, India, New Zealand, Nigeria, Northern Ireland, Republic of Korea, South Africa, Sweden and the United States. At the time of Durrant's analysis (2005) law permitted corporal punishment by parents in all but one of the countries, the exception being Sweden where corporal punishment was abolished in 1979.[1] In reporting prevalence, Durrant defines two levels of severity. Mild punishment includes such practices as smacking, pinching or hitting without the use of an implement and in which no physical injury is sustained. Severe punishment causing physical harm (or likely to cause harm) included such practices as punching, kicking, shaking, burning. Punishments considered severe in this analysis also included repeated or prolonged punishment and may have included the use of implements. Some of the studies examined in the analysis did not specify the level of severity.

For ease of discussion we will cluster the countries into continents: Europe (England, Northern Ireland, Greece, Sweden); Asia (China, Hong Kong, India, Republic of Korea); Africa/Middle East (Nigeria, South Africa, Egypt); Americas (Barbados, Canada, United States of America) and the Pacific (New Zealand).

---

1    In 2007 New Zealand removed a clause from the Crimes Act (1961) which provided a justification for the use of reasonable parental force for the purposes of correction.

- *Europe:* In England a number of studies have identified high levels of corporal punishment with 71–91 per cent of children experiencing mild punishment, and 16–24 per cent severe. In Greece one study identified 61 per cent mild, and 10 per cent severe. In two other Greek studies the level of severity was unspecified (85% and 50% prevalence). In Northern Ireland one study reported an 87 per cent estimated prevalence of mild punishment. Swedish studies reported 8–11 per cent mild, and 0.2–3 per cent severe.

- *Asia:* Studies in China have found a 42 per cent estimated level for mild, and 23 per cent for serious. In two studies where severity was unspecified, prevalence ranged from 10 to 12 per cent. In Hong Kong one study estimated a prevalence of 95 per cent at unspecified severity, while an Indian study identified 56 per cent mild and 44 per cent severe. Two Korean studies were examined with broadly different findings. One found the estimated prevalence to be 9 per cent for mild and 51 per cent for severe. In a reversal, the second study found 67 per cent for mild and 9 per cent for severe.

- *Africa/Middle East:* Two Nigerian studies were examined: one estimated prevalence at 88 per cent for severe and the other 52 per cent. One South African study in which severity was unspecified reported 67 per cent prevalence, and an Egyptian study reported 38 per cent for severe.

- *Americas:* A high level of prevalence of mild corporal punishment was estimated in one American study (97%) while a second study identified 57 per cent for severe and 93 per cent of unspecified severity. Two Canadian studies reported 48 per cent for mild and 7 per cent for severe, and 51 per cent unspecified. Barbados reported one study: 84 per cent for severe.

- *Pacific:* Only one study was included in the analysis from the Pacific. New Zealand reported a high estimated level of 89 per cent prevalence, the severity of which was unspecified.

While it is not always easy to make comparisons across international boundaries, the Swedish findings do appear to stand out among those reported by Durrant. She notes much higher estimations of prevalence for both mild and severe punishment in countries where corporal punishment is legally permissible, Sweden being the one county in her analysis that has abolished the practice.

Aside from Sweden, eleven other countries have fully abolished the corporal punishment of children: Finland (1983), Denmark (explicitly in 1997), Norway (1987), Austria (1989), Germany (2000), Cyprus (1994), Latvia (1998), Israel (2000) Croatia (1999), Iceland (2003) (Smith *et al.* 2004), and most recently, New Zealand (2007). Other countries are currently considering the issue of corporal punishment and exploring whether reform is desirable. In some countries this has been in response to legal action, for example Italy, where the Supreme Court has found corporal punishment to be illegal, but the decision has not yet been reflected in statute (Hindberg 2001). Writers have noted that Swedish changes in the law have also shifted cultural norms with respect to the use of physical punishment (Durrant 2005; Hindberg 2001). Hindberg reports that public approval of corporal punishment has fallen steadily since the law was changed, and that the ban now has the strong support of the Swedish population.

## Physical punishment and rights in practice

Three positions have been identified with regard to the physical punishment debate: the pro-physical punishment lobby, the 'conditional corporal punishment' position, and the anti-physical punishment lobby (Taylor 2005, p.14). Proponents of corporal punishment base their arguments on a firm conviction, whether supported by themes of religiosity or not, that parents have an obligation or duty to correct their children and, in general, support laws that allow a parent to do so (Taylor 2005). The 'conditional' position takes the view that the effect of such punishment is not necessarily negative or positive. It may be negative, or be positive, or both, depending on its circumstances and conditions. Mild smacking, supporters argue, can be beneficial and an effective alternative to other disciplinary practices. The child's response to the punishment, and a belief that its application can have a moderating effect on behaviour, along with its use within a loving nurturing environment, are seen as important within the 'conditional' position. This position has influenced legal responses to physical punishment and countries have clarified in law the limits of reasonable chastisement (Taylor 2005).

Newall (2005), on the other hand, argues that all corporal punishment is a breach of a person's fundamental human rights. Supporters of human rights argue that corporal punishment toward children constitutes inhumane treatment, is degrading, and lacks respect for human dignity (Article 37, UNCROC). Furthermore, it may adversely affect the developing child's acquisition of empathy and make it more likely that the parents will resort to physical violence in the future rather than use non-physical techniques such as persuasion to deal with family conflicts. Respecting freedom rights means accepting that others are entitled to express their disagreements openly and to adopt a contrary viewpoint if they so wish. From a human rights perspective, the use of force is a coercive, aggressive means of controlling children's behaviour, which erodes their sense of agency, dignity and self-esteem. Allowing parents to punish their children by violent means is to privilege their wishes and agency above those of the child and to run the risk of undermining their agency efforts by creating fear, a lack of confidence, and failure to respect themselves and others. In an important sense, children who are hit are being treated as *vehicles* for their parents' wishes, objects to be moulded and shaped according to parental inclinations and interests. This notion of absence of respect has also been identified by young people themselves. When asked how they felt after being physically punished (Saunders and Goddard 2003, p.7) research respondents noted:

> slightly subordinate to adults…I think you should respect all people…I personally don't think it's appropriate for them to physically punish me any more…that should be my say really, 'cause I think I am becoming a bit of a person, not a child anymore. (13-year-old girl)

> Being smacked is like being treated like something very little and not important to the rest of the world. (12-year-old girl)

In addition, the anti-physical punishment lobby consider that it also breaches human rights in the sense that it creates inequality (Article 7, UDHR) under the law (Taylor 2005). Adults have protection in law against assault, and human rights require that children not be treated unequally. In Saunders and Goddard's research (2003, p.9) this notion of equality is captured by one of their 10-year-old respondents:

> [Children and adults] should be treated equally the same, like one shouldn't get more than the other in ways of better treatment, like treat them better just because they're older or younger.

There is no question that international law firmly rejects parental corporal punishment – and indeed corporal punishment in other institutions such as schools and other residences. The International Committee on the Rights of the Child, the UN body which monitors the application of UNCROC, has been very clear in this regard. Newall (2005) further argues that law providing a defence for corporal punishment of children breaches their fundamental rights according to both the Universal Declaration of Human Rights (UDHR) and the International Covenant on Civil and Political Rights (ICCPR). Arguing the cross-cultural universality of human rights he charges the United Nations with an important task:

> The particular task of the United Nations Convention on the Rights of the Child has been to confirm that human rights really are universal, that they do include children: that children, too, are holders of human rights. (Newall 2005, p.26)

Newall argues that reform is inevitable given the degree to which human rights standards have been developed. As we have noted, nearly all countries have become signatories to UNCROC, and given its unequivocal position regarding the physical punishment of children it is likely that state parties to the convention will continue to be influenced by these expectations.

Anticipating children's rights reform and the need for systems to respond to the demands of UNCROC, Power and Hart (2005) have developed a framework for constructive child discipline. They offer seven principles designed to guide constructive practices that they argue have universal relevance (Power and Hart 2005, p.93). We will explore how each of these principles interact with our perspectives on human rights in some detail below.

1. *Respect the child's dignity.* Respect for human dignity is the core justification for possessing human rights. According to Power and Hart it represents the 'golden rule' response: it is the way in which we would all like and expect to be treated. This resonates with our earlier discussion in Chapter 1 where we argued that the violation of human rights occurs when individuals are treated as objects, simply as a means to other people's ends rather than as ends in themselves. In its preamble, UNCROC recognizes the inherent dignity of all people, ipso facto, children. Dignity is noted in several of its provisions. Article 28.2 requires that school discipline not undermine a child's dignity; Article 23.1 requires that children with disability be insured dignity and the enjoyment of a full and decent life; Article 37 (c) requires that young people deprived of liberty be treated with respect consistent with their inherent dignity. In our view a sense of dignity emerges when the child's emerging agency capabilities are respected and their preferences and interests are acknowledged.

   Power and Hart propose the need to protect and respect the physical, psychological, moral and social integrity of all children. This requires that behaviour correction be educative in nature rather than punitive. In this regard adults are seen as having stewardship responsibilities to guide and direct children in the exercise of their rights, thereby recognizing the child's inherent human dignity (see Chapter 4).

2. *Develop pro-social behaviour, self-discipline and character.* Adopting a similar definition of discipline outlined by Smith above, Power and Hart reinforce this in the context of the child's development of pro-social behaviour and character that is inherently relevant to the child's culture. Critical to the development of character is the internalization of values such as compassion, fairness and justice, and the capacity to think critically and be able to make sound judgments and choices. From the point of view of human agency, the possession of such character traits is likely to result in higher levels of well-being and respect for the well-being of others.

   Again Power and Hart see these aspects of human potential being fostered by education to create opportunities for values development, ethical choice-making and behaviour that reflects these. Opportunities for children to develop values of compassion, fairness and justice are particularly emphasized. These, together with support for critical thinking, pro-social skills, empathy and non-violent problem-solving, are seen as critical to the preparation for full citizenship.

3. *Maximize the child's active participation.* Power and Hart argue that participation is critical to 'establishing children as rights-bearing citizens capable of existential thought and choice: persons and not property' (p.100). As noted in Chapter 4, children's rights, and in particular participation rights,

are increasingly at the forefront of public and professional concern. Participation is not only essential for democratic citizenship but also necessary for the child's moral development and, we would argue, for their growing capacity for agency. Across cultures, guided participation has been found to be important in the development of maturity and for self-regulation (Rogoff 2003).

Opportunities for the development of ethical conduct and moral reasoning have been advanced when children are involved in real-life decision-making, problem-solving and the working through of life's dilemmas. In this sense, active participation provides developmental opportunities for children, and promotes self-efficacy, pride and self-dignity.

4. *Respect the child's developmental needs and quality of life.* Linked to (3) above, Power and Hart argue the need to respect the child's development and realization of potential. This is supported by UNCROC, with respect to the child's developing personality, talents and abilities in the context of education (Article 29.1), and their development overall (Article 6.2). In terms of disciplinary practices, these need to be consistent with the child's developmental stage and their growing sense of agency and maturity. Children have a right not to have their development hindered by poor disciplinary practices that could impact on their future life chances. Power and Hart argue 'discipline practices that respect and support these positive conditions at each point in the child's life appear to promote better futures for all involved' (p.101). Arguably, the critical parenting task is that of scaffolding children's developing agency and helping them to acquire the capabilities necessary to function as moral agents and responsible citizens when they reach adulthood. Strategies to advance the child's learning and development are therefore critical. Strengths-based learning and in particular reframing problems as challenges present important opportunities for development.

5. *Respect the child's motivation and life views.* Children approach their world with their own blend of social and cultural thinking (Connolly *et al.* 2006). Understanding childhood cultures as distinct perspectives on life from those of adults is critical to the respectful appreciation of their inherent value. If children are to internalize notions of freedom, peace, tolerance and friendship into their worldview, they need to feel that their own views are equally respected and valued.

Like adult behaviour, a child's behaviour is often motivated by an effort to satisfy basic human needs, physical and/or emotional. Attention-seeking behaviour is a good example of a child's need for connectedness, interpersonal engagement and support. Backing down from a position is never easy, and humans feel a basic need to 'save face', thereby retaining a semblance of pride and/or self-esteem.

Understanding and respecting a child's motivation for their behaviour encourages the development of parental strategies that respect the child's dignity – giving the child somewhere to go if you will, without unnecessary shaming.

6. *Assure fairness and transformative justice.* Justice and fairness are important to human beings. They are values that are given emphasis in UNCROC's preamble, affirming: 'recognition of human dignity and the equal and inalienable rights of all members (including children) of the human family is the foundation of freedom, justice and peace in the world'. Power and Hart (2005, p.103) argue that justice, inextricably linked with freedom and peace, is of supreme value to people across all societies.

The history of human development and behaviour gives strong recognition to the significance of achieving justice – particularly justice that is fair and transformative. Hence, shared respect for legal systems that are just and fair provides individuals with the confidence that they will be treated fairly and equally under the law.

Children are particularly sensitive to injustice when it is applied to them. When something is believed to be unfair, it can significantly influence not only how they perceive the issue, but also how they respond to it. Article 2.1 of UNCROC recognizes the importance of justice for all children and it requires that the rights of children be respected, without discrimination of any kind. According to Power and Hart (2005, p.96): 'Equity and non-discrimination, freedom from capricious and degrading punishment or reward, application of logical and natural consequences respecting the dignity and integrity of persons, and opportunities for appeal and redress should be assured to foster respect for the "rule of law"'.

7. *Promote solidarity.* Humans are relational beings who have needs associated with connectedness, interpersonal affiliation and social support. Connecting with people who share solid moral and ethical values can provide children with an environment within which mutual support and learning can foster peaceful conflict resolution. Supportive parenting cultures in which children and young people can give and receive respect are most likely to provide the kind of learning environment that will help build internal resilience and moral codes that extend beyond the group and guide future behaviour.

This notion of human connectedness brings us back to our earlier discussion of cultural thinking in communities and the ways in which this can be influenced by systems of support within those communities. Earlier we commented on the influence Christianity has had on cultural thinking with respect to corporal punishment. Within the Samoan context Pereira (2004) noted the way in which the Bible lent legitimacy to physical punishment as a means of guiding a child's moral development and future behaviour. Churches can be hugely influential in shaping the way in which communities understand their parenting responsibilities, and Pereira argues that the churches can also be part of the solution:

> It is to the churches I think we should begin in our quest for solutions. It is the place for the conversations around parenting. It is the place for bringing together. It is the place for the culture to show its depth of wisdom and integrity. It is the place for leadership. (Pereira 2004, p.29)

Where the church or cultural community is influential, church leaders and cultural elders can be critical to the strengthening of children's rights within the context of a caring community. In this sense, elders and church leaders can become advocates for children's rights in ways that are consistent with traditional beliefs about respect, authority, honour and responsibility. Modelling non-violent behaviour by respected adults is particularly important in this regard (Power and Hart 2005). When children see authority as being associated with adults who are honest, caring, respectful and reasonable, mutual respect is generated and a sense of partnership is far more likely. Children are drawn to people of integrity and are engaged by the application of logical, fair responses to issues and difficulties. In a bridging of rights-based ideas and the ethics of care, the furthering of rights becomes a process of caring that:

> fosters the growth of those participating in caring relationships, and their willingness to take on open-ended responsibilities in regard to each other. (Meagher and Parton 2004, p.15)

This leads the way for supportive community or church-based services to become 'non-hitting zones' that model respectful relationships between adults and children.

In the same way that cultural leaders can be effective as children's rights advocates, we have argued in Chapter 4 that parents also have a critical stewardship role as defenders of their own children's rights. In the context of the debate over corporal punishment there is no one way of influencing parents to become the guardians of their children's rights (Smith *et al.* 2004). Universal responses have included changes in law and broadly based public educational campaigns. Targeted programmes focusing on constructive or positive child discipline can also contribute significantly to the changing of parental attitudes with respect to violence and the promotion of pro-social family values. Within local communities professionals have significant opportunities to provide support and advice as they interact with families on a day-to-day basis. Parenting values and techniques that support effective discipline focus on parental warmth and involvement. Smith and her colleagues (2004, p.30) note that:

> If children are to become responsible and effective members of society, then disciplinary methods which encourage them to be sensitive to others and to want to please their parents are most likely to be effective.

Children respond positively in the context of warm and supportive relationships where communication is clear and there is also clarity of expectation. Humans learn from their interactions with others, and a child internalizes messages that they receive from their day-to-day interactions with adults. If children are confused about the messages they are receiving, they will not know how best to please their parents and be rewarded by positive responses. Being clear with children and providing reasoned explanations that have logical consequences have been identified as being most effective in terms of child discipline. Building empathy and modelling sensitivity toward others are important to the child's development of pro-social values and behaviour. Again, these are best applied in the context of a warm, loving relationship in which rules and boundaries are clearly articulated and the child understands the consequences of their actions. Consistency goes hand-in-hand with consequences. When children need to learn about consequences, they will do so when consequences are consistently applied. In many respects this presents a reasonably straightforward formula: positive reinforcement follows wanted behaviour; negative reinforcement follows unwanted behaviour. Working with parents around 'what works' helps to avoid simplistic or insulting suggestions that fail to resonate with their particular cultural environment (Fontes 2005). All cultural groups have examples within them of non-violent attitudes and behaviours toward children. It is a question of identifying techniques that work, noting successes, building on strengths, and creating opportunities to talk about non-violent methods of child discipline and the challenges that families face in realizing their aims.

## Conclusions

Raising children is never an easy job for parents, particularly when they are pressured by a range of conflicting messages about how they should bring their children up. A human rights perspective requires that children's rights be central to any discussion about child-rearing practices and child discipline. While we have seen that the issues across cultures are complex, we have also seen examples of non-violent cultural thinking across religious and ethnically diverse societies. Moreover, the benefits of providing opportunities to live non-violent lives and to instil moral values of justice, fairness, compassion and integrity in our children may prove to be more effective in developing caring and supportive communities in which those values are also shared and promoted more widely. One of the best things we can do for our children is to encourage them to respect themselves and others and to understand that fairness and acceptance of self-responsibility (as moral agents) are two of the most important constituents of a just and decent society. Phillips and Alderson (2003, pp.193–194) provide us with a fitting ending for this chapter when they capture the complexity of the changes required to protect children:

Family life is full of complicated paradoxes – power and intimacy, love and violence, public and private concerns. There are, inevitably, both harms and benefits in families trying either to remain static or to change. The effective protection of children, however, like that of women, requires not only legal prohibition of violence against them, but a challenging of prejudice about them and a strengthening of their power position. Adult power and convenience need to be disentangled from assumptions about children's best interests. Adult might is neither right nor a 'right'. The protection of children involves challenging the coercive power of parents and recognizing the moral and practical value of children's own reasoned resistance to parental violence and coercion.

## Chapter 8

# *Respecting Rights: Service-user Rights in Child Welfare*

Over the years family-centred practices have been developing across international service systems in a variety of ways. Indeed, speaking from an American perspective, Pecora and his colleagues (Pecora, Reed-Ashcraft and Kirk 2001) note that family-centred services are some of the fastest growing programme areas in mental health, youth justice and child welfare. Broadly speaking, bringing 'family' back into the child welfare equation has taken the form of family preservation in the United States, family participation in England, and family decision-making in New Zealand (Connolly 1999). Each acknowledge the importance of family to the long-term interests and well-being of children. In their various ways each seeks to mobilize the family to support the care and protection of the children.

However, in recent years writers have also noted the increased intensity of child welfare work internationally (Birmingham, Berry and Bussey 1996; Pecora, Whittaker and Maluccio 1992; Briar-Lawson, Schmid and Harris 1997). Heightened awareness of child abuse has resulted in a significant increase in the reporting of suspected abuse cases to systems of child welfare, placing enormous pressure on the resources of the organizations. Indeed, Barter (2001) maintains that child protection systems as they currently exist are ill equipped to deal with the contemporary realities that confront families and communities, and as a consequence many systems are experiencing multi-dimensional crises. Corollary to this difficult state of affairs, the increased emphasis on child safety and a lower tolerance for the conditions that may be considered issues of care or protection have contributed to a shift to a more interventionist approach in child welfare in recent years. Services, at least in English-speaking nations, have tended to become more risk-averse (Connolly 2004). This brings us to the central issues we consider in this chapter: the relationship between the family and the state, the question of service users' rights to interventions that resonate with their needs, and the ways in which the rights of parents, children and families are negotiated in the context of risk and needs-based state intervention.

# Child protection, risk aversion and the state

Although many systems have acknowledged the importance of family-centred, or family-supportive responses within child welfare, numerous countries continue to struggle with the tension between the dominance of forensic approaches in investigative practice and the need to locate child protection within the broader system of family support. Indeed, this tension has been identified as *the* issue confronting child welfare in the twenty-first century (Tomison 2004). Increasingly high community and political expectations that social workers must protect all children and never miss a single case of abuse have driven social workers toward increasingly forensic investigations that in turn have influenced the general nature and style of practice (Ferguson 2004). Even when countries have family-responsive legal frameworks, a dominant aversion to risk can shift the pendulum from family-centred work toward professionally dominated practice and more adversarial approaches. To understand this pendulum shift in practice over time, and its impact on the rights of service users, it is useful for us to look briefly at the ways in which practice has developed in systems of child welfare.

Countries have different ways of defining abuse and neglect, and they have their own ways of responding to family issues. Systems develop in response to a unique set of social and cultural conditions, and because of this, statutory responses to child care and protection concerns with respect to law, policy and practice can vary considerably cross-nationally. According to Hetherington (2002), three important factors influence the functioning of child welfare systems: structures, professional ideology and culture.

*Structural systems* provide the mechanisms through which services are delivered. These may be organized at a central or regional governmental level, or they may be provided by local non-government systems. The structural system influences both the way in which interventions occur and the thinking behind them. For example, Grevot (2002, p.3) argues that the French child welfare system:

> is rooted in the spirit of the Fifth Republic, with the symbolic alliance between the State and the family for the up-bringing and education of children – child being understood both as a member of a family as well as a citizen to be.

The development of the children's judges system as the 'secular arm of the state' created the structural framework that would influence the French system of child welfare for 50 years. It gave the French system a unique flavour around which services for families have developed.

How structural systems fit together is also important. In England, the call for a 'whole-of-government' approach, providing more integrated systems of welfare, health and education, if successful, will influence the ways in which child protection work will evolve as cross-sectoral relationships develop and are sustained.

*Legal frameworks* contribute importantly to the structural system and also influence levels of state intervention. How the law provides for the needs of children and families in child welfare clearly influences the way in which practice is undertaken. For example, the introduction of the Children, Young Persons and their Families Act (1989) in Aotearoa New Zealand had the effect of changing radically the ways in which children and families are responded to by reinforcing greater family decision-making and signalling less state intervention into family life (Connolly 1999). Equally, the introduction of the Children Act (England and Wales) in the same year provided a platform for partnership work with families.

How systems of welfare develop is also influenced by *professional ideology*. Practitioners have theories that guide their practice and influence their decision-making in child care and protection work. As noted earlier, over the past two decades models of best practice in child welfare have reflected an ideological shift toward a greater commitment to family empowerment and family participation in the processes that concern them. Strengths-based perspectives have also influenced a shift away from more traditional pathology or deficit models. At the same time, risk discourses, including practices that place a greater emphasis on safeguarding children through the use of risk assessment and actuarial tools, have also played their part in shaping practice in a less than constructive way (Parton 2006). In this regard, systems that allow greater use of professional judgment look distinctly different from highly bureaucratized systems with heavily proceduralized requirements. According to Hetherington (2002), while organizational structures, resources, and law provide the influencing environment for child welfare practice, actual decision-making is nevertheless often based on professional knowledge and theory.

Finally, child welfare systems are influenced by the *culture* of the society within which they exist. 'Culture influences and expresses expectations of the various roles that should be played by the state, the family, and by the community in relation to the child' (Hetherington 2002, p.14). Since child welfare encapsulates the complex relationships between state and family, it is significant that the ways in which a society perceives these relationships will influence both philosophy and practice.

Although there would appear to be considerable commonality in terms of the challenges facing child protection systems internationally, writers have identified two distinct ways in which different countries intervene in the lives of families. Spratt (2001), for example, notes a basic 'schism' reflecting opposing positions in child welfare: one that is characterized by a family support orientation and one that is characterized by a child protection orientation. The child protection orientation involves:

> a primary concern to protect children from abuse, usually from parents who are often considered morally flawed and legally culpable. The social work processes associated with this orientation are built around legislative and

investigatory concerns, with the relationship between social workers and parents often becoming adversarial in nature. (Spratt 2001, p.934)

By comparison, the family support orientation sees the nature of the problem differently, 'arising more from family conflict or dysfunction, which, in turn, is seen to stem from social and psychological difficulties which are much more responsive to public aid' (Parton 2006). Countries in continental West Europe (for example, Belgium, Sweden, France, Germany) have been identified as more frequently adopting a family-support approach, while English-speaking nations (e.g. England, Canada, United States, Australia) have tended toward a more adversarial child-protection practice. Although these distinctions are necessarily generalized and to a degree oversimplified, they do provide a context for understanding the ways in which services have developed over time.

Many commentators have expressed concern about the impact of adversarial child protection investigative responses and the ways in which they have the effect of increasing the level of state intrusiveness into the lives of families (Ferguson 2004; Munro 2002; Parton 2006; Scott 2006). Some writers have argued that screening the whole population for at-risk children and undertaking more and more child abuse enquiries has the potential to actually *increase* the risk of child abuse for many children by destabilizing families and by creating an overburdened system that struggles to respond to children who really are at high risk (Scott 2006). Critical of this highly interventionist approach, Scott (p.6) goes on to argue that as a consequence, English-speaking child protection systems have become 'like giant Casualty Departments required to respond to a flood of patients, the vast majority of whom do not require hospitalization and would be much better managed by the local GP'. In addition, recent research looking at the consequences of developing more risk-averse and reactive systems has suggested that the short-term solutions adopted can also have unintended negative consequences for children in the longer term (Mansell 2006).

While much criticism has centred on the way in which state resources have been diverted toward risk management and the delivery of service at the front-end (Doolan and Connolly 2006), Parton's (2006) insightful analysis of 'the preventative state' raises many issues relating to the broadening of state intervention within an early intervention framework. Describing the shifts in service provision over time, Parton notes the significant moves in England toward a greater emphasis on early intervention and the need for a more 'joined-up' system of government to achieve this. A more proactive approach has the potential to achieve multiple benefits:

[by] increasing knowledge of a whole range of individual and social problems…actions could be taken before these problems became chronic. Not only would this be better for the people concerned, but also the financial savings to society over the longer term would be considerable. (Parton 2006, p.91)

In giving life to this proactive approach the government in England has invested significantly in policies that have legitimized early state intervention in the lives of children and families through the broadening of state responsibility and the safety net it provides for children in need. The greater emphasis on children in need, perhaps inevitably, carries with it a state imperative to increase its responsiveness through the building of more complex infrastructures, including the expansion of the surveillance mechanisms it requires to act.

How this level of state surveillance impacts upon effective child protection work we will return to later in the chapter. First, however, we will look in more detail at how state intervention is influenced by professional practice *within* the system itself.

## Cultures of practice and their impact on state intervention

While broader policy initiatives and law influence the ways in which the state intervenes in the lives of children and families, professional cultures also influence statutory workers in the exercising of their professional power. The ways in which professional cultures impact on professionals' day-to-day practice can also influence how the rights of children and families are respected. Cultures of practice relate to Hetherington's notion of professional ideology and the ideas that guide practitioners in their decision-making, which we described earlier in the chapter. Professional cultures generate culturally reflexive responses in practice (Connolly *et al.* 2006) and, as we have seen, child welfare has been variously influenced by broadly defined family support and child protection orientations. In day-to-day practice these positions can be conceptualized along a more finely differentiated continuum from family-led to professionally driven practice models (see Figure 8.1).

The family-led model of the continuum encapsulates the notion of family determination within practice. In this regard it is essentially a rights-based approach which seeks to balance the rights of the child to personal security and material subsistence with the rights of the family to care for their own in the way they believe is in the child's best interest and to participate in decision-making that will impact upon them as a family. It embraces family decision-making and family determined processes and solutions. Within this model, the family, including the extended family and broader kinship system, is acknowledged as having the greatest knowledge of the child, and the commitment required to respond to the child's needs in the longer term. This shifts practice from a focus upon the nuclear family or a parent to a broader conceptualization of family and the family strengths that can be utilized within the broader family system. This responds to some of the concerns that have been expressed regarding the capacity of family members to contribute to decision-making (Banks 2006), as it often provides a larger pool of people from within the kinship network. The professionals take a supportive role in facilitating processes of family decision-making and solution-finding. Because

**Family-led model**

Characterized by:
extended family-driven decision-making following full information access; family solution-focused processes at all phases of the work; family development of plans and family monitoring of safety plans, etc.

**Professionally infused model**

Characterized by:
family-centred processes, but with professional involvement at critical decision-making times. Family is more obviously dependent on professional help, and worker keen to be involved.

**Family-infused model**

Characterized by:
professionally selected family involvement, and/or participation in decision-making processes. Professionally determined processes are likely to be at the level of consultation, for example, with respect to care decision-making.

**Professionally driven model**

Characterized by:
professionally determined assessment and/or investigation, child protection team decision-making followed by professionally determined processes and practices. Often this reflects a heavy reliance on alternative care options.

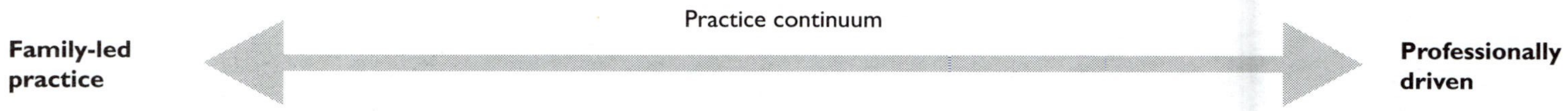

**Family-led practice**

Practice continuum

**Professionally driven**

*Figure 8.1 Continuum from family-led to professionally driven practice*

the family has the key role in deciding what is in the child's best interests and how that can be secured, it is perhaps not surprising that members are more likely to support the child being cared for within the family system, whether this includes state involvement or not. Practice transparency is important, together with family solution-focused processes throughout all phases of the work.

At the other end of the continuum, the professionally driven model is more likely to reflect the characteristics of a child rescue approach to practice. Here we can see elements of traditional practice where professionals determine the nature of the assessment process, dominate decision-making and shape the practice solutions. Professionalized monitoring and a heavy reliance on foster rather than kinship care solutions for children who cannot live with their parents are more likely to be a characteristic of this model. Because child abuse and neglect investigations within this model have the potential to involve legal processes and courts, there is a focus on the proper gathering and management of the evidence of child abuse – the forensic aspects of child protection practice. There is a danger that the risk and forensic focus of child protection work at this end of the continuum will result in an over-use of statutory powers. This approach does not ignore rights. It does emphasize the rights of children to personal security and material subsistence and the legal rights of parents in the context of court action, but it often underemphasizes the rights of children to maintain their connections with their family and culture.

In between we are likely to see practice more or less influenced by the two poles. While generally more strongly located toward the professionally driven practice pole, the family-infused model nevertheless has elements of family involvement, but this is largely determined by the professional. Here we are more likely to see the professional deciding if, where and how the family might be involved in the process. When a child is in state care, the professional is more likely to be at the centre of planning, negotiating the child's access to cross-sectoral resources and making key decisions, for example, placement change.

The professionally infused model, while having more elements of the purer family-led approach, nevertheless has greater professional involvement at critical decision-making times. It can reflect a rights-based orientation in which the family clearly influences professional involvement, but the emphasis here is on a family–state partnership rather than family empowerment. This is an important distinction, for as Banks (2006, p.120) notes, 'Empowerment is also a contested concept'. In this context of our continuum, partnership work with parents characterizes the statutory intervention, with the professional providing support and monitoring as required.

Binary positioning, while useful analytically, tends to reflect differently from human reality. Because practice generally responds to circumstance, it would be unlikely for practice to be consistently at one point along the contin-uum or fully up one end or the other. There will be times when the family-led model may introduce professionally driven elements. Conversely, profession-ally driven practice may at times more fully involve family in the course of the work. Practice can shift along this continuum and families can get more or less of a family-focused response over time. Even systems having family-supportive policy and law are not immune to their services becoming increasingly profes-sionally driven under the pressure of increasing workloads (Connolly 2006b). Despite this, professionals still have the power to affect service intervention along this continuum, and thus determine the level of state involvement in the lives of children and their families. Because of this, Banks' (2006) discussion of 'democratic professionalism' is of significant importance. She argues that:

> Democratic professionalism entails giving more power to service users in the context of the professional relationship, but the focus is on the professional as the one giving the power. So although the service user may be given more rights and be referred to as a 'partner'…it could be argued that it is still the professional that is in control. (Banks 2006, p.116)

Here democratic professionalism can be seen as an attempt to become more responsive to service-user needs and interests, ensuring that they have opportu-nities to participate, but nevertheless retaining some elements of control. In many respects it comes down to the degree of tolerance a jurisdiction has with respect to positioning along the family-led to professionally driven continuum. Some will be able to tolerate, encourage or mandate greater levels of family par-ticipation and empowerment, some less. Yet in some ways, regardless what mandate the system provides, we agree with Banks when she argues 'while laws, policies and procedures can lay the ground rules for service users' rights, they are meaningless if not developed alongside the commitment of agencies and workers to give support and resources for service users to exercise their rights' (p.117). We will return to this issue in Chapter 10.

## Risk-averse practice

Risk aversion is more likely to push practitioners towards the professionally driven end of the practice continuum. The more professionally driven practice becomes the harder it is for families to participate meaningfully in the processes that affect them, and to exercise their right to participation (Theis 2004). A number of drivers have encouraged risk-averse practice over time. Child homicide and the pattern of response to these tragic deaths have been particu-larly influential.

In 1973, the tragic death of Maria Colwell in England brought child homicide to public attention. Maria was seven years old when she was killed by her stepfather. Living in foster care for several years, she had been returned to live with her mother and stepfather when they successfully applied for custody through the court. The review that took place following her death was strongly critical of the English child welfare system and its capacity to keep Maria safe. Since the Colwell enquiry, publicly released death reviews of high-profile tragedies have become increasingly common, and have impacted significantly on the way in which child welfare systems have evolved over time.

In his analysis of risk discourses within child protection work, Ferguson (2004, p.110) identifies the negative effects of the disclosure of child death reviews, the responses of the media to those disclosures, and child death enquiries in recent years:

> With the invariably aggressive attentions of the media, public disclosures of child deaths and inquiries into system 'failures' have played a crucial symbolic role in opening out child abuse and protection services, as well as professional anxiety, to public view.

Each of these – disclosures, media attention, and the enquiries that follow – have impacted on the development of more risk-averse practice over time (see Figure 8.2).

Over the past 30 years child protection work has become increasingly visible to the public. Knowledge about child abuse has increased and child deaths by homicide are graphically reported in the modern media, understandably creating strong community reaction. Calls for accountability follow these deaths, typically involving an enquiry, with expectations of statutory reform. The common response is to introduce new protocols, tools and guidelines to ensure that a tragedy like this will never happen again.

According to Munro (2005, p.378), enquiries into child deaths have generally satisfied community need to find a scapegoat, and to 'meet that need by focusing primarily on whether any professional was at fault'. She identifies three mechanisms that are used to moderate and control professional behaviour:

- punish the culprits and so encourage the others to be more diligent
- reduce the role of individual human reasoning as much as possible by formalizing wherever possible with increasingly precise instructions to the human operators
- increase the monitoring of practice to ensure compliance with instructions.

(Munro 2005, p.378)

It is likely that these three mechanisms will resonate with practitioners who daily confront the dilemmas and anxieties of child protection work. Even though they may not have experienced the death of a child themselves, most will have followed the protracted processes of formal enquiry and noticed the blaming process that it has become. They will also be aware that reflecting on practice in hindsight invariably provides insights that are not always clearly available to practitioners responding in the here and now.

While Ferguson (2004, p.122) notes the relative rarity of child homicide, he is nevertheless struck by the increased anxiety that the risk of child death produces:

The paradox is that social workers' fears and anxieties have multiplied at a time when the actual phenomenon of child death in child protection is such an extremely rare experience that only a tiny fraction of professionals will ever encounter it.

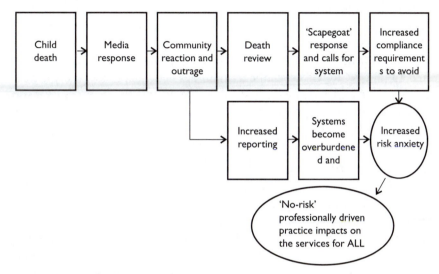

Figure 8.2 Impact of child death on child welfare service systems

Where a climate of blame exists, supported by the application of the three mechanisms outlined by Munro above, it is perhaps not surprising to find child protection workers practising risk management more conservatively in contemporary child protection practice.

It is clear that an increasingly sensationalist media in recent years has had a key role in shaping public perception of child abuse and the systems that respond to it (Parton 2006). Research into media attention and the impact it has on the reporting of children at risk by the public suggests a close correlation between the two. Mansell (2006) found that periods of high media attention coincided with periods of higher notifications for abuse to statutory services, and extreme growth in reporting of abuse also follows very intensive media attention. Ferguson (2004, p.195) remains pessimistic about the way forward:

> The relentless focus on professional 'failure' to protect means that scandal politics, social anxiety and the questioning of expertise has not only expanded into every aspect of child welfare services but also shows no signs of abating.

This is a particularly significant issue as we come to consider in more detail the relationship between the state and the family, and the issue of service-user rights in the context of child welfare. Rights-based practice in child protection is inextricably linked to greater service-user participation and, again using Beresford's words, 'meeting their different self-defined needs in the way they, ensured full knowledge, support and choice, prefer' (Beresford, cited in Smith

2005, p.102). Because of the emphasis on service-user autonomy and participation, rights-based perspectives will resonate more strongly toward the family-led end of the practice continuum. Professionally driven practice tends to be highly interventionist in nature, and we would argue that the further along the continuum you move toward professionally driven practice, the less likely practice will accommodate the full range of relevant human rights, particularly those associated with ensuring continuity of connection with family and culture (Article 29 (c) UNCROC) as well as the rights of parents (Articles 5 and 14 (2) UNCROC). Given the relationships between professionally driven processes, state interventionism and risk-averse systems, the more risk-averse a professionally driven system becomes, the less room there will be to negotiate service-user rights during interventions.

## State intervention in family life

Resting at the heart of this issue is the nature of the relationship between the family and the state, the rights of the family, and the role the state plays in the protection of children.

In Chapter 4 we discussed the 'Limited Parental Rights' in which parents have significant but limited rights to raise their children according to what they perceive to be in the children's best interests. This is generally consistent with what has been termed the 'liberal standard' – a prescription that state interference in the family can only be justified when there is a serious risk of harm for the child:

> The liberal seems to countenance breaching familial privacy only *after* there is a reason to believe the child is being exposed to serious harm, and not to establish that such harm is occurring…once the mistreatment of the child has become public then its protection can include measures which override family privacy. (Archard 1993, p.128)

Archard's viewpoint implies a distinction between the state intervening on the basis of believing that a child has been harmed, and the state having a more general surveillance role which may pick up evidence of harm or need. We will come back to this issue in the context of early intervention strategies later in the chapter. Nevertheless, the 'liberal standard' has generally sought to accommodate both the protection needs of the child and the right of the family not to be unjustifiably intruded upon by the state. One could also argue, on the grounds of both protection needs and human rights, that the child should be able to grow up without being exposed to precipitant or unnecessary action by the state (Article 9.1 UNCROC).

This brings us back to the nature and threshold of statutory intervention, and the impact of more risk-averse responses by the state on the rights of children and their families in matters of child protection.

It is clear that many systems of child welfare have, for a variety of reasons, become increasingly risk-averse, resulting in more and more families being tangled up in the statutory net (Scott 2006). Further, Ferguson (2004) has argued that 'conveyer belt social work', a characteristic of overburdened, risk-averse systems, is more concerned with meeting targets and getting families through the system than being responsive to family needs and the promotion of child safety and healing. Clarifying and respecting families' rights under these circumstances can easily be undermined. It is not that professionally driven practice necessarily lacks an emphasis on service-user rights; indeed parents are likely to be made fully aware of their legal rights as professionals exercise their statutory powers. But such adversarial responses are more likely to result in parents responding defensively or legalistically. What professionally driven practice may lack, however, is recognition of the moral and human rights of families to meaningful participation (Article 9.2 UNCROC) and self-determination, and the suppleness to manage risk, child safety and family support.

Many countries have recognized the negative impact of risk-averse systems that concentrate their efforts at the investigatory front-end of the child protection process. Risk-averse practice cultures are, nevertheless, difficult to shift. That said, England has been at the forefront in its efforts to refocus child protection services toward more family-supportive responses. The introduction of the Assessment Framework in 2000 was effective in broadening the role of statutory services in this regard, and in 2003 the government green paper, *Every Child Matters*, set out the most significant child welfare reform packages seen in England for 30 years. The major inquiry into the murder of eight-year-old Victoria Climbié provided the impetus for the change, and following an extensive process of consultation on the document, a set of proposals to strengthen early intervention systems, improve accountability and foster cross-agency work was put in place. Child protection would no longer be seen in isolation; rather, it was to be seen within the context of broader concerns relating to children's well-being. Hence the emphasis shifted from the state providing protective services for children at risk of abuse, to also embracing children in need. Paradoxically, it is this refocusing on well-being and need that has created a new set of dynamics relating to rights and responsibilities, and has once again reshaped the relationship between the family and the state.

Perhaps inevitably, state responsiveness to need increases the number of children and families becoming entangled with the state in the context of child care and protection. The state threshold for intervention is lowered to ensure that children who are not having their needs met will not slip under the bar. According to Parton (2006, p.173), this creates more porous boundaries between those children identified as vulnerable, those in need, and the rest of the nation's children: 'every child, and anyone who is or might be responsible for children is implicated where there might be a "cause for concern"'.

While the rationale for early intervention by the state is laudable and important for the long-term outcomes for children, there are nevertheless a set of consequences that impact on the role the state plays in family matters and diminish family autonomy, thereby compromising family rights. Increased effort by the state to identify and support children in need requires a greater infrastructure of system support and surveillance (Parton 2006). The expectation that no child in need will fall through the cracks places huge pressure on systems to transform themselves in ways that will withstand future criticism. Increasing procedural expectations and expanding the monitoring of children requires more sophisticated methods of surveillance. Safeguarding children therefore becomes an even more complex endeavour in which the sharing of information relating to a much larger group of families becomes necessary. In the shift from the 'liberal standard', rather than the state intervening only when 'there is a reason to believe the child is being exposed to serious harm', its more general surveillance role will pick up evidence of need which will trigger some form of intervention. Perhaps ironically, rather than ensuring a shift away from a culture of risk-aversion, a system that tries to catch every situation of need in its net may begin to share elements of risk-driven child protection cultures:

> Because the systems are so extensive, the definitions of concern so broad and the fact that the professionals who have responsibilities for children are held so (publicly) accountable (if things go wrong), there is a huge potential that worries about children's vulnerabilities will lead to a huge explosion of activity which only tangentially relates to the concerns of children and young people themselves. (Parton 2006, p.185)

In this situation opportunities to protect the core human rights of children at risk can become swamped by the task of monitoring all children and responding to a plethora of needs.

Overburdened systems can be dangerous for children. Scott (2006, p.1) argues in reference to Australia and New Zealand that 'trawling through escalating numbers of low-income families to find a small minority of cases in which statutory intervention is necessary and justifiable' has the potential to actually increase the risk of child abuse by destabilizing families and creating an overburdened system that finds it increasingly difficult to respond to children who really are at risk. Such systems struggle to meet the expectations of their communities, or the children and families they serve. While Scott is writing here about risk-averse child protection systems, her criticisms nevertheless sound a note of caution for systems contemplating or actually trawling for need. It is not unusual for the reforms of one era to vex society in the next.

This brings us finally to the issue of recognizing and respecting children's rights in the context of greater state interventionism.

## State interventions and respecting children's rights

Systems of child welfare can be very adult focused, with decision-making generally being the purview of adults who believe they act in the child's best interests. As writers have noted, however, the meaningful participation of children in matters that concern them is important from a number of perspectives:

> Participation by children matters, not only because it is an acknowledgement of their civil rights but because without listening to children and understanding how they experience their world, how can we begin to determine what will ensure their protection and enable them to grow into healthy adults? (Schofield and Thoburn 1996, p.1)

It has also been argued that involving children is important because children themselves are better able to suggest ways of implementing their rights that will respect their dignity. In eliciting children's views directly adults show respect for children as persons (Morrow 2004). Although attention to children's rights may seem like a loss of power for parents and other adults, Morrow (2004, p.166) notes in her research that children themselves appreciate the complexity of becoming fully self-determining beings:

> They want to be talked to and consulted, and given information, and to be able to give their point of view and have their opinions taken into account. Even quite young children saw decision-making as potentially problematic and could see this from others' perspectives.

Cashmore (2002) argues that children are not necessarily seeking to control decision-making, but that they do want to be informed about and involved in the process.

It is clear that UNCROC expects children to be actively consulted in matters that concern them, as Article 12 of the Convention notes:

> State Parties shall assure to the child who is capable of forming his or her own views the right to express those views freely in all matters affecting the child, the views of the child being given due weight in accordance with the age and maturity of the child.

Writers have argued that this article is critical to our understanding of children's rights in child welfare as it demands a shift from a paternalistic approach to one where children are seen as stakeholders in decisions. Children have a right to have input rather than merely being the object of concern or the subject of decision (Cashmore 2002).

Summarizing research on the perspectives of children reveals several themes that are important from a human rights perspective: the child's lack of knowledge of the circumstances leading up to their entry into care; their lack of participation and consultation in the decision-making process; their low level of satisfaction with their experiences of being in care; their lack of contact with their biological families; and their erratic relationship with the social workers (Connolly 2004). A growing body of research indicates that systems of child welfare could do much more to incorporate a children's rights perspective in their service responses. What is sometimes difficult to conceptualize, however, is what more responsive systems might look like.

A useful way of visualizing levels of children's participation in child welfare systems has been presented by Shier (2001). Influenced by Hart's 'ladder of participation' (1992), Shier provides a tool that helps practitioners to explore increasing levels of participation by children. Five levels of participation are conceptualized in the model: children being listened to, children being supported to express their views, children's views being taken into account, children being involved in decision-making processes, and children sharing decision-making power and responsibility. In each level of participation, Shier identifies three aspects of engagement: openings, opportunities and obligations. Openings focus on the practitioner's willingness to consider children's participation – a signal of intent if you will. Opportunities describe the possibilities that exist within the child welfare system. Obligations identify any policy that dictates that staff should function at that level (see Figure 8.3).

At the very basic level (level 1) the view of the child, once expressed, is listened to by responsible adults and policy reflects this requirement. At level 2, the expectation is that the child's view is actively sought out, and that they are supported to express their view. Level 3 requires that the child's view is given due weight in decision-making, and that there are processes in place to enable this. Shier notes that level 3 is the minimum level required to comply with the demands of UNCROC. Levels 4 and 5 represent the highest levels of participation: level 4 expects that children are actively involved in decision-making processes, and level 5 expects that children will share power and responsibility for that decision-making. Thus the movement from level 1 to 5 is likely to reflect children's development as they increasingly acquire the capabilities needed to exercise agency. Considerable scaffolding is necessary at earlier ages until children acquire the freedom and well-being goods necessary to function as independent moral agents. As we noted in earlier chapters the human rights of children are usefully seen as protective capsules that maximize the degree to which their interests are actively factored into decisions that directly impact on their lives.

The 'pathways to participation' model is useful in clearly identifying the commitment required to meet the expectations of UNCROC. It also explores the state's level of interest in, or tolerance for, more intensive participation by children. Giving effect to increased levels of participation in systems of child welfare has been identified as a major challenge (Parton 2006). Parton argues that it takes a degree of organizational maturity, a greater tolerance of risk, and less complex systems for monitoring children to embrace more participatory practices. Indeed, in developing more and more complex systems to monitor children, we may be in danger of further losing sight of children's rights. Over the next decade the rights of children are likely to be at the forefront of professional and community concern. As we reform systems of child welfare, we need to future-proof services by taking into account children's rights in the here and now.

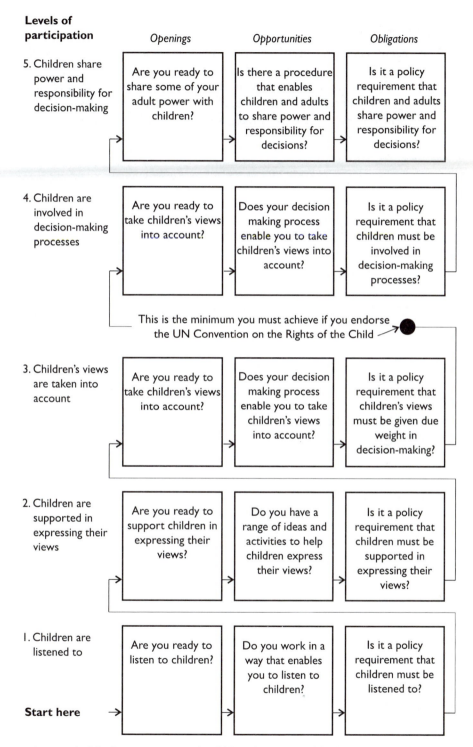

| Levels of participation | Openings | Opportunities | Obligations |
|---|---|---|---|
| 5. Children share power and responsibility for decision-making | Are you ready to share some of your adult power with children? | Is there a procedure that enables children and adults to share power and responsibility for decisions? | Is it a policy requirement that children and adults share power and responsibility for decisions? |
| 4. Children are involved in decision-making processes | Are you ready to take children's views into account? | Does your decision making process enable you to take children's views into account? | Is it a policy requirement that children must be involved in decision-making processes? |

This is the minimum you must achieve if you endorse the UN Convention on the Rights of the Child

| | | | |
|---|---|---|---|
| 3. Children's views are taken into account | Are you ready to take children's views into account? | Does your decision making process enable you to take children's views into account? | Is it a policy requirement that children's views must be given due weight in decision-making? |
| 2. Children are supported in expressing their views | Are you ready to support children in expressing their views? | Do you have a range of ideas and activities to help children express their views? | Is it a policy requirement that children must be supported in expressing their views? |
| 1. Children are listened to<br><br>Start here | Are you ready to listen to children? | Do you work in a way that enables you to listen to children? | Is it a policy requirement that children must be listened to? |

*Figure 8.3 Shier's 'Pathways to Participation' model (2001). Reprinted with kind permission from the author and the publisher.*

## Conclusions

This chapter completes Part Two of this book in which we have navigated various practice domains using a rights perspective to guide us. In doing so we have clarified the rights that service users can expect to have recognized and respected. We will now broaden our analysis and look at the ways in which rights perspectives can be actively integrated into the delivery of services

# Part Three
# Integrating Rights-based Ideas

## Chapter 9

# Rights-based Values in Practice Frameworks

Practice within the human services area is essentially values-based and is generally rooted in a core set of values that give purpose, meaning and direction to the work. Non-discrimination, democracy, human rights, client participation and integrity are important values that resonate in codes of practice internationally. Nevertheless, integrating rights-based values into practice is a complex endeavour particularly, as we have seen in earlier chapters, when the rights of different parties are perceived to be in conflict.

In this final section of the book we consider the ways in which rights-based values and ideas can be integrated into human service work. In this chapter we explore practice systems themselves and how the principles of inclusiveness, participation and shared responsibility shift us toward a greater emphasis on rights within practice.

## Why integrate rights-based ideas into practice?

In this book we have talked about the way in which agency, self-determination and participation impact on the potential for people to achieve good lives. Increasingly the need to involve service users has been connected to the realization of good outcomes:

> Service users should be regarded as active participants with a right to effect support, but equally, with responsibilities to take up support...and play an active role in improving their outcomes...lack of control over one's own life is a key contributory factor to poor outcomes. (Department for Education and Skills 2007, pp.86–87).

Having an 'outcomes orientation' requires that we think about how services impact on the future lives of service users, and how interventions contribute to their longer-term outcomes. This means supporting people to become healthy and thriving members of a society which they feel valued by and connected to. The next decade will require an increasing responsiveness by practitioners within a constantly changing environment. Practice will always need to evolve as it confronts contemporary needs. As illustrated in Chapters 2 and 3, migrant populations are changing the face of human service work. Workers are also encountering much more complex family systems with multiple maternal and paternal parenting and step-parenting arrangements. These require a further consideration of how rights and perceptions of rights play themselves out in family and community systems, and how services need to develop richer frameworks to respond to contemporary need and emergent rights.

While we agree that incorporating rights-based values, such as inclusiveness, self-determination and participation, has the potential to support better outcomes, we would also argue that it is important because it is ethically the right thing to do. We agree with Skegg (2005) when she discusses the benefit of rights-based approaches on the basis of entitlement, rather than charity. Entitlement within a rights-based approach, she suggests, increases empowerment and when utilized well can strengthen practice.

In the context of working with children, there has also been recent encouragement for governments to consider children as full human beings as well as participating members of families and broader kinship networks (Henricson and Bainham 2005). In Chapter 7 we noted that professional and community attention to the rights of children is increasing, and argued the need to future-proof services by taking children's rights into account now.

## Integrating rights-based values and ideas into practice frameworks

While we support the greater emphasis on rights-based values and ideas in practice, we nevertheless acknowledge that this requires the development of supple frameworks that balance competing needs and interests while at the same time upholding the rights of all the individuals involved. In Chapter 4 we discussed a youth justice practice framework that integrated needs- and rights-based approaches within the context of restorative justice practice. The framework takes into consideration the needs and rights of young people who offend against the law, the needs and rights of victims, and the broader participatory rights of families, and also bridges the gap between welfare and justice orientations. It is this type of framework that we would suggest provides the greatest potential for rights-based values and ideas to influence the practice of workers in ways that are sensitive to both rights and needs. We will now look at a similar New Zealand practice framework that has been developed to support work with children and families in child welfare, and end the chapter by looking at the ways in which these ideas could also be incorporated into work with offenders.

## Care and protection practice framework: rights and needs

Organizations attempt to shape practice in a variety of ways. For example, the Assessment Framework that has been introduced in Britain (discussed in Chapter 8) provides a systematic approach for analyzing information about children and families. The framework has a number of dimensions that are explored during an assessment relating to the child's developmental needs, the ability of caregivers to respond to those needs, and the impact of external factors on the parents' abilities and the child's well-being (Department of Health 2000). Recent research suggests that the Assessment Framework is, indeed, influencing the way in which families are responded to by practitioners (Cleaver and Walker 2004). This is an important development that will clearly influence practice with children and families in child welfare. These kinds of initiatives also raise the possibility of embedding rights-based ideas within frameworks that support good outcomes for children.

The New Zealand care and protection practice framework developed by Connolly (2006a) weaves a set of rights- and evidenced-based driving principles through the phases of the work in order to achieve desired outcomes for children. Like the youth justice framework discussed in Chapter 4, the metaphor used to capture the interwoven nature of the framework is that of a Maori *kete*, representing, in this context, a basket of knowledge, the woven strands making the practice stronger (see Figure 9.1).

Three philosophical strands, each linked to rights-based ideas, provide the basis of the framework: the *child-centred* perspective, the *family-led and culturally responsive* perspective, and the *strengths- and evidence-based* perspective. These three perspectives influence practice across the three phases of the New Zealand care and protection process: *assessment and engagement, seeking solutions,* and *securing safety and belonging.*

The first strand of Connolly's framework – the *child-centred* perspective – is embedded in a human rights orientation and is also supported by the research and literature that informs this perspective. Central to this strand is the United

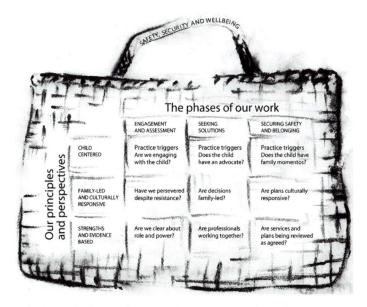

*Figure 9.1 The New Zealand Care and Protection Practice Framework (Connolly 2006a, p.4). Reproduced with kind permission of the British Journal of Social Work*

Nations Convention for the Rights of the Child (UNCROC), and its underlying theme of children's entitlement to special care, provision, protection and participation (Office of the Commission for Children 2005), the principles of which also underpin child welfare legislation in the UK. Within the New Zealand context, the welfare and interests of the child are of primary importance, as is the child's right to preserve their own identity, and to enjoy their own culture, religion and language. While one might assume that child protection work is, by definition, child-centred, 'practice tends to operate from an adult point of view, with little reference to childhood cultures and the need for children to be involved in the processes that concern them' (Connolly *et al.* 2006, p.60). Research also indicates that children and young people have the capacity to participate in decisions that affect them and therefore have the right to be listened to (Cashmore 2002; Littlechild 2000). In addition to children's rights, the child-centred strand of the framework also addresses the attachment needs of the child, and the application of attachment theory to child abuse and neglect. Stability of care and attachment has been found to be critical to child well-being (Cassidy and Shaver 1999; Watson 2005) and the framework recognizes the need to bring together rights- and needs-based ideas in practice. In essence, the framework captures the most relevant research and best practice ideas and uses them to reinforce children's rights and child advocacy practice. In addition, as we shall see, the framework also places importance upon the rights of families to participate in child welfare matters that concern them. From a human rights perspective, a critical role of the family is to *scaffold* children's developing agency – to help them explicitly develop the capabilities to identify and act in the service of their own (evolving) interests.

The *family-led and culturally responsive* strand of the framework reinforces the need to work with family cultures and to support families in their primary role of carers and protectors of their children. The driving principles of family empowerment and the collective (extended family) responsibility for children rest at the heart of the framework and guide practice toward more family-responsive approaches. This strand of the framework reinforces the right of families to be involved in matters that concern them and to be the key decision-makers with respect to their children. The need to strengthen families is also recognized, and realized through fostering practice partnerships, and includes processes that involve families in decision-making. Research supporting participatory practice models indicates that families, including extended families, do respond positively when invited to take the lead (Burford 2005; Titcomb and LeCroy 2003), that they can develop rich and diverse plans to support their children when given the opportunity (Thoennes 2003), and that such systems compare favourably in terms of child safety measures (Crampton 2003; Gunderson *et al.* 2003). There are also indications that family-led plans have the potential to provide greater stability for the child (Gunderson, Cahn and Wirth 2003; Wheeler and Johnson 2003). Harnessing the collective strengths of the family for the care and safety of children also recognizes the rights and responsibilities of the extended family and broader kinship systems. Of course, it is imperative that families do not view children simply as means through which they realize their own conceptions of a good life, and therefore run the risk of distorting their children's developing agency. Failure to recognize the scaffolding role of parenting may result in dependent and stunted adults when children mature and effectively amounts to a denial of their fundamental human rights to freedom and well-being.

Supporting the cultural context of the family is also central to this strand of the practice framework. Building alliances with communities and working positively with cultural supports require reflexive social work practice in the context of culturally responsive solutions. While this makes demands upon workers both personally and professionally, it has the potential to strengthen good outcomes for children and families (Webb, Maddocks and Bongilli 2002). As we saw in Chapter 2, human rights and the goods they protect are applicable to different cultures but it is imperative that practitioners make the effort to translate them into meaningful local norms.

The final strand in the framework relates to *strengths- and evidence-based* practice. Understanding what works in practice increases the skill repertoire of workers and, according to Trotter (2004), makes them more likely to be effective than if they rely selectively on limited, idiosyncratic sources of knowledge. With respect to rights-based ideas, Trotter's research is particularly relevant here. His summary of his own and others' research suggests that best practice occurs in the context of role clarity, collaborative problem-solving, pro-social modelling, and sound worker/service-user relationships. When workers respect the human dignity of service users by being clear about their role and being transparent and honest with them, they have been found to be more effective. In supporting collaborative problem-solving, effective workers are able to encourage and support the extended family's agency over plans and decisions relating to their children. Fundamentally, this research supports strengths-based approaches in which good outcomes flow from dialogue and collaboration (Saleebey 1992). In essence, it respects the dignity of service users and their right to formulate their own life plans based upon their beliefs and preferences.

The New Zealand practice framework provides a set of *practice triggers* within an accessible visual model that remind workers of the links between theory and practice, and of the rights-based ideas that are captured within the framework. Each phase of the work has a set of practice triggers (reminders) that have been drawn from the supporting research and practice literature. There are many practice triggers within the framework beyond those focused on rights-based practice (for a fuller discussion of the framework and its practice triggers see Connolly 2006a). Here we will briefly consider those practice triggers that are particularly relevant to rights-based practice across the phases of the care and protection process.

## Engagement and assessment phase

This phase of the work begins with notification and corresponds to the investigative phase in many systems of child welfare. In developing the framework the New Zealand child welfare system aimed to move away from the strong investigative/forensic focus that had previously characterized the work, toward a more engagement-focused practice. By changing the practice language from the previously named 'intake and investigation' phase to 'engagement and assessment', the framework also sought to influence the way in which practitioners perceived the task and therefore the way in which the investigations were undertaken.

Each perspective strand has generated several rights-based triggers.

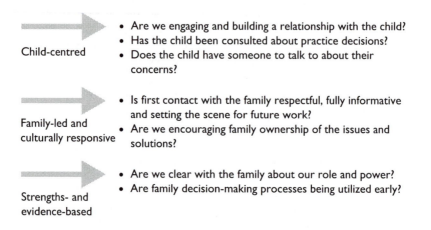

**Child-centred**
- Are we engaging and building a relationship with the child?
- Has the child been consulted about practice decisions?
- Does the child have someone to talk to about their concerns?

**Family-led and culturally responsive**
- Is first contact with the family respectful, fully informative and setting the scene for future work?
- Are we encouraging family ownership of the issues and solutions?

**Strengths- and evidence-based**
- Are we clear with the family about our role and power?
- Are family decision-making processes being utilized early?

*Figure 9.2 Rights-based practice triggers in the engagement and assessment phase*

As we have already seen, the child-centred strand of the model is designed to ensure that practitioners consider the needs and rights of the child when making decisions that impact on their lives. In the first phase of the work the critical task is to establish a relationship with the child, and by doing so to respect their dignity as a human being. In addition, the child's viewpoint needs to be actively canvassed and practitioners must work hard to clearly explain the difficulties confronting the child and family in a way that is accessible and meaningful to them. In order to help the child make sense of what is happening in their world it is important to provide them with a person with whom they can discuss their fears and concerns. These strategies are designed to *scaffold* the child's ability to exercise agency-related rights and to openly express their opinions. The practice triggers thus revolve around issues of engagement, consultation and communication (see Figure 9.2).

The family-led and culturally responsive strand places a priority on ensuring that the rights of family members are acknowledged and factored into the process of decision-making. This is really a matter of respecting the dignity of family members and accepting that despite their difficulties they are likely to have been trying to live the best lives they can. Sadly, as is often the case, histories of abuse and deprivation or even just unforeseen events can result in significant parental problems that make it difficult for them to appreciate the needs of their children. It is important for workers to address explicitly the concerns of family members and take on board their views but at the same time always ensure that the rights of the child are kept in mind. A family has group rights (see Chapter 2) in the sense that it is an entity with specific needs and responsibilities, and often requires considerable resources to develop the capabilities to function as an adaptive entity. The practice triggers revolve around respectful contact and family ownership of the issues and solutions.

Finally, practitioners have a responsibility to base their assessment and engagement processes on reliable and valid procedures. Research literature on what works, relevant theory (e.g. strengths model) and practice guidelines should be utilized when seeking to assess a family's vulnerabilities and strengths. The rights-related triggers of the strengths- and evidence-based strand revolve around the adoption of transparent and valid procedures and attendance to family decision-making processes.

## *Seeking solutions phase*

This phase of the work begins once the social worker has formed a belief that the child is in need of care and/or protection, and work therefore needs to be done toward developing a solution that addresses those needs. Within New Zealand, this would typically involve bringing the family together, including the extended family, in a solution-focused forum: the Family Group Conference (Connolly 1999).

From the child-centred perspective, practitioners need to ensure that the child has been actively involved in the decision-making that affects them. Furthermore, children often struggle to understand the reasons for interventions into family life and their role within them. The concept of scaffolding is also relevant in this phase and it is worth ensuring that children are presented with relevant information about the intervention and its likely impact. Failure to attend to the scaffolding task may cause a child undue distress, adversely influence the family and ultimately jeopardize chances of successful outcomes. Essentially it is a question of respecting the child's developing agency and dignity attendant on being listened to and having input into life-changing decisions. The practice triggers for this strand centre on the inclusion of the child in intervention decision-making and ensuring that the child has an advocate who actively supports their viewpoint and scaffolds their agency attempts (see Figure 9.3).

From the family-led and culturally responsive perspective the key tasks are to make certain that the family is fully informed and involved in decision-making processes and any interventions that follow. Ensuring that all family members have an opportunity to contribute to discussions, and the formulation and implementation of an action plan, is vital and will safeguard their agency while at the same time address the needs and interests of the children involved. In a sense, practitioners can also scaffold the agency attempts of families by facilitating the structuring of safety solutions around the family's core interests and by encouraging members to take the lead at every opportunity. The practice triggers evident in this strand focus on collaborative decision-making and encouraging families to take ownership of intervention plans.

From the strengths- and evidence-based perspective the main objective is to ensure that families possess the knowledge they need to protect their child and themselves when future flashpoints occur. Practitioners need to equip families with sensible strategies for dealing with high-risk situations and link them with appropriate community agencies and supports. In addition, any interventions used should be empirically supported and be implemented by qualified and trained workers. The practice triggers focus on incorporating family strengths and resources into the implementation plan and making sure that families have the necessary information to make good decisions.

## Securing safety and belonging

Once plans are developed, the third phase of the work commences: *ensuring safety* and securing a sense of *belonging* for the child. This may involve support for the family with the child remaining at home, or it may involve a change of placement for the child, either with another family member (kin care) or with alternative care-givers (foster care).

From the child-centred perspective practitioners need to think carefully about the consequences of placing children outside the home. The implemen-

**Child-centred**
- Has the child been actively involved in decision-making processes?
- Are decisions respectful of the child's timeframes?
- Does the child have an advocate?

**Family-led and culturally responsive**
- Is the family fully involved in the process of decision-making?
- Are all family members having an opportunity to contribute?
- Are the decisions family-led?

**Strengths- and evidence-based**
- Does the family have all the information necessary to make sound decisions?
- Are decisions and plans linked to family strengths and resources?

*Figure 9.3 Rights-based practice triggers in the seeking solutions phase*

tation of the plan developed in the previous phase should be directly linked with protecting the child's core interests and, in a sense, be a realization of their human rights to well-being goods. To ensure that freedom rights are not violated, practitioners should confirm that the child is still able to make significant choices despite the changes to their life. The practitioner also needs to ensure that the child grasps how the plan relates to their core interests and experiences a sense of being consulted and listened to. The relevant practice triggers are based on ensuring understanding, seeking placement permanency and monitoring stability.

From the family-led and culturally responsive perspective it is important that the needs of the family are taken into account and that regular contact is maintained with the child if that is at all possible. This will help the child to maintain sense of belonging and connectedness and therefore contribute to their well-being rights. Of course, family contact may need to be carefully monitored and problems identified as early as possible in order to strengthen the functioning of the family and its ability to accommodate the core interests of all members. It goes without saying that the implementation of the care plan should be culturally responsive and meaningful and translate human rights values into acceptable (and justifiable) local norms. The practice triggers revolve around family contact, family input into on-going decision-making, and culturally sensitivity (see Figure 9.4).

Finally, from the strengths- and evidence-based perspective it is crucial that professional relationships are working positively to safeguard service users' rights. Writers agree that coordinated responses provide more effective interventions, reducing the potential for duplication and more targeted services based on what the family actually needs (Bell 1999; Hallett and Birchall 1992; McIntosh 2000). It is also important that service providers are familiar with the relevant codes of practice and intervention protocols and have a deep understanding of the nature of human rights and their justification. It is the responsibility of practitioners to make certain that families have access to the cross-sectoral services they are entitled to, that the service providers communicate well with each other, and that the services are as effective as they can be. The practice triggers are concerned with supporting service users' rights and effective cross-sectoral functioning.

Practice triggers are designed to challenge practitioners. Within each phase of the work, the worker is encouraged to take on board all three perspectives in order to reinforce the importance of maintaining a child-focused, family-based, culturally responsive, and empirically sound intervention. By placing an emphasis on the rights of all service-users during each phase of the work, the framework encourages practitioners to uphold children's rights as well as the human rights of all family members. Inevitably there will be times when there is a conflict of interests. Used as a practice tool in supervision the framework provides a context within which these tensions can be explored and

**Child-centred**
- Does the child understand about care decisions and what is happening?
- Is permanency a priority and is placement stability being closely monitored?

**Family-led and culturally responsive**
- Are family members having regular contact with the child?
- Is the family at the centre of care decision-making?
- Are plans culturally responsive?

**Strengths- and evidence-based**
- Are professional relationships working positively to support service user's rights?
- Are the service user's getting the cross-sectoral services they are entitled to?

*Figure 9.4 Rights-based practice triggers in the securing safety and belonging phase*

worked through. Primarily, the practice triggers function to reinforce the essential ideas of each of the philosophical strands.

We will now explore the development of a similar rights-based practice framework for working with offenders.

## A framework for working with offenders: rights and needs

In recent years there has been a movement within the correctional system that seeks to combine strengths-based and risk management approaches to therapeutic work with offenders (Ward and Maruna 2007). In retrospect, this work fits nicely with a human rights perspective and could easily be seen as an example of rights-based practice. In brief, a rights-based framework can provide an ethical scaffold for offender treatment that goes well beyond traditional approaches by virtue of its emphasis on the importance of primary human goods and the capabilities required to achieve them. It draws out the ethical assumptions often implicit in standard treatment programmes and links them to the agency efforts of the individual in a way that is likely to motivate offenders and also reduce their level of risk. The lack (or distortion) of the internal and external conditions needed to acquire human rights goods (similar to Ward's 'primary human goods' in his Good Lives Model – see Ward and Maruna 2007; Ward and Stewart 2003) can be conceptualized as criminogenic needs (i.e. dynamic risk factors that if modified will reduce the risk of future offending). Therefore, a standard treatment approach that focuses on dynamic risk factors is also likely to promote human rights because of its capability-building emphasis.

Using the rights-based ideas outlined in this book, rights-based practice in offender work needs to (a) reduce risk to the community and (b) promote offenders' core interests and goods. The capability building aspect of treatment focuses on attending both to skills acquisition (e.g. intimacy skills, emotional regulation skills) and value orientation (the need for offenders to understand what their own real interests are, and how they can be realized whilst also responding to the well-being needs and rights of others). Human rights serve a dual purpose in treatment. First, human rights can be used to guide the construction of a framework for examining the therapist's own interactions and responses to offenders. Second, human rights can be used as a clinical tool to educate offenders and help with the design and delivery of treatment.

The Offender Practice Framework (OPF) which we will develop in this chapter provides a useful rights-oriented structure for integrating the risk management and goods promotion aspects of therapy for offenders. As stated above, human rights provide an ethical scaffold for treatment that fuses the skills that offenders learn with the values they acquire into a single, simple idea: pursue your own core goals and legitimate interests in ways that respect the human rights of others.

There are three strands to the framework: the *justice and accountability* perspective, the *offender-focused* perspective, and the *strengths- and evidence-based* perspective. Like the earlier framework, these three philosophical perspectives are considered at each of the three phases of intervention: *engagement, assessment and planning, changing offender behaviour,* and *sustaining lifestyle changes* following the completion of therapy. We will now consider each of the three phases in turn, explicitly addressing the human-rights-based practice triggers derived from each perspective (see Figure 9.5).

As this is a newly developed framework we will explore the rationale behind the inclusion of each of the various practice triggers, even though some of them may not be directly connected with human rights issues.

## *Engagement, assessment and planning*

The *justice and accountability* strand is an important part of correctional rehabilitation and its primary aim is to ensure that offenders have begun the process of value reorientation and capability acquisition that will help then to desist from crime and build a more satisfying 'good life' (Ward and Maruna 2007). The practice triggers for the engagement phase of therapy revolve around three core activities (see Figure 9.5): (a) collaborating in the estimation of risk of reoffending and self-harm, (b) ensuring the offender understands the treatment and assessment process, and (c) ensuring the offender understands the reasons for being in treatment and their need to actively engage in the process of behaviour change. This entails the offender being as honest as they can about their problems and being assured that their human rights will be a major focus alongside those of the other individuals. The collaborative approach of Ward's Good Life Model involves a genuine commitment by the therapist to working transparently and respectfully with the offender, and to emphasize that the client's best interests are to be served by the assessment process. Potential issues

| Framework strands | Phases of the work | | |
|---|---|---|---|
| | Engagement and assessment | Changing behaviour | Life-style change |
| Justice and accountability ➤ | • Has the risk assessment been collaborative? <br> • Does the offender understand the assessment and treatment process? <br> • Does the offender know his/her rights? | • Are we reinforcing both duties and rights? <br> • Is the offender taking responsibility? <br> • Are we receptive to their need for redemption/ transformation? | • Does the environment/ community support offender rehabilitation? <br> • Is the offender sensitive to community concerns? <br> • Have we got the balance right re offender needs and community protection? |
| Offender focused ➤ | • Are we linking needs and offending behaviour, and do we understand the offender's primary values? <br> • Are 'good life' opportunities identified? <br> • Are conditions of agency in place? | • Are we building agency capabilities? <br> • Are we encouraging an alternative 'good life' identity? <br> • Have we listened to the offender's hopes/goals? | • Does the plan pay attention to offender goods? <br> • Are there meaningful opportunities for a good life? <br> • Is the plan a meaningful one for the offender? |
| Strengths- and evidence- based ➤ | • Have we assessed for risk-taking behaviour and safety? <br> • Do we have a therapeutic alliance? <br> • Are we using instruments that are ethically sound? | • Are we using interventions that reduce risk? <br> • Are we using interventions that meet criteria for effective therapy? <br> • Are we building on the offender's strengths and agency? | • Are services familiar with and supportive of the 'good lives' plan? <br> • Does the offender have the right service support? <br> • Are risk monitoring systems in place? |

Figure 9.5 The Offender Practice Framework

of risk and need are presented to the offender as areas for collaborative investigation.

From the *offender-focused* perspective it is critical that the function of the offending is established through the identification of the primary goods that are directly or indirectly linked to the abusive actions. In addition, the identification of the *overarching good* or value around which the other goods are oriented should be ascertained. The 'overarching good' informs the worker about what is most important in a person's life and hints at the offender's fundamental commitment. It is strongly constitutive of personal identity and is a useful way of illuminating how the person sees themselves and the world. The therapist then focuses on a 'good life' treatment plan for the offender based on the above considerations and information. Thus, taking into account the kind of life that would be fulfilling and meaningful to the individual, the clinician notes the capabilities or competencies the offender requires to have a reasonable chance of putting the plan into action. A treatment plan is then developed. Thus the key practice triggers of this strand relate to grasping the offender's motivating value and its role in the offending, constructing a 'good life' plan, and ensuring that the capabilities necessary to achieve that plan are in place and resonate with the offender's own priorities, thus respecting their agency.

From the *strengths-* and *evidence-based* perspective workers need to be cognizant of the research evidence on offender readiness and the engagement process. For example, working collaboratively with offenders in developing treatment goals results in a stronger therapeutic alliance (Mann and Shingler 2006), and therapist features such as displays of empathy and warmth, as well as encouragement and rewards for progress, positively facilitate the change process. In addition, practitioners have obligations to always use assessment measures appropriately, ensure they are trained in their administration, and make certain that at the end of the assessment process they have a holistic, empirically sound and integrated case formulation that is based around the individual's unique features alongside those they share with other offenders (Ward, Mann and Gannon 2007; Ward and Maruna 2007). Thus the practice triggers for the third strand in the engagement, assessment and planning phase revolve around the need to assess effectively risk and safety, construct a sound therapeutic alliance, and to engage in an ethical and scientifically rigorous assessment process.

## Changing behaviour

In the second phase the offender enters a therapy programme of some kind and as a consequence of this is subject to personally challenging and anxiety generating experiences. From the *justice and accountability* perspective a significant consideration concerns the attitude of the therapist to the offender and the importance of respecting the offender's human rights by adopting a constructive, humanistic approach. If offenders are viewed as people attempting to live meaningful worthwhile lives in the best way they can in the specific circumstances confronting them, then workers need not view offenders as amoral beings. That is, individuals who commit offences act from a set of goals that they share in common with other human beings. Like other members of society offenders should be treated fairly, acknowledging that they have the capacity to change and atone for their behaviour. They warrant our respect for their capacity to change and the fact that their offending will have been directly or indirectly related to their pursuit of the ingredients of a good life. Furthermore, a critical therapeutic task is ensuring that both the rights and duties of offenders are sufficiently addressed during treatment. This means the offender must take at least some responsibility for the change process and begin to grasp the significance of others people's interests alongside their own. Thus the practice triggers ensure that intervention is balanced between promoting the offender's core interests and securing those of the community's; stress the necessity that the offender functions as a moral agent (i.e. assumes responsibility for actions); and finally, encourage the workers to be receptive to the offender's desire for redemption and transformation.

From the offender-focused perspective on the change process, a critical therapeutic task involves managing the delicate balance between the 'approach goal' of promoting offender goods and the 'avoidance goal' of reducing risk. Erring on the side of either goal can result in disastrous social and personal consequences for the offender and victims. Simply seeking to increase the well-being of an offender without regard for their level of risk may result in a happy but dangerous individual. Alternatively, attempting to manage an offender's risk without concern for goods promotion or well-being could lead to rather punitive practices and a disengaged and hostile client. According to the assumptions about well-being underpinning our approach to human rights, human beings are complex, multifaceted creatures who seek to realize a plurality of goods in their lives. A worthwhile life requires the presence of all the goods in some form, although typically individuals weight some of the primary goods more highly than others. The overarching good(s) in effect reflects a person's basic commitment and thus their personal identity (Ward and Maruna 2007). These facts about human nature mean that therapy needs to be holistic and take into account a wide range of interests and needs. Although the different goods are individually important, in reality they interact in a dynamic way and tend to come in clusters – in effect, lifestyles.

In essence, the rehabilitation of offenders is an evaluative and capability-building process that is concerned with promoting primary goods and managing risk. At the heart of this process is the construction of a more adaptive narrative identity and the acquisition of capabilities that enable offenders to secure important values in their post-release environments. The practice triggers of the offender-focused strand involve the development of agency, the acquisition of a more adaptive identity, and taking seriously the offender's hopes and goals.

From the strengths- and evidence-based perspective the aim is to ensure that interventions are delivered in ways that are likely to reduce risk and to enhance offender well-being. Therapy is therefore seen as an activity that should *add to* an offender's repertoire of personal functioning, rather than an activity that simply *removes* a problem or is devoted to *managing* problems, as if a lifetime of grossly restricting one's activity is the only way to avoid offending (Ward *et al.* 2007). From a human rights perspective, offender treatment should aim to return individuals to as normal a level of functioning as possible, and should only place restrictions on activities that are highly related to problematic behaviour. Thus, a man who raped an adult woman might be encouraged to avoid certain situations in his future life, but should not be expected to give up any hopes of developing an intimate relationship by being told to avoid all situations where single women might be present.

In other words, a more holistic treatment perspective is taken, based on the core idea that the best way to reduce risk is by helping offenders live more fulfilling lives. In addition, therapy is tailored to each offender's 'good lives' plan while still being administered in a systematic and structured way. It is envisaged that offenders need only undertake those treatment activities that provide the ingredients of their particular plan. In addition to this focus on a better fit between therapy and the offender's specific issues, abilities, preferences, and contexts, greater attention is also paid to the development of a therapeutic alliance and the process of therapy. Furthermore, risk factors are regarded as internal and external obstacles that make it difficult for an individual to implement a 'good lives' plan in a socially acceptable and personally fulfilling manner. Thus, a major focus is on the establishment of the skills and competencies needed to achieve a better kind of life, alongside the management of risk.

A final requirement of effective treatment in the correctional arena is that it proceed according to a number of therapeutic principles. The most important of these are the risk, needs and responsivity principles (Andrews and Bonta 1998). The *risk principle* is concerned with the match between level of risk and the actual amount of treatment received, and proposes that the intensity and type of interventions should be dependent on the offender's assessed level of risk. The higher the level of risk presented by an individual, the greater amount of therapy they should receive. Second, according to the *needs principle*, programmes should primarily target criminogenic needs, that is, dynamic risk factors associated with recidivism that can be changed. By contrast, non-criminogenic needs are considered non-essential or discretionary treatment targets. Third, the *responsivity principle* is concerned with a programme's ability to actually reach and make sense to the participant for whom it was designed. In other words, the aim is to ensure that the offender is able to understand the content of the programme and subsequently change their behaviour. As stated above, a human rights approach stipulates that alongside the reduction of risk, offender goods must also be promoted.

The practice triggers derived from the strengths- and evidence-based perspective cluster around the necessity of establishing that the interventions are likely to reduce both risk and enhance well-being, build on the offender's strengths and agency, and are delivered in a way that maximizes effectiveness (i.e. attend to both risk and offender goods).

## Sustaining life-style changes

In the final phase of the work the aim is ensure that the gains made in therapy transfer into the offender's daily life and persist into the future, and that offenders are fully equipped to deal with the demands that will be placed upon them during high-risk situations. Initially, this involves the individual (with the help of workers, and other group members) developing a safety plan that helps to strengthen their awareness of how personal risk factors contribute to their own offending and enables them to articulate the strategies that they have learned over the previous weeks to manage those situations. Typically this plan will include individualized external supports and monitoring needs that will have emerged through the treatment process.

The *justice and accountability* strand is concerned with ensuring that offenders are sensitive to the demands of the community, and that the balance of risk management and offender goods promotion is right. Furthermore, it is necessary to ensure that the community will be supportive of the offender's rehabilitation plans and efforts. From the vantage point of a human rights approach, the treatment for offenders is essentially about equipping them to live rewarding lives that do not result in harm to others. Offenders are viewed as moral agents who have directly or indirectly sought certain goods through abusive or other illegal behaviours. The goal of this phase is to help individuals articulate their significant goals, and taking into account their preferences, priorities, abilities and context, develop a life-style plan that is likely to result in the formation of a new personal identify and a more satisfying life. The worker then needs to ensure that the offender acquires the *internal* and *external* conditions they require in order to put their plan into action; it is essentially about designing a new life. The major stress will have been on the selection of suitable secondary or instrumental goods (e.g. type of work, training, relationships, hobbies, and so on) to be utilized by the person in order to realize certain primary goods (e.g. mastery, relatedness). The practice triggers derived from this strand include making sure there is good offender–environment match, that the offender is aware of the constraints and needs associated with living in the community, and that the balance of risk management and goods promotion is correct. In terms of human rights, the latter trigger is essentially a matter of dealing with offender rights and duties in an appropriate and ethically defensible manner.

From the *offender-focused* perspective, it is important to customize individuals' treatment plans so that they focus more on their positive or approach goals (i.e. instituting good lives) rather than simply avoiding relapse. More accurately, the argument is that a life-style plan should reflect both goods promotion and risk management strategies. Developing a plan that manages risk using the language of approach goals has proved to be useful, and preliminary results of adopting this approach are encouraging (see Ward and Maruna 2007). Practice triggers include ensuring that the life-style plan is meaningful to the offender and revolves around his or her core values and interests (i.e. goods), and contains genuine opportunities for a good life.

Finally, from the *strengths- and evidence-based* perspective of the OPF, a life-style plan should focus on two related although distinct goals: (a) the implementation of a 'map' for living within a specific community under particular circumstances that possesses all of the conditions required for a good life, and (b) the identification of strategies for responding to problematic situations in which the smooth functioning of the offender's post-release life is disrupted or threatened in some manner. In terms of the latter, the presence of acute risk factors that are salient for a given individual, such as relationship conflict, emotional distress, or a significant life event, should be viewed as markers indicating problems in the conditions required to live a good life. These conditions are likely to be external but may sometimes signal difficulties in aspects of a person's psychological functioning. The skills, beliefs, attitudes and resources acquired during therapy can then be used to (a) reflect on the nature of the disruption threat, (b) construct an action plan to resolve the threat or problem, and (c) implement the plan and evaluate its effectiveness. All the time the offender needs to be careful to ensure they keep in mind the importance of maintaining approach goals and risk management strategies in any modification to their life-style plan. The danger of making ad hoc adjustments that restrict access to important goods is that a route to reoffending may be reopened. Service providers should be knowledgeable about an offender's risk profile and treatment progress, and be responsive to needs if a crisis occurs. The practice triggers include the degree to which service providers are aware and supportive, the kinds of services implemented and their utility, and the presence of explicit risk monitoring plans.

## Conclusions

The practice frameworks we have described in this chapter we believe provide an effective means through which rights-based ideas can be introduced into practice. In providing three framework examples, the youth justice framework (in Chapter 4), the care and protection framework, and the offender practice framework, we suggest the potential for the development of similar rights-based frameworks across other fields of practice. Refocusing attention on rights, and building this upon a sound body of knowledge, creates opportunities for practice to be both more responsive to service users and knowledge-based. In our next chapter we will look at how policy and law also provide opportunities for the reinforcement of rights-based ideas.

*Chapter 10*

# Embedding Rights-based Ideas

Law and policy provide the environment within which ideas and beliefs are sanctioned and supported in practice. They provide the overarching mission and goals for child welfare services (Pecora, Whittaker and Maluccio 2006), and they can provide the impetus for innovative change and development. For example, the Children Act 1989 (England and Wales) has been innovate in taking a developmental approach in responding to children, and also requires that statutory services take the views of children into account when working with them (Rose, Gray and McAuley 2006). New Zealand's Children, Young Persons and Their Families Act, also introduced in 1989, was similarly innovative when it created the Family Group Conference, thereby enshrining a model family-decision-making process in law (Connolly 1999). Given their important role in service development, law and operational policy can be catalysts for furthering service users' rights in child welfare. Despite being useful mechanisms for shaping service in this way, it is also interesting to see how easily human rights that are embedded in law and policy can nevertheless be undermined by other pressures within a system. As Hart (2003, p.36) notes from a family court perspective:

> The rights of the child embodied in UNCROC can be avoided by signatory nations... Rights...are easily subverted by the overriding needs and interests of the child's caregivers. Current adversarial processes, in effect, support rights-based conflicts that focus on the needs and interests of parents, not those of the children.

In the context of child welfare where the state also has an interest in the child and perceptions about what is in the child's best interests, the dynamics of intervention and decision-making can also impact on the assertion of rights, both with respect to children and their families.

In this chapter we will consider the role that government policies and law have played in furthering (or otherwise) practice that respects human rights. We will look in some detail at examples of child welfare systems that illuminate human rights issues well. Finally, we will consider some of the challenges involved in shifting practitioners toward human rights-based practice and how they can be addressed. First, though, we will look again at the duty of the state to support human rights.

## Rights and responsibilities: the role of the state

In defining rights Dworkin (1970, p.13) argued the importance of governments protecting the freedom of its citizens based on the familiar idea of political equality:

> weaker members of a political community are entitled to the same concern and respect of their government as the more powerful members have secured for themselves, so that if some men [sic] have freedom of decision whatever the effect on the general good, then all men must have the same freedom.

Rights are essentially to do with fairness, and the duty of the government is to support equity, fair treatment and other rights necessary to protect a person's human dignity.

According to Theis (2004, p.3) the state also has a duty to 'respect, protect and fulfil rights'. In *respecting* the rights of its citizens, Theis argues that state laws, policies, programmes and practices should not violate human rights, nor should they interfere with the individual's pursuit of their rights. The state should also *protect* rights by preventing rights violation by others. In *fulfilling* rights the state is expected to take positive action to frame rights in law, policy and practice. While the state cannot be expected to be responsible for everything, Theis (2004, p. 3) argues that the state nevertheless:

> has an obligation to create the conditions that enable other duty bearers, such as parents, private sector, local organisations, donors and international institutions, to fulfil their responsibilities.

This is an inclusive approach to fostering rights-based initiatives through the formation of duty-bearer alliances around a common vision and goals.

That the vast majority of countries have become signatories to the United Nations Convention on the Rights of the Child (UNCROC) is an indication of the commitment that state parties have to the furthering of children's rights. Conventions are treaties endorsed by states (or organizations) acting together (Veerman 1992). Unlike declarations, which are not considered to be binding documents, conventions carry specific obligations, and ratifying implies that the state must take active steps to meet those expectations. In ratifying a convention the state therefore accepts its obligations. While declarations are considered 'soft' international law, conventions are considered to be 'hard' international law. In becoming a signatory to UNCROC, therefore, a state makes an important commitment to meet its expectations under the convention and also subjects itself to criticism if it does not comply.

Yet the relationship between law, operational policy and practice in the human services is a complex one and it is not always clear how enabling current laws and policies are for practitioners wanting to utilize a rights-based approach (Williams 2004).

Initially, however, we will consider how state responses to indigenous peoples and cultural practices have evolved over time (see also Chapter 3) as this illuminates the ways in which policies and practice can impact both positively and negatively on the rights of individuals and cultures.

## Indigenous peoples and the state

In recognition of the issues confronting indigenous people, governments internationally have striven to develop child welfare initiatives that are more equitable and culturally responsive to the needs of disadvantaged communities. For example, over many years the Canadian government has worked with First Nation communities to establish agreements for delivering services to Aboriginal children and families (Thompson, Maxwell and Stroick 1999). In Australia too, state governments have begun to work in more constructive partnerships with indigenous communities (Stanley, Tomison and Pocock 2003). These and other initiatives notwithstanding, responses to indigenous communities have nevertheless struggled to stem the numbers of children coming into the care of statutory child welfare services. Indeed, speaking from a Canadian perspective Blackstock (2006) states that there are more First Nation children in state care now than there have ever been throughout Canadian history.

### Canada: the First Nation experience

From a rights perspective, historical Canadian responses to First Nation peoples makes for grim reading. Policies supporting residential schools, which were run by the Canadian federal government in partnership with Christian churches, have been denounced as a 'deliberate assault on the Aboriginal family' (Bennett, Blackstock and De La Ronde 2005, p.18). During the nineteenth century children were uplifted from their families and placed in residential schools, often some distance from their home communities. In a purposeful attempt to isolate them from their parents and their broader cultural community, all aspects of indigenous culture were suppressed in those institutions. In common with other residential services at the time, abuse and neglect was a frequent occurrence. Many children also died of preventable diseases. From an historical perspective there is little evidence of any state efforts to address these abuses (Blackstock et al. 2004). While the residential schools began to close in the 1940s, their doors did not completely close until 1996, five years after Canada became a signatory to UNCROC. According to Blackstock and her colleagues (2004, p.154):

> Residential schools had a profound effect on disrupting child care knowledge and practice and introduced multi-generational dysfunction as community members tried to cope with the trauma often with little or no resources.

During the period that residential schools were being phased out, provincial and territorial governments began developing child welfare services for reservation communities. The shift toward the local provision of services provided an opportunity for Aboriginal families to be supported to look after their own children. It was an opportunity lost, however, as the services uplifted thousands of children from their homes, often without their parents' knowledge or consent (Sinclair 2007). From the 1960s to the mid-1980s, the mass adoption of Aboriginal children into largely non-Aboriginal homes has become known as 'the sixties scoop'.

While it is clear that Canadian governments have become more progressive in working toward the development of culturally responsive service for First Nation people in recent years (Libesman 2004), they have continued to struggle to reduce the overrepresentation of indigenous children caught up within the child welfare system net. Sadly commentators have noted:

> the involvement of the child welfare system is no less prolific in the current era. Dr Lauri Gilchrist of Lakehead University noted that given current child welfare statistics, the 'Sixties Scoop' has merely evolved into the 'Millennium Scoop' and Aboriginal social workers, recruited into the ranks of social services and operating under the umbrella of Indian Child and Family services, are now the ones doing the 'scooping'. (Sinclair 2007, p.67)

In response to this enduring disadvantage, in February 2007 the Assembly of First Nations and the First Nations Child and Family Caring Society of Canada filed a formal complaint with the Human Rights Commission against the Canadian federal government (Blackstock 2007). In making the complaint they contend that the government funding policy discriminates against First Nation children because it knowingly provides them with unequal funding, and therefore benefit, under child welfare law. More equitable funding, they argue, would enable First Nation agencies to provide essential preventative services for their families:

> The most critical missing component is prevention, or the ability of the agencies to link families with support services that will ensure child safety and enable the family unit to remain intact whenever possible. It should be noted that investment in prevention will not realize its full potential if not accompanied by investing in core services such as information management and professional development. (Assembly of First Nations 2007)

Arguing on the grounds of human rights, the complainants maintain that the lack of funding has resulted in children being denied the services that would have supported them to remain in their home environment. It could be argued that this denies them critical developmental resources and the opportunity to acquire some of the core capabilities necessary to function as purposive agents who can effectively pursue their own conception of a good life in adulthood. If we use Theis' (2004) analysis of the state's responsibilities as discussed earlier in the chapter, it could be argued that the state has not provided equitable conditions that would enable other duty-bearers (i.e. the First Nation service providers) to fulfil their responsibilities to their own people.

## Australia: the Aboriginal experience

Common to the experience of First Nation peoples, cultural and spiritual oppression have also been identified as important aspects of the Australian Aboriginal experience:

> Indigenous people generally have been profoundly affected by the erosion of their cultural and spiritual identity and the disintegration of family and community that has traditionally sustained relationships and obligations and maintained social order and control. (Robertson 2000, p.xii)

Mirroring the Canadian experience, the forcible removal of thousands of Australian Aboriginal children from their homes to institutions and missions has been variously described as 'cultural genocide', or conversely as an initiative to advance the 'welfare' and 'interests' of the children themselves (Van Krieken 2005). Like the indigenous children in Canada and roughly over the same time period, Australian Aboriginal children also experienced high levels of abuse and neglect in the care of the state (Weber and Lacey 2005). An enquiry into what is now referred to as the 'Stolen Generation', conducted by the Australian Human Rights and Equal Opportunity Commission in 1995 found:

> that many indigenous children were physically assaulted, brutally punished and sexually abused and that conditions in missions, government institutions and children's homes were often very poor with insufficient resources to cover clothing, food, education and shelter. (Weber and Lacey 2005, p.54)

The federal government, however, has maintained throughout the last decade that the forcible removal of Aboriginal children was not a violation of human rights, leaving indigenous people little recourse but through legal challenge. Weber and Lacey argue that by working closely within a legal perspective only, the government has avoided the need to explore its moral responsibilities and the state's moral duty to support the principles of autonomy, non-malfeasance (official non-misconduct), beneficence (doing the right thing) and justice.

Given this history, it is not surprising that Australian Aboriginal communities continue to be highly sensitive about the removal of children:

> there is a deep distrust of state welfare organizations and great concern about the numbers of indigenous children still being removed from their families on the basis of abuse and neglect. (Parkinson 2003, p.165)

This emerged as an issue again more recently when the Australian government, influenced by developments in Britain and the United States, proposed promoting adoption as the preferred permanency option for children in state care (Parkinson 2003). The proposal was ultimately defeated, but in the process raised a number of important issues regarding the ways in which responses can be shaped by differing ideological approaches.

At the heart of the debate lay two competing ideological positions: the importance of state partnership with families with respect to the care of children, and the need for children to have security of care when they are at risk at home. Although both views are clearly important to the care and protection of children, in the debate they were increasingly perceived as polarized positions, one reflecting family support and partnership, the other children's rights.

The proposal took the drive for children's permanency to a different level when it advocated that adoption be discussed in all cases whenever a care order is sought. This was a significant move from seeing adoption as an important but last resort for children. Here adoption was seen as providing the child with the right to a permanent and secure home. In the context of the proposal, it was promoted as an initiative in support of children's rights (Parkinson 2003).

The alternative ideological position (partnership with family) had become established as an important practice principle within international child welfare jurisdictions in the latter part of last century. The emphasis was on the right of the family to continue to be involved, even if the child was placed permanently elsewhere:

> Involving the family in decision-making concerning the children and in continuing to be involved in the children's lives following removal are means of trying to maintain some family ties and beneficial aspects of family involvement despite the need to remove the children. (Parkinson 2003, p.151)

In a different take on children's rights, Parkinson argues that maintaining familial linkages was also supporting the human right of a child to relationship continuity. Article 9.3 of UNCROC states that: 'State parties shall respect the rights of the child who is separated from one or both parents to maintain personal relations and direct contact with both parents on a regular basis...' In this context it is also clear that from an indigenous perspective this is inextricably connected to cultural identity and tribal continuity. This presents an alternative to the earlier expression of adoption as being supported in the name of children's rights. Arguably it is access to familial and cultural resources that will enable individuals to realize their conception of what constitutes a good life and to acquire a sense of meaning, and ultimately achieve a state of well-being. According to our analysis of human rights both freedom and well-being are the necessary conditions for agency. The separation of children from their family of origin and culture may significantly limit their access to important constituent well-being goods (e.g. relatedness, a sense of belonging, cultural connectedness) and thereby impair their ability to function as independent human beings in adulthood.

Had the move to implement the proposal been successful, it would have undoubtedly had ramifications for Australia's indigenous communities. Because Aboriginal children continue to be over-represented in state care, any new law that places a greater emphasis on adoption would have certainly resulted in greater numbers of Aboriginal children being placed in out-of-family adoptive homes, severing permanently their relationships with their families of origin.

## Aotearoa New Zealand: Maori experiences

While there are some parallels, Maori experience of colonization in Aotearoa has differed markedly from the experiences of First Nation peoples in Canada and Australia. In the early years of European settlement Maori people transformed themselves to meet the challenges and opportunities of cultural interaction with Europeans:

> Maori turned out to be capable and competitive entrepreneurs who could grow, produce and harvest commodities such as flax and timber on a large scale...In addition to coastal contact with Europeans via harvesting and trading, there was another source of interaction between Maori and Pakeha in which Maori did, literally, discover the rest of the world. Having come themselves from a highly maritime culture...Maori turned out to be excellent crew members on European ships. (King 2003, p.128)

Hence, initially at least, Maori-Pakeha[1] contact was mutually advantageous, and characterized by trading and protective cooperation (Orange 1987).

In 1840 a treaty with the British Crown was signed by over 500 Maori chiefs. The *Treaty of Waitangi* established an agreement between the two parties and addressed issues of sovereignty, possession of land and other resources, and citizenship. Since that time there have been long periods when both the spirit and the words of the Treaty have been ignored, and there have been extensive arguments about its relevance in modern society. In recent years, however, Aotearoa New Zealand has attempted to grasp the meaning and realise the intent of the treaty, and Maori have made successful claims against the Crown when it has been established that they were prejudicially affected by practices that were inconsistent with the treaty (Stenson 2004).

In the decades immediately following the signing of the treaty, however, as the numbers and institutions of the Pakeha began to dominate, the position of the indigenous people became one of increasing dispossession and deprivation. Maori were perceived as needing to be assimilated into Pakeha society, and for Maori this process of 'modernization' resulted in the systematic dismantling of their traditional society. In the report *Puao te Ata tu* this process is described:

> Policies aimed at redefining land ownership, converting a communal culture to an individualistic one, fostering new forms of leadership and educating Maori children out of their essential Maoriness were rooted in the concept of 'assimilation'. The underlying idea of assimilation was that Pakeha culture and ways were 'modern' and 'forward-looking' and therefore superior as compared with 'traditional' Maori ways which were no longer 'relevant'. (Ministerial Advisory Committee on a Maori Perspective for the Department of Social Welfare 1986, p.5)

1    Pakeha is a New Zealander of European descent.

New land ownership laws were passed that advanced Pakeha interests and dis-advantaged those of Maori, and large areas of Maori land were acquired by Pakeha settlers. Maori were excluded from accessing low-interest loans under the Advances to Settlers Act of 1894. The Old Age Pension Act of 1898 provided a pension of £18 per year but Maori were excluded. The 1907 Sup-pression of Tohunga Act outlawed the spiritual and educational role of the tohunga (priestly expert), and the Native Health Act of 1909 prevented Maori from using traditional systems for adopting children. In 1840, the Maori popu-lation is estimated to have been about 200,000 and there were only a few thousand Pakeha. By 1910 the Maori population had dropped to an historical low of less 50,000, whereas the Pakeha population had risen to nearly one million. Maori people were increasingly becoming alienated from their land, and major health and welfare issues were emerging.

This legacy of disadvantage still shows itself strongly within New Zea-land's system of child welfare. In common with other indigenous experience, Maori children have been, and still are, overrepresented in welfare statistics. During the 1980s there was considerable dissatisfaction with the negative effects that care practices were having on a growing number of Maori children. These children were frequently being placed outside their kinship network, and many Maori felt the effects of this loss of cultural and familial identity.

Ironically, just as law was used to deny Maori their essential Maoriness in the early twentieth century, so too law was now used to strengthen Maori cultural practices within the modern child welfare system:

> There was a feeling of determination that the Department would actually lead the way in re-orientating itself...from a mono-cultural department into a department that was there for Maori. (Connolly 2006c, p.2)

The introduction of the Children, Young Persons and Their Families Act in 1989 demanded a different approach to practice with children and their families in New Zealand. The legislation brought with it new and different ways of thinking about family rights, including the rights of children.

Perhaps most significant from a rights perspective is the way in which the legislation introduces a model of family decision-making, captured within the mechanism of the Family Group Conference (FGC). Based on Maori decision-making practices, the FGC is convened whenever a child is assessed to be in need of care or protection. It brings together extended family and the pro-fessionals in a family-led decision-making forum. As such, it provides the family with an opportunity to hear the concerns that the professionals have for the child and to then make decisions to resolve the issues. Family members in the broadest sense, including the kinship network, are legally entitled to attend the conference. The Act's general principles clearly articulate the importance of family and the right of the family to participate in decision-making:

wherever possible, a child's or young person's family, whanau, hapu, iwi,[2] and family group should participate in the making of decisions affecting the child or young person. (s.5 [a])

Essentially the FGC has three phases: information sharing, private family deliberation and reaching agreement. In the first phase the coordinator of the conference is required to provide the family group with information relating to the professional concerns for the child, the assessment that has been undertaken and any subsequent findings. The emphasis the legislation places on the process of decision-making being family-led is captured in the second phase of the FGC, the private family deliberation:

> No person…is entitled to be present at any family group conference during any discussions or deliberations held among the members of the family, whanau, or family group of the child or young person in respect of whom the conference is held, unless those members request any such person to be present. (s.22 [2])

In practice this means that once full information has been provided for the family, the professionals are required to withdraw, allowing the family privacy to discuss the concerns and arrive at decisions and plans to ensure the child's future care and safety. The final phase involves the professionals rejoining the family and together reaching agreement on the family plan. With respect to this process of reaching agreement, the professionals are guided by the principle that the child 'should be removed from his or her family, whanau, hapu, iwi, and family group only if there is a serious risk of harm' (s.13 [e]).

While the legislation clearly intends the process of decision-making to be family-led, the right of the child to be protected, to participate, and be involved in decision-making is also clearly supported in law. With respect to protection, s.6 ensures that the welfare and interests of the child shall be the first and paramount consideration. With respect to participation and decision-making, the child, as an entitled member of the FGC, has the right to attend the meeting, and to agree or disagree with any decisions or plans that are developed during private family time. If it is inappropriate for the child to be at the meeting in person, the coordinator of the meeting is required to ascertain the child's views and ensure that they are communicated to the family group.

Essentially the introduction of the legislation changed the way in which professionals responded to families in New Zealand's system of child welfare. Unlike the previous legislation, the Act supported the ideology of family responsibility and empowerment, giving the family the right not only to be

---

2     Whanau, hapu, and iwi do not translate readily to western concepts of what constitutes family, but most closely approximate a range of meanings from extended family to tribal affiliation, and comprise the familial kinship structure upon which Maori society is based.

involved but also to influence critically what happens for themselves and their children. As noted in Chapter 8, it captured the key elements of family-led practice, and provided an opportunity for the family to determine their own way forward. While it probably goes further than most other jurisdictions in terms of enshrining family decision-making into law, it nevertheless shares a vision, common to many other legislative frameworks, that seeks to increase family participation in child welfare matters.

That said, despite evidence of an international movement toward legal provision for greater partnership with families over recent years, we have seen evidence in Chapter 8 which suggests that legal frameworks alone are unlikely to be enough to sustain family-led practice and the furthering of human rights-based ideas. Returning to Hart's (2003) earlier assertion, despite legislative requirements, rights can indeed be subverted in the context of competing interests.

## Challenges when embedding rights-based ideas

There is no question that in recent years a growing recognition of the issues confronting indigenous peoples has spurred governments to develop initiatives that are more culturally responsive and meet the particular needs of their disadvantaged communities. Yet, despite many progressive initiatives in Canada, Australia and Aotearoa New Zealand, state governments still struggle to address the continuing over-representation of indigenous people in negative statistics that ultimately represent the outcomes of their efforts.

In the context of demanding and complex child welfare practice, the interpretation of the intent of progressive legislation can shift over time. As we noted in Chapter 8, practice positioning across the ideological continuum from family-led to professionally driven practice can be strongly influenced by how sympathetic the worker is to the rights of children and families. A good example of this can be found in New Zealand practice. Research indicates that the FGC in practice is not always the empowering process that was so clearly envisioned by the legislation:

> It means that quite often it's a process that's gone through in order to get it to court. We're going to conference in order to get this outcome...the families feel very disempowered, and often voice that: 'What have you got us all here for – you've already decided what will happen'. (Coordinator quoted in Connolly 2006b, p.530)

How often such professional pre-judgment occurs in FGC practice is unclear. However, it serves to illustrate how legal intent can be subverted when the vision and principles of the legislation are no longer strongly embedded in the practice culture of the professionals involved, or are not reinforced strongly in the practice policy, guidelines and training of the organization.

Regardless of the intent of the legislation, practitioners and organizations are likely to have differing degrees of commitment to family empowerment, and the right of family members to participate in the generating of solutions. In Chapter 8 we discussed Shier's (2001) conceptual model for practitioners which helps to explore differing levels of children's potential participation (see Figure 8.3). It is a useful way of visualizing levels of participation and can also be adapted to encompass family participation. Here, then, we will take the liberty of adapting Shier's three strands of engagement (openings, opportunities and obligations) to provide a visual picture of levels of family participation (see Figure 10.1). Again *Openings* focuses on identifying the degree to which the practitioner is willing to consider and commit to the notion of family participation in decision-making. *Opportunities* describes the possibilities that exist within the practice system – to what extent does the organization's service design accommodate family participation in decision-making? And *Obligations* explores the extent to which policy directions require practitioners to involve the family actively in decision-making (see Figure 10.1).

There are five levels of participation:

- *Level 1: Parents are consulted and their views are taken into account.* This is the most basic level of commitment to the ideal of family participation in decision-making. To tease out practitioner and organizational commitment to family consultation the model asks a set of simple questions. First, is the practitioner ready to listen to and consult with families? One way of developing listening skills is to talk less and find out what is helpful. Second, does the practice system facilitate this kind of interaction, for example, is there a culture of practice that supports these ideas? Is time allowed for properly engaging the family? Third, does operational policy demand that the family be consulted and listened to? This places an obligation on staff to listen to families and take notice of their views.

- *Level 2: Parents and families are encouraged to contribute solutions.* In this next level, the questions test out practitioner and organizational receptiveness to allowing the family to contribute possible solutions. First, in order to commit to this kind of practice, the practitioner must believe in it – does the practitioner have confidence that families can be trusted to develop good solutions? Second, does the service design, and practice system support, the fostering of family-led solutions; for example, does the agency support the ideal of family-led practice or is it more orientated toward professionally driven practice (see Figure 9.1). Third, in policy directives is the requirement for family-led problem-solving made explicit?

- *Level 3: Parent and family feedback on service delivery is proactively sought.* Here the model asks whether the practitioner is receptive to family feedback on the services that are being provided. It does not really matter how many service-user feedback forms are completed; unless the practitioner is receptive, the feedback will not contribute constructively to the improvement of services. This brings us to the organizational system and whether there are learning mechanisms in place to make the best use of collated service-user feedback. Finally, does operational policy require that service feedback is sought?

- *Level 4: Parents and families are directly involved in decision-making.* This higher level of participation marks the transition from indirect involvement in decision-making (*consultation, contribution* and *feedback*) to *direct participation*. It reflects a shift in the power relationships and the need for professionals to examine whether they are able to commit to a set of core values that may be at odds with previous professional experience, and ask themselves whether they are ready to embrace the involvement of family in the actual decision-making. Furthermore, does the service design of the organization – its practice frameworks – support this level of practitioner commitment, or are there structural barriers from the practitioner's perspective? Finally, does policy lend support to family involvement in decision-making, or does it have elements that prevent or inhibit a worker from making this higher level of commitment?

- *Level 5: Families share responsibility for implementing decisions.* This is the highest level of commitment with respect to family participation. Here families work with the practitioner to implement decisions – for example, monitoring plans and the provision of support for members of an extended family group. Such a partnership requires a level of trust that family resources can be mobilized around the needs of the child, and works on the basis that supporting the family's right to exercise agency with respect to decisions that affect their children is more likely to produce a greater investment in actions that will result in successful outcomes. Using this logic, if the professional makes the decisions and provides the solutions, the professional will have a greater investment in the outcomes. Unfortunately professional investment rarely provides the best incentive for family change, but in contrast this highest level of commitment to family participation empowers families with respect to both decision-making and outcomes.

It will be apparent that for practitioners to practise confidently at higher levels of family participation in decision-making and solution implementation, the sanctioning of family empowerment in operational policy and guidelines is critical, and an appropriately supportive service design would also be helpful. As Croft and Beresford (1994, p.58) put it, 'a more participatory practice is unlikely to be possible without more participatory agencies'.

In adapting Shier's model to the concept of family participation, we have been struck by the range of factors that can influence the way a practitioner views the rights of a family to be involved and participate in matters that concern them. Inevitably the practitioner is influenced by their own views and beliefs about the rights of children and families, and their contestability in this complex area of practice. The concept of the *personal self* provides an important

**Levels of participation**

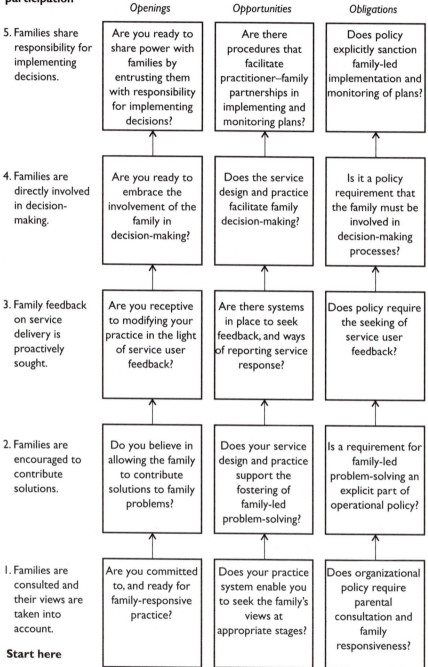

|  | *Openings* | *Opportunities* | *Obligations* |
|---|---|---|---|
| 5. Families share responsibility for implementing decisions. | Are you ready to share power with families by entrusting them with responsibility for implementing decisions? | Are there procedures that facilitate practitioner–family partnerships in implementing and monitoring plans? | Does policy explicitly sanction family-led implementation and monitoring of plans? |
| 4. Families are directly involved in decision-making. | Are you ready to embrace the involvement of the family in decision-making? | Does the service design and practice facilitate family decision-making? | Is it a policy requirement that the family must be involved in decision-making processes? |
| 3. Family feedback on service delivery is proactively sought. | Are you receptive to modifying your practice in the light of service user feedback? | Are there systems in place to seek feedback, and ways of reporting service response? | Does policy require the seeking of service user feedback? |
| 2. Families are encouraged to contribute solutions. | Do you believe in allowing the family to contribute solutions to family problems? | Does your service design and practice support the fostering of family-led problem-solving? | Is a requirement for family-led problem-solving an explicit part of operational policy? |
| 1. Families are consulted and their views are taken into account.<br><br>**Start here** | Are you committed to, and ready for family-responsive practice? | Does your practice system enable you to seek the family's views at appropriate stages? | Does organizational policy require parental consultation and family responsiveness? |

*Figure 10.1 Pathways to family participation (adapted from Shier 2001)*

focus for a rich analysis of reflexive reactions, enabling the practitioner to identify the personal beliefs that inevitability influence professional action (Connolly *et al.* 2006).

It is clear to us that the way a worker practices will also be influenced by the professional system within which they work. Service designs, frameworks and policies can support rights-based approaches to practice. Professional cultures can adopt human rights theories and values that will influence the way in which a professional system, and the practitioners working within it, perceive the rights of the people with whom they work. Finally, as we have previously noted, human rights enshrined in legislation can also influence practice. Here, though, law can be interpreted in ways that can be supportive of rights-based ideals, or as we have seen, it can be subverted by competing interests. The way in which risk aversion influences practice toward increasingly professionally led processes and interventions is an example of this (see Chapter 8).

We believe it is important to bring together the elements of practice, operational policy and law in an integrated conceptual framework that will provide the broad-ranging reinforcements that we consider essential to the embedding and maintenance of rights-based practice.

## Creating an integrated framework to support rights-based ideas

As we draw toward the close of this book it has become clear to us that focusing on discrete elements of a human service is unlikely to have the kind of impact needed to strengthen rights-based practice. We do not consider that focusing on practitioners' views, for example, will be sufficient to further human rights-based practice without rights-based ideas being reinforced by other elements of the service – service design, operational policy and legislation. Nor do we think that law or policy or the practice system alone can provide sufficient reinforcement to embed rights-based ideas. We believe that it is necessary to bring together the potential influence of each of these components in order to mutually reinforce a coherent vision within which rights-based practice will flourish.

There are times when practitioners struggle to appreciate the purpose of operational policies, partly because operational policy is at times developed in an ad hoc way in response to external pressure from politicians or the media. Such developments do not always resonate with the way practitioners view and experience the world in which they work, and indeed, some policies are perceived to be obstacles to good practice and may actually be so. Conversely, policy analysts and legal professionals may be concerned about the way in which practice can evolve in the absence of clear policy guidelines and/or research evidence on what works well.

We contend that applying a coherent human rights perspective to service design, operational policy development and legislative review, as the opportunities occur, has the potential to influence strongly good outcomes for service users. In our view, the more focused the practitioner is on the service user's human rights, the more likely it is that an environment will be created which fosters positive change. We therefore see a focus on rights-based ideas, including those that impact on the relationship between practitioners and service users, as central to achieving good outcomes: 'meeting their different self-defined needs in the way they, ensured full knowledge, support and choice, prefer' (Beresford, cited in Smith 2005, p.102).

Human beings have the right to realize their full potential and to experience the best outcomes that they can for themselves and their families. Linking human rights to outcomes encourages practitioners to think about how practice influences longer term outcomes for the people they work with, and how nurturing human agency is critical to the realization of good outcomes. This means that practitioners need to support and at times scaffold people's agency efforts to live a 'good life' which is in accord with their cherished goals and values, and in doing so become healthy and thriving members of a society in which they feel valued and connected. Building practice frameworks that are rights-based and outcome-focused (for example, the youth justice practice framework we discussed in Chapter 4 and the child welfare and offender frameworks we discussed in Chapter 9) will reinforce practice behaviours that are consistent with a rights-based perspective. When operational policy and guidelines are developed or reviewed this provides an opportunity to embed relevant human rights-based principles, such as inclusion, participation, provision and protection, in the field of child protection, which will further reinforce human rights-based practice. Finally, when a revision of the relevant legislation occurs, the human rights principles in international treaties such as the United Nations Convention on the Rights of the Child or the United Nations Conventions on the Rights of Persons with Disabilities need to be incorporated into the legislation of those countries that have ratified the particular treaty. The inclusion of specific human rights in the relevant legislation will reinforce the importance of rights-based practice as practitioners work with service users, and it will also influence the development of operational policies and guidelines.

If we conceptualize these three elements (service design, operational policy and statutory provision) as the key factors which influence practice with clients, then if all three reflect right-based ideas in an integrated way they will mutually reinforce rights-based practice (see Figure 10.2). As such they are they primary reinforcers of rights-based practice.

A strategy that involves developing systems that mutually reinforce critical ideas will be more likely to have the kind of depth of influence required to shift practitioners toward human rights-based practice and ensure its endurance over time. These are not the only important reinforcers, however. As practice develops around a coherent set of rights-based ideas it becomes important to reinforce this through other systemic processes such as supervision, quality

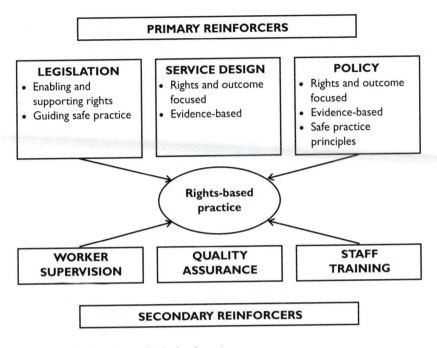

*Figure 10.2 Mutual reinforcers of rights-based practice*

assurance/improvement and training. These secondary reinforcers can also play a critical role when marshalled toward a collective rights-based vision and purpose.

## Conclusions

We have explored how service design, policy directives and legislative provisions can work together to mutually reinforce rights-based practice in the field of child protection, but the same approach can be successfully applied to other fields of practice such as mental health, offender treatment and elderly care.

In our view, human rights are ethical scaffolds that connect the different strands of human life in ways that respect the integrity of persons and need for social justice. Rights are protective capsules that function to safeguard the essential conditions for agency, freedom and well-being. They are constructs that can only exist in supportive political, social and personal networks where human dignity is valued and the life of each individual treasured. Human rights remind us that we all require scaffolding by the efforts of others at one time or another in our lives and that an effective way to create a healthy community is to attend to the needs of the individuals that comprise it. Rights-based practice is simply another entrance into a world where the interests of clients are viewed as pivotal and the task of practitioners is to help them to create a space where their lives can be lived in ways that reflect their deep commitments and momentary concerns. This is a world where each person counts as much as the next and none are held to be inherently superior or singularly deficient. It is a place of dreams and possibilities, but one rooted in the simple conviction that there is a basic threshold of living below which no one should be allowed to fall. And if they do, then we are individually diminished and collectively accountable.

# Concluding Thoughts

In writing this book we set out to understand better the implications of human rights for practice. We found that the issues are complex, and the ideas are challenging from personal, professional and broader systems perspectives. In a way, though, focusing on human rights has the potential to make some things simpler. Once rights are acknowledged as fundamental to the development of fair and equitable human services, we have no option but to address them comprehensively. This has the potential to integrate aspects of multi-layered systems that impact on the lives of so many in ways that improve outcomes for people. That said, as we have noted in this book, how we interpret and respond to human rights issues in day-to-day practice often requires a balancing of ideas – weighing up rights in the context of competing interests and claims.

Moral claims cover a wide range of entitlements and obligations that are related to moral status, but human rights clarify the minimal conditions required for individuals to have a chance to lead a worthwhile life – a 'good life'. At the heart of such a life reside individual judgments about what is worthwhile and important, and these are reflected in the projects that people engage in as they pursue their goals. It is the exercise of this agency that bestows dignity on human beings, the fact that people are able to translate their ideals and dreams into effective action in the world, and by doing so, give their lives shape and meaning.

Too often the codes of ethics adopted by human services operate as blunt instruments, a set of inflexible rules that are mindlessly applied. They also function to restrict and control the actions of practitioners which ultimately impacts upon the services provided for service users. In our experience, ethical codes are regarded as backstops for effective work in human services – bottom-line considerations to ensure that gross injustices are not inflicted on vulnerable people and that workers and agencies are protected from litigation and charges of gross misconduct. While we do not want to minimize the value of existing codes and some of the functions they serve, in our view they do not go far enough. A truly comprehensive ethical resource ought to be a tool that can be used to promote the well-being of clients as well as prevent them from coming to harm. Human rights can provide much more comprehensive guidance in this regard. A human rights perspective can provide practitioners with an ethical scaffold that enables them to select interventions and to deliver services in ways that are responsive to the unique issues and needs of individuals as well as their rights.

As we have seen in this book, the core values of freedom and well-being that underpin human rights, and the various human rights goods associated with each value, can be utilized as conceptual tools for dealing with a broad range of issues across multiple practice domains. This is possible because of the fundamental relationship between human rights goods and purposive agency. The core idea of our approach is that ensuring individuals possess the internal and external goods (capabilities) required to enable them to pursue cherished goals will result in higher levels of well-being and freedom, thus respecting their human dignity, which is the raison d'être of rights. This approach to human rights will enable practitioners to work with clients in multifaceted ways.

Our model of the structure of human rights also supports the development of practice frameworks which explicitly seek to ensure that individuals possess the goods necessary to function as purposive agents, formulating and implementing their own conception of a good life. The implications of these rights-based practice frameworks, particularly in the context of offender work, are at once quite radical and a little unsettling. We have placed ethical and humanistic concerns directly at the centre of the work and argued that values and capability-building are the twin pillars of effective practice. Adopting a human rights perspective unifies the treatment of offenders with the broader ethical concerns of nations and communities, strengthening individuals' capacities to pursue their own vision of a good life in a manner that is personally meaningful and respectful of the interests and rights of others.

Human rights have too frequently been regarded as excessively individualistic and antagonistic to communitarian concerns. We have seen that cultural critics have claimed that human rights treaties are instruments of western propaganda, hopelessly biased and insensitive to the needs of minority cultures and ethnic groups. We believe, however, that a suitably enriched model of human rights is able to preserve values such as personal freedom, human dignity and respecting judgment, whilst also advocating respect for the richness of different cultures and recognizing the needs and rights of communities and families. We are interdependent beings and the exercise of individual agency is only possible within a social context where other people either respect or actively support our attempts to realize our own vision of a good life. Human rights are at once social constructs and vehicles for individual choice.

On a final note, in writing this book we have once again been struck by the huge impact human service systems have on the lives of service users and on whether they are able to assert their human rights. Nigel Parton's insightful analysis of 'the preventative state' in Chapter 8 raises many issues relating to the broadening of state intervention within an early intervention framework and the perceived need for increased surveillance to ensure the well-being of children. Munro (2007, p.42), writing also from a UK perspective, raises a set of questions relating to power and the relationship between the state and the family – and how this can be affected by systems reform:

> Who needs preventative help and what type of help do they need? Who decides what is in the child's best interests? Should help be available universally or targeted on specific groups? Should it be available on a voluntary basis for those families who want to take up a service or should the need for a service be determined by professional assessment followed by encouraging, or even coercing, the family to accept the service?

Developments in e-technology add another dimension to the debate. Technological advances have enabled child welfare systems to explore ways in which huge quantities of information can be efficiently gathered to enable early identification and monitoring of children at risk. While this has been claimed to be a means through which services can be better targeted in a preventative way, critics have questioned the human rights and privacy implications of monitoring a whole population in order to identify children in need (Munro 2007; Munro and Parton forthcoming). The relationship between human rights, early intervention, and the perceived need for public surveillance mechanisms to further preventative aims is a complex one. It is, however, one that is likely to rest at the heart of future human rights debate as human services seek to take advantage of developments in technology and governments seek to balance meeting the interests/needs of individuals with addressing the broader interests and concerns of society.

In this book we have explored a wide range of issues that impact on or are affected by human rights. In doing so, we hope that the ideas we have put forward will resonate with people who work in or support the delivery of human services. We believe it is important to think about rights, and to think deeply about them. It is an obligation we share because we are human.

# References

Abramowitz, M. Z. (2005) 'Prisons and the human rights of persons with mental disorders.' *Current Opinion in Psychiatry 18*, 525–529.

Ahdar, R. (2003) 'Indigenous spiritual concerns and the secular state: Some New Zealand developments.' *Oxford Journal of Legal Studies 23*(4), 611–637.

Andrews, D. A. and Bonta, J. (1998) *The Psychology of Criminal Conduct* (second edition). Cincinnati, OH: Anderson.

Andrews, D. A. and Bonta, J. (2003) *The Psychology of Criminal Conduct* (third edition). Cincinnati, OH: Anderson.

Andrews, D. A., Bonta, J. and Hoge, R. D. (1990) 'Classification for effective rehabilitation: Rediscovering psychology.' *Criminal Justice and Behavior 17*, 19–52.

Andrews, D. A., Bonta, J. and Wormith, J. S. (2006) 'The recent past and near future of risk and/or need assessment.' *Crime and Delinquency 52*, 7–27.

Archard, D. (1993) *Children: Rights and Childhood*. London: Routledge.

Archard, D. (2007) Children's rights and juvenile justice. In M. Hill, A. Lockyer and F. Stone (eds) *Youth Justice and Child Protection*. London: Jessica Kingsley Publishers.

Archard, D.W. (2003) *Children, Family and the State*. Aldershot: Ashgate.

Assembly of First Nations (2007) *First Nations Child and Family Services – Questions and Answers*. Accessed on 15 March 2007 at: www.afn.ca/article.asp?id=3372

Banks, S. (2006) *Ethics and Values in Social Work* (third edition). New York, NY: Palgrave.

Barter, K. (2001) 'Building community: A conceptual framework for child protection.' *Child Abuse Review 10*(4), 262.

Bauman, H-D. L. (2005) 'Designing deaf babies and the question of disability.' *Journal of Deaf Studies and Deaf Education 10*(3), 311–315.

Baylies, C. (2002) 'Disability and the notion of human development: questions of rights and capabilities.' *Disability and Society 7*, 725–739.

Becker, H., Dumas, S., Houser, A. and Seay, P. (2000) 'How organizational factors contribute to innovations in service delivery.' *Mental Retardation 38*(5), 385–394.

Bell, L. (1999). A comparison of multi-disciplinary groups in the UK and New Jersey. Child Abuse Review, 8(5), 314-324.

Bennett, M., Blackstock, C. and De La Ronde, R. (2005) *A Literature Review and Annotated Bibliography on Aspects of Aboriginal Child Welfare in Canada* (second edition). Ottawa, ON: First Nations Child & Family Caring Society of Canada.

Berger, R.L., McBreen, J.T. and Rifkin, M.J. (1996) *Human Behavior: A Perspective for the Helping Professions* (fourth edition). New York, NY: Longman.

Birgden, A. (2004) 'Therapeutic jurisprudence and responsivity: Finding the will and the way in offender rehabilitation.' *Psychology, Crime and Law 10*(3), 283–295.

Birgden, A. and Ward, T. (2003) 'Pragmatic psychology through a therapeutic jurisprudence lens: Psycholegal soft spots in the criminal justice system.' *Public Policy, Psychology and the Law 9*(3), 334–360.

Birmingham, J., Berry, M. and Bussey, M. (1996) 'Certification for child welfare protective services staff members: "The Texas initiative".' *Child Welfare 75*(6), 727.

Blackstock, C. (2006) *Wen:de, We are Coming to the Light of Day: National Policy Review of First Nations Child and Family Services*. Joining Hands Across the World for Indigenous Children; An International Indigenous Knowledge Symposium. Ottawa, ON: First Nations Child & Family

Caring Society of Canada. Accessed on 15 March 2007 at: www.fncfcs.com/docs/JoiningHands_FinalFeb2006.pdf

Blackstock, C. (2007) A Chance to Make a Difference for First Nation Children: Background on the Human Rights Complaint on First Nations Child Welfare. Accessed on 15 March 2007 at: www.fncfcs.com/docs/CommitteeOnHumanRightsFeb2005.pdf

Blackstock, C., Clarke, S., Cullen, J., D'Hondt, J. and Formsma, J. (2004) *Keeping the Promise: The Convention on the Rights of the Child and the Lived Experiences of First Nation Children and Youth.* Ottawa, ON: First Nations Child & Family Caring Society of Canada.

Blyth, E. and Farrand, A. (2004) 'Anonymity in donor-assisted conception and the UN Convention on the Rights of the Child.' *The International Journal of Children's Rights 12,* 89–104.

Blyth, E. and Landau, R. (2005) 'Introduction.' In E. Blyth and R. Landau (eds) *Third Party Assisted Conception Across Cultures: Social, Legal and Ethical Perspectives.* London: Jessica Kingsley Publishers.

Blyth, E. and Speirs, J. (2004) 'Meeting the rights and needs of donor-conceived people: The contribution of a voluntary contact register.' *Nordisk Sosialt Arbeid 24*(4), 318–330.

Bowpitt, G. (1998) 'Evangelical Christianity, secular humanism, and the genesis of British Social Work.' *British Journal of Social Work 28,* 675–693.

Bradley, V. (1994) Evolution of a new service paradigm. In V. Bradley, J. Ashbaugh and B. Blaney (eds) *Creating Individual Supports for People with Developmental Disabilities: A Mandate for Change at Many Levels* (pp.11–32). Baltimore, MD: Brookes.

Bradley, V. (2000) 'Changes in services and supports for people with developmental disabilities: New challenges to established practices.' *Health and Social Work 25*(3), 191–203.

Bray, A. (2003) *Definitions of Disability.* Dunedin, NZ: Donald Beasley Institute.

Brennan, S. and Noggle, R. (1997) 'The moral status of children: Children's rights, parents' rights, and family justice.' *Social Theory and Practice 23*(1) Spring.

Briar-Lawson, K., Schmid, D. and Harris, N. (1997) 'The partnership journey: First decade.' *Child Welfare 55*(2), 4.

Brierley, P. (2000) 'Religion.' In A.H. Halsey and J. Webb (eds) *Twentieth-century British Social Trends.* New York, NY: St. Martin's Press.

Broad, B., Hayes, R. and Rushforth, C. (2001) *Kith and Kin: Kinship Care for Vulnerable Young People.* York: Joseph Rowntree Foundation.

Brown, S. C. (2001) 'Methodological paradigms that shape disability research.' In G. L. Albrecht, K. D. Seelman and M. Bury (eds) *Handbook of Disability Studies* (pp.145-170). Thousand Oaks, CA: Sage.

Burford, G. (2005) 'Families: Their role as architects of civil society and social inclusion.' *Practice 17*(2), 79–88.

Buss, D. M. (1999) *Evolutionary Psychology: The New Science of the Mind.* Boston, MA: Allyn and Bacon.

Butts, J., Mayer, S. and Ruth, G. (2005) *Focusing Juvenile Justice on Positive Youth Development, Issue Brief,* #105. Chicago: Chapin Hall Centre for Children/University of Chicago, www.chapinhall.org.

Canada, E. and Furman, L. (1999) *Spiritual diversity in social work practice: The heart of helping.* New York, NY: Free Press.

Carrabine, E. (2006) 'Punishment, rights, and justice.' In L. Morris (ed.) *Rights: Sociological Perspectives* (pp. 191–208). Oxford: Routledge.

Casanova, J. (1994) *Public Religions in the Modern World.* Chicago, IL: University of Chicago Press.

Cashmore, J. (2002) 'Promoting the participation of children and young people in care.' *Child Abuse and Neglect 26,* 837–847.

Cassidy, J. and Shaver, P.R. (eds) (1999) *Handbook of Attachment: Theory, Research and Clinical Applications.* London: Guilford.

Chappell, D. (2004) 'Protecting the human rights of the mentally ill: Contemporary challenges for the Australian criminal justice system.' *Psychiatry, Psychology and Law 11,* 13–22.

Charter of Human Rights and Responsibilities Act 2006 (Vic). Accessed on November 19 2006 at: www.justice.vic.gov.au/humanrights/

Child, Youth and Family (CYF) (2002) *The Youth Justice Plan.* Wellington NZ: CYF.

Churchill, R.P. (2006) *Human Rights and Global Diversity.* Upper Saddle River, NJ: Pearson Prentice Hall.

Cleaver, H. and Walker, S. (2004) *Assessing Children's Needs and Circumstances: The Impact of the Assessment Framework.* London: Jessica Kingsley Publishers.

Cnaan, R.A., Boddie, S. and Danzig, R.A. (2005) 'Teaching about organized religion in social work: Lessons and challenges.' *Social Work and Divinity 24*(1), 93–110.

Connolly, M. (1999) *Effective Participatory Practice: Family Group Conferencing in Child Protection.* New York, NY: Aldine de Gruyter.

Connolly, M. (2001) 'The art and science of social work.' In M. Connolly (ed.) *New Zealand Social Work: Contexts and Practice.* Auckland: Oxford University Press.

Connolly, M. (2004) *Child and Family Welfare: Statutory Responses to Children at Risk.* Christchurch: Te Awatea Press.

Connolly, M. (2006a) 'Practice frameworks: Conceptual maps to guide interventions in child welfare.' BJSW Advance Access published online on June 16, 2006, *British Journal of Social Work,* doi:10.1093/bjsw/bcl049

Connolly, M. (2006b) 'Fifteen years of family group conferencing: Coordinators talk about their experiences in Aotearoa New Zealand.' *British Journal of Social Work 36*, 523–540.

Connolly, M. (2006c) *Learning from the Past and Repositioning the Future: The FGC in Contemporary Practice,* Plenary address at the International Conference on the Family Group Conference 'Coming Home Te Hokinga Mai', Wellington, New Zealand, 27-29 November 2006.

Connolly, M. (2007a) *Looking after Children in Care: What will the Future Look Like?* Plenary address, IFCO XV Biennial International Foster Care Conference, Hamilton, New Zealand, 11-16 February 2007.

Connolly, M. (2007b) 'Youth justice social work: Developing frameworks to support practice with youth at risk.' *Social Work Now 36*, 18–27.

Connolly, M., Crichton-Hill, Y. and Ward, T. (2006) *Culture and Child Protection: Reflexive Responses.* London: Jessica Kingsley Publishers.

Coyle, A. (2002) *A Human Rights Approach to Prison Management: Handbook for Prison Staff.* London: International Centre for Prison Studies.

Coyle, A. (2003) 'Editorial: A human rights approach to prison management.' *Criminal Behaviour and Mental Health 13*, 77–80.

Crampton, D. (2003) 'Family group decision making in Kent County, Michigan: The family and community compact.' *Protecting Children 18*(1&2), 81–83.

Croft, S. and Beresford, P. (1994) 'A participatory approach to social work.' In C. Hanvey and T. Philpot (eds) *Practising Social Work.* London: Routledge.

Daly, L. (2006) *God and the Welfare State.* Cambridge US: Massachusetts Institute of Technology.

Davies, S. (2005) 'Power and knowledge: The making and managing of the "unfit".' In J. Bessant, R. Hil and R. Watts (eds) *Violations of Trust: How Social and Welfare Institutions Fail Children and Young People.* Aldershot: Ashgate.

Deci, E. L. and Ryan, R. M. (2000) 'The "what" and "why" of goal pursuits: Human needs and the self-determination of behavior.' *Psychological Inquiry 11*, 227–268.

Denny, D. (2005) *Risk and Society.* London: Sage.

Department for Education and Skills (2007) *Policy Review of Children and Young People: A discussion paper.* London: HM Treasury.

Department of Health, UK (2000) *Framework for the Assessment of Children in Need and their Families.* London: The Stationery Office.

Dominion Post (2007) *Turbines Weaken Hills' Life Force, say Maori.* Dominion Post, Saturday March 17, 2007.

Donnelly, J. (2003) *Universal Human Rights in Theory and Practice* (second edition). London: Cornell University Press.

Doolan, M. (1988) *From Welfare to Justice (Towards New Social Work Practice with Young Offenders: An Overseas Study Tour Report).* Wellington: Department of Social Welfare.

Doolan, M. and Connolly, M. (2006) 'Getting the balance right: Assessing risk and supporting families.' In K. McMaster and L. Bakker (eds) *Will They Do It Again?: Assessing and Managing Risk.* Christchurch: HMA Books.

Drewitt, A. Y. (1999) 'Social rights and disability: the language of "rights" in community care politics.' *Disability and Society 14*, 115–128.

Dunn, T. and Wheeler, N. J. (1999) (eds) *Human Rights in Global Politics.* Cambridge: Cambridge University Press.

Durrant, J.E. (2005) 'Corporal punishment: Prevalence, predictors and implications for child behaviour and development.' In S.N. Hart (ed.) with J. Durrant, P. Newell and F. C. Power *Eliminating Corporal Punishment: The Way Forward to Constructive Child Discipline*. Paris: UNESCO.

Dworkin, R. (1970) 'A special supplement: Taking rights seriously.' *New York Review of Books 15*(11), December 17, 1970.

Ehrle, J. and Geen, R. (2002) 'Children cared for by relatives: What services do they need?' *Assessing the New Federalism*, Series B, No B-47, June. Washington, DC: The Urban Institute.

Emerson, E. (1992) 'What is normalisation?' In H. Brown and H. Smith (eds). *Normalisation: A Reader for the Nineties* (pp. 1–18). London: Routledge.

Ferguson, H. (2004) *Protecting Children in Time: Child Abuse, Child Protection and the Consequences of Modernity*. Basingstoke: Palgrave Macmillan.

Finkel, N. J. and Moghaddam, F. M. (2005) (eds) *The Psychology of Rights and Duties*. Washington, DC: American Psychological Association.

Fiske, A. P. (2002) 'Using individualism and collectivism to compare cultures – a critique of the validity and measurement of the constructs: comment on Oyserman *et al.* (2002).' *Psychological Bulletin 128*(1), 78–88.

Fontes, L.A. (2005) *Child Abuse and Culture: Working with Diverse Families*. New York, NY: Guilford Press.

Fontes, L.A. (2006) *Working with Cultural Minority Parents on Issues of Physical Discipline and Abuse*. VISTAS 2006 Online. Accessed on 3 April 2007 at: http://counselingoutfitters.com/ Fontes.htm

Fox, W. (2006) *A Theory of General Ethics: Human Relationships, Nature, and the Built Environment*. Cambridge, MA: MIT Press.

Freeden, M. (1991) *Rights*. Minneapolis, MN: University of Minnesota Press.

Freeman, M. (2002) *Human Rights*. Cambridge: Polity Press.

Freeman, M. (2004) 'The future of children's rights.' In M. Freeman (ed.) *Children's Rights*, Volume II. Aldershot: Ashgate Publishing.

Fulcher, J. and Scott, J. (1999) 'Religion in modern society.' In J. Fulcher and J. Scott (eds) *Sociology*. New York, NY: Oxford University Press.

Furman, L.D., Benson, P.W., Grimwood, C. and Canda, E. (2004) 'Religion and spirituality in social work education and direct practice at the millennium: A survey of UK social workers.' *British Journal of Social Work 34*, 767–792.

Garland, D. (2001) *The Culture of Control: Crime and Social Order in Contemporary Society*. Chicago, IL: University of Chicago Press.

Gearty, C. (2006) *Can Human Rights Survive?* Cambridge: Cambridge University Press.

Geen, R. (2000) 'In the interest of children: Rethinking federal and state policies affecting kinship care.' *Policy and Practice of Public Human Services. 58*(1), 19.

Germain, C.B. (1991) *Human Behavior in the Social Environment: An Ecological View*. New York, NY: Columbia University Press.

Gewirth, A. (1981) *Reason and Morality*. Chicago, IL: University of Chicago Press.

Gewirth, A. (1996) *The Community of Rights*. Chicago, IL: University of Chicago Press.

Gewirth, A. (1998) *Self-fulfillment*. Princeton, NJ: Princeton University Press.

Glaser, B. (2003) 'Therapeutic jurisprudence: An ethical paradigm for therapists in sex offender treatment programs.' *Western Criminology Review 4*(2), 1–16.

Gleeson, J.P. (1999) 'Kinship care as a child welfare service.' In R. Hegar and M. Scannapieco (eds) *Kinship Foster Care: Policy, Practice and Research*. New York, NY: Oxford University Press.

Grevot, A. (2002) 'The plight of paternalism in French child welfare and protective policies and practices.' *Partnerships for children and families project, June 2002*. Accessed on 28 August 2004 at: www.wlu.ca/docsnpubs_detail.php?grp_id=1288&doc_id=7203

Griffiths, D. M., Owen, F., Grosse, L., Stoner, K., Tardif, C. Y., Watson, S., Sales, C. and Vyrostko, B. (2003) 'Human rights and persons with intellectual disabilities: An action-research approach for community-based organizational self-evaluation.' *Journal of Developmental Disabilities 10*, 25–42.

Grundy, E. and Henretta, J.C. (2006) 'Between elderly parents and adult children: A new look at the intergenerational care provided by the "sandwich generation".' *Aging and Society 26*, 707–722.

Grundy, E., Murphy, M. and Shelton, N. (1999) Looking beyond the household: Intergenerational perspectives on living kin and contacts with kin in Great Britain. *Population Trends 97*(19), 27.

Gunderson, K., Cahn, K. and Wirth, J. (2003) 'The Washington State long-term outcomes study.' *Protecting Children 18*(1&2), 42–47.

Hallett, C. and Birchall, E. (1992) *Coordination and Child Protection: a Review of the Literature.* Edinburgh: HMSO.

Handley, P. (2000) 'Trouble in paradise – a disabled person's right to the satisfaction of a self-defined need: some conceptual and practical problems.' *Disability and Society 16*, 313–325.

Hanson, R.K. (1998) 'What do we know about sex offender risk assessment?' *Psychology, Public Policy and Law, 4*(1/2), 50–72.

Hart, A.S. (2003) 'The silent minority: The voice of the child in family law.' *Children Australia 28*(4), 31–38.

Hart, R.A. (1992) *Children's Participation, from Tokenism to Citizenship.* Florence: UNICEF.

Haugaard, J.J. and Avery, R.J. (2002) Termination of parental rights to free children for adoption. In B. Bottoms, M. Bull Kovera and B. McAuliff (eds) *Children, Social Science, and the Law.* Cambridge: Cambridge University Press.

Hayden, P. (Ed.) (2001) *The Philosophy of Human Rights.* St Paul, MN: Paragon House.

Healy, K. (2005) *Social Work Theories in Context: Creating Frameworks for Practice.* New York, NY: Palgrave.

Henricson, C. and Bainham, A. (2005) *The Child and Family Policy Divide: Tensions, Convergence and Rights.* York: Joseph Rowntree Foundation.

Herr, S. S., Gostin, L. O. and Koh, H. H. (eds) (2006) *The Human Rights of Persons with Intellectual Disabilities.* New York, NY: Oxford University Press.

Hetherington, R. (2002) 'Learning from difference: Comparing child welfare systems.' *Partnerships for Children and Families Project, June 2002.* Accessed on 27 August 2004 at: www.wlu.ca/docsnpubs_detail.php?grp_id=1288&doc_id=7203.

Hindberg, B. (2001) *Ending Corporal Punishment: Swedish Experience of Efforts to Prevent all Forms of Violence against Children – and the Results.* Stockholm: Ministry of Health and Social Affairs and Ministry of Foreign Affairs.

HM Treasury (2007) *Policy Review of Children and Young People: A Discussion Paper.* HM Treasury and the Department for Education and Skills. London: The Stationery Office.

Hodge, D.R., Baughman, L.M. and Cummings, J.A. (2006) 'Moving toward spiritual competency: Deconstructing religious stereotypes and spiritual prejudices in social work literature.' *Journal of Social Service Research 32*(4), 211–231.

Hohfeld, W. N. (1919) *Fundamental legal conceptions.* New Haven, CT: Yale University Press.

Hudson, B. (1988) 'Do people with a mental handicap have rights?' *Disability, Handicap and Society 3*, 227–237.

Hudson, B. (2001) 'Human rights, public safety, and the Probation Service: Defending justice in the risk society.' *The Howard Journal 40*, 103–113.

ICESCR, (1994) Cited in Rioux, M. and Carbert, A. (2003). 'Human rights and disability: the international context.' *Journal on Developmental disabilities 10*, 1–13.

Ife, J. (2001) *Human Rights and Social Work: Towards Rights-Based Practice.* Cambridge: Cambridge University Press.

Ishay, M. R. (2004) *The History of Human Rights.* Berkley, CA: University of California Press.

Joseph, M.V. (1998) 'Religion and social work practice.' *Social Casework 69*, 443–452.

Kekes, J. (1989) *The Morality of Pluralism.* Princeton, NJ: Princeton University Press.

King, M. (2003) *The Penguin History of New Zealand.* Auckland: Penguin Books.

Kiro, C. (2004) 'Child rights and physical punishment in Aotearoa New Zealand.' *Childrenz Issues 8*(2), 16–21.

Kitayama, S. (2002) 'Culture and basic psychological processes – toward a system view of culture: comment on Oyserman *et al.* (2002).' *Psychological Bulletin 128*(1), 89–96.

Kitayama, S., and Markus, H. R. (1999) 'Yin and yang of the Japanese self: The cultural psychology of personality coherence.' In D. Cernone and Y. Shoda (eds) *The Coherence of Personality: Social Cognitive Bases of Personality Consistency, Variability, and Organization* (pp. 242–302). New York, NY: Guilford Press.

Korbin, J.E. (1991) 'Cross-cultural perspectives and research directions for the 21st century.' *Child Abuse and Neglect 15*, 67–77.

Kymlicka, W. (1996) *Multicultural Citizenship: A Liberal Theory of Minority Rights*. New York, NY: Oxford University Press.

Lazarus, L. (2006) 'Conceptions of liberty deprivation.' *Modern Law Review 69*, 738–769.

Leveratt, M. and Pargeter, D. (2001) 'Church and state: Where do the boundaries lie?' VCOSS Social Policy Congress: Developing visions for new ways forward, Melbourne.

Levy, N. (2002) 'Deafness, culture, and choice.' *Journal of Medical Ethics 28*, 284–285.

Lewis, S. (2005) 'Rehabilitation: Headline or footnote in the new penal policy?' *Probation Journal 52*, 119–136.

Li, A. (2006) *Ethics, Human Rights, and Culture*. Basingstoke: Palgrave MacMillian.

Libesman, T. (2004) 'Child welfare approaches for indigenous communities: International perspectives.' *National Child Protection Clearinghouse, Issues Paper 20*. Melbourne: Australian Institute of Family Studies.

Liebling, A. (2004) *Prisons and their Moral Performance: A Study of Values, Quality, and Prison Life*. Oxford: Oxford University Press.

Lippke, R. L. (2002) 'Toward a theory of prisoners' rights.' *Ratio Juris 15*, 122–145.

Littlechild, B. (2000) 'Children's rights to be heard in child protection processes: Law, policy and practice in England and Wales.' *Child Abuse Review 9*(6), 403–415.

Lomasky, L. E. (1987) *Persons, Rights, and the Moral Community*. New York, NY: Oxford University Press.

Luckasson, R. and Spitalnik, D. (1994) 'Political and pragmatic shifts of the 1992 AAMR definition of mental retardation.' In V. Bradley, J. Ashbaugh and B. Blaney (eds) *Creating Individual Supports for People for Developmental Disabilities: A Mandate for Change at Many Levels*, pp. 81–95. Baltimore, MD: Brookes.

Luckasson, R., Coulter, D., Polloway, E., Reiss, S., Schalock, R., Snell, M., Spitalink, D. and Stark, J. (1992) *Mental Retardation: Definition, Classification and Systems of Supports*. Washington, DC: American Association on Mental Retardation.

Magito-McLaughlin, D., Spinsoa, T. and Marsalis, M. (2002) 'Overcoming barriers: Moving toward a service model that is conducive to person-centered planning.' In S. Holburn and P. Vietze (eds) *Person-centered planning: Research, practice and future directions*, pp. 127–150. Baltimore, MD: Paul Brookes.

Maldonado, M. (2005) *Cultural Issues in the Corporal Punishment of Children*. Kansas Association for Infant Mental Health. Accessed on 3 April 2007 at: www.kaimh.org/corporal.htm

Mann, R. E. and Shingler, J. (2001) *Collaborative Risk Assessment with Sexual Offenders*. Paper presented at the National Organisation for the Treatment of Abusers, Cardiff, Wales, September 2001.

Mann, R.E. and Shingler, J. (2006) 'Collaboration in clinical work with sexual offenders: Treatment and risk assessment.' In W.L. Marshall, Y.M. Fernandez, L.E. Marshall and G.A. Serran (eds) *Sexual Offender Treatment: Controversial Issues*, pp.225–239). Chichester: John Wiley.

Mansell, J. (2006) 'The underlying instability in statutory child protection: Understanding the system dynamics driving risk assurance levels.' *Social Policy Journal of New Zealand 28*, 97–132.

Marks, S.P. (2005) 'Human rights in development: The significance for health.' In S. Gruskin, M. A. Grodin, G.J. Annas and S. Marks (eds) *Perspectives on Health and Human Rights*. New York, NY: Routledge.

Marshall, W.L., Serran, G.A., Fernandez, Y.M., Mulloy, R., Mann, R.E. and Thornton, D. (2003) 'Therapist characteristics in the treatment of sexual offenders: Tentative data on their relationship with indices of behaviour change.' *Journal of Sexual Aggression 9*, 25–30.

Maruna, S. (2001) *Making Good: How Ex-convicts Reform and Rebuild their Lives*. Washington, DC: American Psychological Association.

Matravers, M. (2000) *Justice and Punishment: The Rationale of Coercion*. Oxford: Oxford University Press.

Maxwell, G., Robertson, J., Kingi, V., Morris, A. and Cunningham, C. (2004) *Achieving Effective Outcomes in Youth Justice: An Overview of Findings*. Wellington: Ministry of Social Development.

Maxwell, G.M. (2005) 'Alternatives to prosecuting for young offenders in New Zealand.' In T.W. Lo, D. Wong and G. Maxwell (eds) *Alternatives to Prosecution: Rehabilitative and Restorative Models of Youth Justice*. Singapore: Marshall Cavendish Academic.

Maxwell, G.M., Lo, T.W. and Wong, D.S.W. (2005) 'Introduction: The changing themes in youth justice.' In T. W. Lo, D. Wong and G. Maxwell (eds). *Alternatives to prosecution: Rehabilitative and restorative models of youth justice*. Singapore: Marshall Cavendish Academic.

McFadden, E.J. (1998) 'Kinship care in the United States.' *Adoption and Fostering 22*(3), 7.

McIntosh, J. (2000) 'Where service paths cross: Potential for innovative practice.' In *Proceedings of 'the Way Forward: Children, Young People and Domestic Violence National Forum, April 2000*, pp.87–88. Barton, ACT: Office of the State of Women for Partnerships Against Domestic Violence.

McNeill, F. (2006) 'A desistance paradigm for offender management.' *Criminology and Criminal Justice 6*, 39–62.

Meagher, G. and Parton, N. (2004) 'Modernising social work and the ethics of care.' *Social Work and Society 2*(1), 10–27.

Melton, G. B. (1992) 'The law is a good thing (psychology is, too): Human rights in psychological jurisprudence.' *Law and Human Behaviour 16*(4), 381–398.

Melville, R. and McDonald, C. (2006) '"Faith-based" organizations and contemporary welfare.' *Australian Journal of Social Issues 41*(1), 69–85.

Miller, M. and Morris, N. (1988) 'Predictions of dangerousness: An argument for limited use.' *Violence and Victims 3*, 263–283.

Ministerial Advisory Committee on a Maori Perspective for the Department of Social Welfare (1986) *Puao-te-ata-tu (Daybreak)*. Wellington: Department of Social Welfare.

Modood, T. (2005) *Multicultural Politics: Racism, Ethnicity and Muslims in Britain*. Minneapolis, MN: University of Minnesota Press.

Monahan, J. and Steadman, H.J. (1996) 'Violent storms and violent people: How meteorology can inform risk communication in mental health law.' *American Psychologist 51*, 931–938.

Morris, A. and Maxwell, G. (2001) *Restorative Justice for Juveniles: Conferencing, Mediation and Circles*. Oxford: Hart Publishing.

Morris, L. (2006) (Ed.) *Rights: Sociological Perspectives*. Oxford: Routledge.

Morrow, V. (2004). '"We are people too": Children and young people's perspectives on children's rights and decision-making in England.' In M.Freeman (ed.) *Children's Rights*, Volume II. Aldershot: Ashgate.

Muncie, J. (2002) 'Children's rights and youth justice.' In B. Franklin (ed.) *The New Handbook of Children's Rights: Comparative Policy and Practice*. Oxford: Routledge.

Munro, E. and Parton, N. (forthcoming) 'Mandatory reporting in child welfare: Developments in England.' *Child Abuse Review*

Munro, E. (2002) *Effective Child Protection*. London: Sage.

Munro, E. (2005) 'Improving practice: Child protection as a systems problem.' *Children and Youth Services Review 27*, 375–391.

Munro, E. (2007) 'Confidentiality in a preventive child welfare system.' *Ethics and Social Welfare 1*(1), 41–55.

Nagi, S. Z. (1979) 'The concept and measurement of disability.' In E. D. Berkowitz (ed.) *Disability Politics and Government Programs*, pp.1–25. New York, NY: Praeger.

Newell, P. (2005) 'The human rights imperative for ending all corporal punishment of children.' In S.N. Hart (ed.) with J. Durrant, P. Newell and F. C. Power *Eliminating Corporal Punishment: The Way Forward to Constructive Child Discipline*. Paris: UNESCO.

Nickel, J. W. (2007) *Making sense of human rights* (second edition). Oxford: Blackwell.

Nirje, B. (1969) 'The normalisation principle and its human implications.' In R. Kugel and W. Wolfensberger (eds) *Changing Patterns in Residential Services for the Mentally Retarded*, pp. 179–195. Washington: President's Committee on Mental Retardation.

Nirje, B. (1980) The normalisation principle. In R. Flynn and K. Nitch (eds) *Normalisation, Social Integration and Human Services* (pp. 31–50) Baltimore, MD: University Park Press.

Noddings, N. (1984) *Caring: A Feminine Approach to Ethics and Moral Education*. Berkeley, CA: University of California Press.

Nussbaum, M. C. (2000) *Women and Human Development: The Capabilities Approach*. New York, NY: Cambridge University Press.

Nussbaum, M. C. (2006) *Frontiers of Justice: Disability, Nationality, and Species Membership*. Cambridge, MA: Belknap Press.

Office of the Commissioner for Children (2005) *The United Nations Convention on the Rights of the Child*. Wellington: Office of the Commissioner for Children.

Office of the High Commissioner for Human Rights (1985) *United Nations Standard Minimum Rules for the Administration of Juvenile Justice ('The Beijing Rules')*. Adopted by General Assembly resolution 40/33 of 29 November 1985: www.unhchr.ch/html/menu3/b/h_comp48.htm

Orange, C. (1987) *The Treaty of Waitangi.* Wellington: Bridget Williams.

Orend, B. (2002) *Human Rights: Concept and Context.* Ontario, ON: Broadview Press.

Parekh, B. (2006) *Rethinking Multiculturalism: Cultural Diversity and Political Theory* (second edition). Basingstoke: Palgrave MacMillan.

Parkinson, P. (2003) 'Child protection, permanency planning and children's right to family life.' *International Journal of Law, Policy and the Family 17*(2), 147–172.

Parton, N. (2006) *Safeguarding Childhood: Early Intervention and Surveillance in Late Modern Society.* Basingstoke: Palgrave Macmillan.

Pecora, P.J., Reed-Ashcraft, K. and Kirk, R. (2001) 'Family-centered services: A typology, brief history, and overview of current program implementation and evaluation challenges.' In E. Walton, P. Sandau-Beckler and M. Mannes (eds) *Balancing Family-centered Services and Child Well-being: Exploring Issues in Policy, Practice, Theory, and Research.* New York, NY: Columbia University Press.

Pecora, P.J., Whittaker, J.K. and Maluccio, A.N. (1992) *The Child Welfare Challenge: Policy, Practice, and Research.* New York, NY: Aldine de Gruyter.

Pecora, P.J., Whittaker, J.K. and Maluccio, A.N. (2006) 'Child welfare in the US: Legislation, policy and practice.' In C. McAuley, P. Pecora and W. Rose (eds) *Enhancing the Well-being of Children and Families through Effective Interventions: International Evidence for Practice.* London: Jessica Kingsley Publishers.

Pereira, F.T. (2004) 'A Pacific perspective on physical punishment.' *Childrenz Issues 8*(2), 27-29.

Perlin, M. L. (2005). '"With faces hidden while the walls were tightening": Applying international human rights standards to forensic psychology.' *Paper presented at the 15th European Law and Psychology Conference*, Vilnius, Lithuania, July 2005.

Petrunik, M. (2003) 'The hare and the tortoise: Dangerousness and sex offender policy in the United States and Canada.' *Canadian Journal of Criminology and Criminal Justice 45*, 43–57.

Phillips, B. and Alderson, P. (2003) 'Beyond "anti-smacking": Challenging violence and coercion in parent–child relations.' *International Journal of Children's Rights 11*, 175–197.

Power, F.C. and Hart, S.N. (2005) 'The way forward to constructive child discipline.' In S.N. Hart (ed.) with J. Durrant, P. Newell and F. C. Power *Eliminating Corporal Punishment: The Way Forward to Constructive Child Discipline.* Paris: UNESCO.

Quayle, E., Erroga, M., Wright, L., Taylor, M. and Harbinson, D. (2006) *Only Pictures? Therapeutic Work with Internet Sex Offenders.* Dorset: Russell House Publishing.

Rasmussen, D. B. and Den Uyl, D. J. (2005) *Norms of Liberty: A Perfectionist Basis for Non-perfectionist Politics.* University Park, PA: Pennsylvania State University Press.

Renteln, A. D. (2003) 'Cross-cultural perceptions of disability: Policy implications of divergent views.' In Herr, S. S., Gostin, L. O. and Koh, H. H. (eds) *The Human Rights of Persons with Intellectual Disabilities*, pp.58–81. New York, NY: Oxford University Press.

Rescher, N. (1993) *A System of Pragmatic Idealism. Vol II: The Validity of Values.* Princeton, NJ: Princeton University Press.

Rioux, M. and Carbert, A. (2003) Human rights and disability: the international context. *Journal on Developmental Disabilities 10*, 1–13.

Robertson, B. (2000) *The Aboriginal and Torres Strait Islander Women's Task Force on Violence Report.* Department of Aboriginal and Torres Strait Islander Policy and Development, Queensland.

Roche, D. (2006) 'Dimensions of restorative justice.' *Journal of Social Issues 62*(2), 217–238.

Rogoff, B. (2003) *The Cultural Nature of Human Development.* Oxford: Oxford University Press.

Rose, W. Gray, J. and McAuley, C. (2006) 'Child welfare in the UK: Legislation, policy and practice.' In C. McAuley, P. Pecora and W. Rose (eds) *Enhancing the Well-being of Children and Families through Effective Interventions: International Evidence for Practice.* London: Jessica Kingsley Publishers.

Saleebey, D. (1992) *The Strengths Perspective in Social Work Practice.* New York, NY: Longman.

Saleebey, D. (2001) *Human Behavior and Social Environments: A Biopsychosocial Approach.* New York, NY: Columbia University Press.

Saunders, B.J. and Goddard, C. (2003) 'Parents' use of physical discipline: The thoughts, feelings and words of Australian children.' *Paper presented at the Ninth Australasian Conference on Child Abuse and*

*Neglect (ACCAN)*, Sydney NSW. Accessed on 1 April 2007 at: www.community.nsw.gov.au/documents/accan/papers/2S4E-2.pdf

Scannapieco, M. (1999) 'Kinship care in the public child welfare system: A systematic review of the research.' In R.L. Hegar and M. Scaannapieco (eds) *Kinship Foster Care: Policy, Practice and Research.* New York, NY: Oxford University Press.

Schofield, G. and Thoburn, J. (1996) *Child Protection: The Voice of the Child in Decision-making.* London: Institute for Public Policy Research.

Schone, J. M. (2001) 'The short and painful death of prisoners rights.' *The Howard Journal 40*, 70–82.

Scott, D. (2006) 'Sewing the seeds of innovation in child protection.' *Paper presented at the Tenth Australasian Conference on Child Abuse and Neglect*, Wellington, NZ. February 2006.

Shakespeare, T. (2006) *Disability Rights and Wrongs. Oxford: Routledge.*

Sheridan, M.J. and Amato-von Hermert, K. (1999) 'The role of religion and spirituality in social work education and practice: A survey of student views and experiences.' *Journal of Social Work Education 35*(1), 125–141.

Shier, H. (2001) 'Pathways to participation: Openings, opportunities and obligations.' *Children and Society 15*, 107–117.

Sinclair, R. (2007) 'Identity lost and found: Lessons from the sixties scoop.' *First Peoples Child and Family Review 3*(1), 65–82.

Singer, P. (1979) *Practical Ethics.* Cambridge: Cambridge University Press.

Skegg, A. (2005) 'Human rights and social work: A western imposition or empowerment to the people?' *International Social Work 48*(5), 667–672.

Smith, A. B. (2004) 'What do children learn from being smacked: Messages from social science theory and research.' *Childrenz Issues 8*(2), 7–15.

Smith, A.B., Gollop, M.M., Taylor, N.J. and Marshall, K.A. (2004) *The Discipline and Guidance of Children: A Summary of Research.* Report published by the Children's Issues Centre, University of Otago and the Office of the Children's Commissioner, June 2004.

Smith, R. (2005) *Values and Practice in Children's Services.* New York, NY: Palgrave Macmillan.

Smith, S.R. and Sosin, M.R. (2001) 'The varieties of faith-related agencies.' *Public Administration Review 61*, 651–670.

Spratt, T. (2001) 'The influence of child protection orientation on child welfare practice.' (Electronic version) *British Journal of Social Work 31*, 933–954.

Stanley, J., Tomison, A.M. and Pocock, J. (2003) *Child abuse and Neglect in Indigenous Australian Communities.* National Child Protection Clearinghouse, Issues Paper 19. Melbourne: Australian Institute of Family Studies.

Stenson, M. (2004) *The Treaty: Every New Zealander's Guide to the Treaty of Waitangi.* Auckland, NZ: Random House.

Stolle, D. P., Wexler, D. B., Winick, B. J. and Dauer, E. (2000) 'Integrating preventive law and therapeutic jurisprudence: A law and psychology approach to lawyering.' In D.P. Stolle, D. B. Wexler and B. J. Winick (eds) *Practicing Therapeutic Jurisprudence: Law as a Helping Profession*, pp. 5–44). Durham, NC: Carolina Academic Press.

Stratford, B. (1991) 'Human rights and equal opportunities for people with mental handicap – With particular reference to Down's syndrome.' *International Journal of Disability, Development & Education 38*, 3–13.

Talbott, W. J. (2005) *Which Rights Should be Universal?* New York, NY: Oxford University Press.

Tangenberg, K. (2004) 'Spirituality and faith-based social services: exploring provider values, beliefs, and practices.' *Journal of Religion and Spirituality in Social Work 23*(3), 3–23.

Tangenberg, K. (2005) 'Faith-based human services initiatives: Considerations for social work practice and theory.' *Social Work 50*(3), 197–207.

Taylor, N. (2005) 'Physical punishment of children: International legal developments.' *New Zealand Family Law Journal 5*(1), 14–22.

Theis, J. (2004) *Promoting Rights-based Approaches: Experiences and Ideas from Asia and the Pacific.* Bangkok: Save the Children Sweden.

Thoennes, N. (2003) 'Family group decision making in Colorado.' *Protecting Children 18*(1&2) 74–80.

Thompson, J. R., Hughes, C., Schalock, R. L., Silverman, W., Tasse, M. J., Bryant, B., Craig, E. M. and Campbell, E. M. (2002) 'Integrating supports in assessment and planning.' *Mental Retardation 5*, 390–405.

Thompson, S., Maxwell, J. and Stroick, S.M. (1999) *Moving Forward on Child and Family Policy: Governance and Accountability Issues.* CPRN Discussion Paper No. F. 08 December 1999.

Titcomb, A. and LeCroy, C. (2003) 'Evaluation of Arizona's family group decision making program.' *Protecting Children 18*(1&2), 58–64.

Tobin, J. (2004) *The Convention on the Rights of the Child: The Rights and Best Interests of Children Conceived through Assisted Reproduction.* Melbourne: Victorian Law Reform Commission.

Tomison, A.M. (2004) *Current Issues in Child Protection Policy and Practice: Informing the NT Department of Health and Community Services Child Protection Reviews.* National Child Protection Clearinghouse. Melbourne: Australian Institute of Family Studies.

Trotter, C. (2004) *Helping Abused Children and Their Families.* Crows Nest, NSW: Allen and Unwin.

United Nations (1948) 'Universal declaration of human rights.' In J. P. Martin and R. Rangaswamy (1984) (eds) *Twenty-five Human Rights Documents.* New York, NY: Columbia University for the Study of Human Rights.

United Nations (1989) *Convention on the Rights of the Child (UNCROC).* Accessed on 4 December 2006 at: ww0w.unhchr.ch/html/menu3/b/k2crc.htm

United Nations (1993) *Standard rules on the equalisation of opportunities for persons with disabilities.* New York, NY: United Nations.

United Nations (2006) *Convention on the Rights of Persons with Disabilities (CPRD).* New York, NY: United Nations.

UPIAS (1976) *Fundamental Principles of Disability.* London: UPIAS.

Valette, D. (2002) 'AIDS behind bars: Prisoners rights guillotined.' *The Howard Journal 41*, 107–122.

Van Krieken, R. (2005) 'Trust, liberal governance and civilization: The stolen generations.' In J. Bessant, R. Hil and R. Watts (eds) *Violations of Trust: How Social and Welfare Institutions Fail Children and Young People.* Aldershot: Ashgate.

Veerman, P.E. (1992) *The Rights of the Child and the Changing Image of Childhood.* Dordrecht: Martinus Nijhoff.

Verhellen, E. (2004) The Convention on the Rights of the Child. In A. Weyts (ed.) *Understanding Children's Rights: Collected Papers Presented at the Seventh International Interdisciplinary Course on Children's Rights.* Ghent: Children's Rights Centre, University of Ghent.

Vess, J. (2005) 'Preventive detention versus civil commitment: Alternative policies for public protection in New Zealand and California.' *Psychiatry, Psychology and Law 12*, 357–366.

Walgrave, L. (2004) 'Restoration in youth justice.' *Crime and Justice: A Review of Research 31*, 543–597.

Wallbank, J. (2004) 'The role of rights and utility in instituting a child's right to know her genetic history.' *Social and Legal Studies 13*(2), 245–264.

Ward, T. and Brown, M. (2004) 'The good lives model and conceptual issues in offender rehabilitation.' *Psychology, Crime and Law 10*, 243–257.

Ward, T. and Gannon, T. (2006) 'Rehabilitation, etiology, and self-regulation: The Good Lives Model of sexual offender treatment.' *Aggression and Violent Behavior 11*, 77–94.

Ward, T. and Marshall, W. L. (2004) 'Good lives, aetiology and the rehabilitation of sex offenders: A bridging theory.' *Journal of Sexual Aggression: Special Issue: Treatment and Treatability 10*, 153–169.

Ward, T. and Maruna, S. (2007) *Rehabilitation: Beyond the risk paradigm.* London: Routledge.

Ward, T. and Stewart, C. A. (2003) 'The treatment of sex offenders: Risk management and good lives.' *Professional Psychology: Research and Practice 34*, 353–360.

Ward, T. and Vess, J. (2007) *The Ethics of Risk Assessment.* Manuscript in preparation.

Ward, T., Mann, R. and Gannon, T. (2007) The Good Lives Model of Offender Rehabilitation: Clinical Implications. *Aggression and Violent Behavior 12*, 87–107.

Warren, M. A. (1997) *Moral Status.* Oxford: Oxford University Press.

Watson, S. (2005) 'Attachment theory and social work.' In M. Nash, R. Munford and K. O'Donoghue (eds) *Social Work Theories in Action.* London: Jessica Kingsley Publishers.

Webb, E., Maddocks, A. and Bongilli, J. (2002) 'Effectively protecting black and minority ethnic children from harm: Overcoming barriers to the child protection process.' *Child Abuse Review 11*(6), 394–410.

Weber, R. and Lacey, S. (2005) 'Trust us: Indigenous children and the state.' In J. Bessant, R. Hil and R. Watts (eds) *Violations of Trust: How Social and Welfare Institutions Fail Children and Young People.* Aldershot: Ashgate.

Wexler, D. B. (1990) *Therapeutic Jurisprudence: The Law as a Therapeutic Agent.* Durham, NC: Carolina Academic Press.

Wheeler, C.E. and Johnson, S. (2003) 'Evaluating family group decision making: The Santa Clara example.' *Protecting Children 18*(1&2), 65–69.

Williams, J. (2004) 'Social work, liberty and law.' *British Journal of Social Work 34*, 37–52.

Winick, B. J. (1998) 'Sex offender laws in the 1990's: A therapeutic jurisprudence analysis.' *Public Policy, Psychology and the Law, 4*(1/2), 505–570.

Winthrop, R. (2002) 'Exploring cultural rights: An introduction.' *Cultural Dynamics 14*(2), 121–42.

Wong, D. B. (2006) *Natural Moralities: A Defense of Moral Pluralism.* New York, NY: Oxford University Press.

Working Group on Human Needs and Faith-Based Community Initiatives (2003) *Harnessing Civic and Faith-based Power to Fight Poverty.* Accessed on March 19 2007 at:
www.community-wealth.org/_pdfs/articles-publications/anchors/book-sider-lynn.pdf

www.therapeuticjurisprudence.com (2006). Accessed on November 19 2006 at:
www.therapeuticjurisprudence.org

Yancey, G., Rogers, R., Singletary, J., Atkinson, K. and Thomas, M.L. (2004) 'Public-private partnerships: Interactions between faith-based organizations and government entities.' *Social Policy Journal 3*(4), 5–16.

Young, D. A. and Quibell, R. (2000) Why rights are never enough: rights, intellectual disability and understanding. *Disability and Society 15*, 747–764.

# Subject Index

# Author Index